Sir Olateru Olagbegi KBE
The Legendary King

Dr. Olusola Oloidi

Copyright © 2021 Dr. Olusola Oloidi

All rights reserved

No part of this book may be reproduced, or stored in a retrieval system, or transmitted in any form or by any means, electronic, mechanical, photocopying, recording, or otherwise, without express written permission of the publisher.

ISBN-13: 978-978-993-827-8

Cover design by: Infinite Intel Consult

Coutesy– Chief Olu Fadairo's Private Library

Second Edition Reprinted in the United States of America

Copyright © 2021 Dr. Olusola Oloidi

FOREWORD

The subject of this biography, Sir Olateru Olagbegi, is someone whom I have had personal relationship with for so many years. Yet I must admit he is an intriguing personality deserving of close study to unravel the strength of character that make up his being.

Sir Olateru Olagbegi is an enigma, indeed a legend of a sort. For how many people have gone through almost 25years of tribulation and yet be able to stand their feet to claim the glory of victory. Perhaps not many And Sir Olagbegi is among the few ones. What an honour and impeccable record! This record needs to be noted in the ***Guinness Book of Records***

That the problem came after 25years of epoch making achievements on the throne was enough to kill most hopeful spirits, but the then government at that time, along with a lot of his subjects, misunderstood his good intentions and this caused his being removed from throne for 25 solid years. Yet Sir Olagbegi remains for all time a formidable pillar of strength in the mist of misunderstanding.

It is in this light that I commend the author for putting together this book in record time. This book is a biographical account of Sir Olagbegi, a committed and patriotic Nigerian, a first class traditional ruler. A strong believer in the cause of natural justice, a humanist and a renowned pan Africanist, is aptly titled **"*Sir Olateru Olagbegi – The Legendary King*"**.

This book, which contains ten chapters, delves into the history of Obaship in the historic and very ancient Owo town from the 9th Century, the disagreement between some of his subjects and Sir Olateru Olagbegi, his dethronement and his eventual re-enthronement. No doubt the book is a good material for historians, research students and the entire populace.

This book is compulsively readable. It reveals all you want to know about Sir Olateru Olagbegi. It is a must for all and sundry.

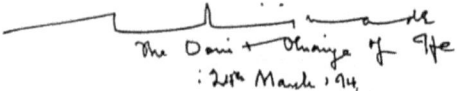

Alaiyeluwa Oba Okunade Sijuwade Olubuse II.
The Ooni & Oluaiye of Ife
The Aafin, Ile-Ife,
Osun State, Nigeria.

OLUSOLA OLOIDI

PREFACE

This project started out of curiosity in order to know who is Sir Olateru Olagbegi? With so many wives and children, how does he manage? What are the secret of his doggedness despite all tribulations? Is his dethronement justifiable? 25 years after dethronement, he is now back as the natural ruler of Owo. What are the reasons?

We tried to do a thorough research on this illustrious son of Nigeria and one of the powerful Obas during the first Republic so that readers could know more about this enigma of a man

This book in ten chapters therefore captures the life and times of Sir Olagbegi, with particular attention devoted to his twenty seven years on the throne, his twenty five years outside the throne, the struggle to regain the throne and the dramatic return to the Owo throne.

Readers will find in this book a lot of materials hitherto unexposed in the long battle of a man to regain what he rightly felt was wrongly taken away from him. The first two chapters contain a cursory look at the historical background of the Owo people and landmark events in the annals of the people's history.

Chief Tokunbo Osuporu, the Personal Assistant to Sir Olagbegi for more than three decades contribution is in the form of being a repository of the vital documents and historical papers of the Olowo which he released for the project while Dupe Onabanjo, a journalist, assisted in research and interview for the book.

The book also contains a good number of memorable pictures obtained from the personal library of the king and they are stories on their own

This book would have achieved its aim if it has assisted in shedding light on the life and struggles of one of the last generation of powerful Obas in Yoruba land, who had the rare luck of being a participant in both the ancient and modern times of traditional rulership.

Olusola Oloidi

New Jersey, 2021

CONTENTS

Foreword

Preface

Acknowledgements

Introduction

1	Owo: The Roots	1
2	Landmark in Owo History	14
3	Parentage, Birth And Early Life	24
4	His Administration and Achievements	41
5	Owo Crisis And Deposition	68
6	80th Birthday Celebration	98
7	What People Say About Him	116
8	Agitations For Reinstatement	123
9	The Return of the Legend	171
10	Sir Olateru In The Eyes Of ThePress	211
11	Epilogue	262

ACKNOWLEDGMENTS

In the process of writing this book, many people rendered one assistance or the other. First and foremost, our most sincere appreciation to Papa Sir Olateru Olagbegi for his fatherly assistance during the collations of the materials. He gave us unhindered access to his library and allowed us to interview him at odd hours sometimes without prior appointments. I am grateful to the three eldest sons, i.e. Omo-ori-ite: Princes Fola Olateru-Olagbegi, Banji Olateru-Olagbegi and Yanju Olateru- Olagbegi. They provided useful information and suggestions. Prince Yanju's personal assistance is greatly appreciated.

We acknowledge and recognize the contributions of an historian, lawyer and a literary analyst of all times, Her Excellency Mercy Ayoade Omoyeni (Nee Olateru - Olagbegi) to the success of this book.

We also recognize the unflinching supports and contributions of all the children of Kabiyesi both home and abroad. Without people like you, this book may not see the light of the day. You are highly appreciated. Prince Lafo was awesome he acted as valuable contact with the Olagbegis.

The support and contributions of Chief Tokunbo Osuporo and Mrs Dupe Onabanjo are well noted, appreciated and recognized.

There are many other contributors to the book – I specially thank Mr Akin Ogunrinde the then News Editor of National Concord for his valuable suggestions and proof reading of the manuscripts.

Many articles and news stories were culled from various newspapers and magazines, we are grateful to the publishers and editors of these publications.

I wish to commend the efforts of Mr Laja Shoniran, Chief Executive Officer of the publishing outfit INFINTE INTEL CONSULT for his valuable contribution and input into the book, and to his company for making this second edition a reality. Last but not the least, I thank my wife Bunmi Oloidi for her love, support and encouragement, my children and grandchildren. You're awesome.

INTRODUCTION

This book, Sir Olateru Olagbegi 11, KBE...The Legendary King is a most engaging biography of one of Nigeria's last generation of powerful traditional rulers in Nigeria, the largest black nation in the world.

It is a story of a sweet and bitter life struggle of a king caught in the whirlwind of political cum traditional intigues. After almost 27 eventful years on the throne as Olowo of Owo, one of the ancient towns in Nigeria, Sir Olateru Olagbegi was deposed in controversial circumstances only to return to the throne 25 years after his dethronement. He succeeded the man who took over after his dethronement.

The story of Olateru Olagbegi which is captured in this book is a classical study in the power struggle between an entrenched traditional power-base and emerging political elite in post independent Nigeria.

A masterpiece for those who are keen to know about the power-play between the king and the political leaders of this period in the history of the Western Region of Nigeria immediately after independent

Chapter 1

OWO: THE ROOTS

Some one hundred and sixty kilometers east of Ile-Ife, the acclaimed cradle of the Yoruba race is a town called RESPECT. Owo is the Yoruba word for respect and the town that is so named has the proud heritage of having produced distinguished paramount rulers or Obas all through its chequered existence.

But apart from Chief M.B. Ashara's 1951 publication on the history of Owo, the fascinating origins of this wonderful town remains an untold tale, a tale about the triumph of people and the exploits of their Obas who are offsprings of Oduduwa, the pre-eminent pioneer of the Yorubas.

Ojugbelu, the first king of Owo (Olowo or Lord of Owo), is known to have established his domain at about 1019 A.D., having left Ile-Ife, the home-base of Oduduwa, his father.

The first Olowo: Recounting Ojugbelu's departure from Ile-Ife to establish Owo, Chief Ashara explained in his book that Ojugbelu returned from one of his hunting expeditions one day to find all his brothers (fellow siblings of Oduduwa) absent.

All of them had left their ancestral home to break new grounds, having received special blessings and the most precious of Oduduwa's possessions as parting gifts.

The misfortune of Ojugbelu's absence at that moment of blessing was attributed, in history, to his arrogant disposition to a particular maid-servant who had rashes on her skin. Out of this resentment, Ojugbelu would always give only the remnant of his meal to the servant while one of his brothers (who later became the Oba of Benin) allowed the afflicted girl to eat with him from the same bowl.

Consequently, the maid-servant was so pleased with Ojugbelu's brother that she pronounced her blessing on him and it was believed that this was why the Oba of Benin and his other brothers got all the blessings and left home in Ojugbelu's absence.

So when Ojugbelu returned from his expedition, he met his father, Oduduwa, who felt very sorry for him. But out of love, and in appreciation of Ojugbelu's handsome look and polite disposition, Oduduwa named him "Ọmọ-Owó," or respectable Prince. Thenceforth this became Ojugbelu's name.

Odùduwà afterwards told Omo-Owo that he had offered all he had to his departed brothers with the exception of Edun, Adanigjo, Upe, Imemeowa, Ado and a Crown. He gave these things to Omo-Owo, offered some blessings and assured him that he would be fortunate in his journeys.

Thus Omo-Owo went in haste after his brothers. Luckily, he met them within a short distance where they had been stranded. When Ojugbelu got there with his Edun, Adanigjo, Ada (State Sword) he mapped out a road for them. But before he could allow his brothers to pass, Omo-Owo forced them to pay him something. So he got some beautiful clothes from them and afterwards, they departed from each other.

When the Olowo went a little further, he too lost his way and from there, he, with his people, were led by an Edun (Enchanted

Monkey) to Upafa. (This explains why members of the Owo royalty are forbidden from eating monkeys).

Ojugbelu and his entourage remained, in the meantime, at Upafa and made a home for themselves there. The Oluwa, the War Minister fought fiercely against Ojugbelu. Peace was later restored among the two parties. And after the invasion, they took an oath of allegiance that they would never leave the town. The Oludanre made boundary with Ojugbelu when he wanted to wage war against him.

Ojugbelu died at Upafa shortly after, and his son, Imade, reigned in his stead.

It is on record that Ojugbelu, alias Omolaiye or Arere, had a lovely time in his old age. Today, at Upafa, most of the dilapidated walls can still be seen in mounds (Chief Ashara's book 1951).

There have been about 31 Olowos since then, but it was Imade, Ojugbelu's son, who actually came to settle at Owo, about 110 kilometers north of Benin.

PAST OLOWOS: After Olowo Ojugbelu, and through the ages, there have been a long line of succession with each Olowo making his own mark in an age of intense inter and intra tribal wars, an age when 'might' was 'right'. Each Olowo had his own fair share of warfare, apart from other socio-economic achievements. Below is a resume of these noble rulers of yore.

1. OLOWO IMADE: 1070: Left Upafa for Oke-Made and settled some of his subjects at Okiti-Asegbo, a place which is still at Owo today. Twelve Igbare Iloros (High Chiefs), who were known to have come from Ile-Ife with Olowo Ojugbelu, are responsible for the burial and installation of Olowos.

2. OLOWO KODO: 1106: During his reign, clay lamps were invented in place of Agunran and Agudugbe (native candles). About 500 pots were made and with the size of Owo then, this was adequate for the full "electrification" of the town. He introduced the Iron gown.

3. OLOWO AGWOBOJORO: 1156: (Alias Atekuta): He was tall like a giant. During his reign, the Ogun (God of Iron) festival commenced and it was celebrated yearly.

4. OLOWO DONDON: 1209: Unfortunately he was reported to have become a cripple some years after his appointment as the Olowo.

5. OLOWO ADEGBERIN: 1260: During his reign, the "Oja Ceremony" (god of hunters) commenced and was marked annually by hunters with Agberebe dance. Sacrifices were usually offered during the festival.

6. OLOWO OBA: 1305: It was during his reign that the Elefene title was proscribed. Chief Elefene had settled at Okiti-Asegbo before the Owos came. He undermined the Olowo's authority and was duly punished.

7. OLOWO ASUNSOLA: 1332: There was remarkable peace and plenty during his reign.

8. OLOWO RERENGENJEN: 1340: His reign witnessed many significant developments -

> (a) Olowo moved from Okiti-Asegbo to the present palace, and the Iloros to their present quarter.

> (b) The slaves were made to reside at Isaipen quarters by the Iloros.

> (c) The Oronsen festival now known as Igogo festival started. The full story of the festival will be rendered in latter pages.

9. OLOWO ASUNSOME: 1346: He was said to have misruled the people. The Olusherepe Dancers for the Olowo and Chiefs were appointed during this period.

10. OLOWO OJEJA: 1386: He abolished the title of Elefene altogether and started a palace expansion project which extended to Oke-Igbala and Uluoja. A straight road was built to link Isuada.

11. OLOWO IMAGELE: 1430: Many customary traditions commenced as the town developed. For instance, any girl or maid of Olowo's choice was earmarked for marriage by putting pins in her hairs by Omode-Owa (State Sword Bearers). A death penalty was instituted against adultery (Ogun Odi). The Oro or Ogbor (Secret Society) was introduced. This was usually celebrated in the night when no lights or woman must be seen outside.

12. OLOWO ALAMUREN: 1481: During his reign, the Eduma (by the Chief Priestto the Olowo) performed every nine days was introduced. The Ijase (Ujase) masquerades festival started.

13. OLOWO OMASAN: 1539: An age-old idea of confiscating the properties of dead persons was abandoned during his tenure. Instead, the eldest children of such families were made chiefs.

14. OLOWO OMARO: 1578: The popular Uka masquerade started under him.

15. OLOWO OSHOGBOYE: 1600: As a prince, Oshogboye was brought up by the Oba of Benin who did not want him to go back to Owo. But Oshogboye cleverly adopted some historic methods to come back to Owo to reign. During his reign, State Umbrellas and State drums, like Umoba drums andAgunokun were introduced.

16. OLOWO ALUBIOLOKUN: 1648: During one of the

intertribal wars of his time, the Ifons came from Ifon-Ile near Oshogbo.

17. OLOWO OTUTUBOSUN: 1690: There was "peace and plenty" during this period. A town, Ọba-Àkókò, located itself in its present site with inhabitants from Oba-Iso. The Ale of lkare led his people to bring presentations to the Olowo.

18. OLOWO AJAGBUSI-EKUN: 1719: He was a great warrior. He captured Oka, Efira, Arigidi, Ora and other towns in Owo Division.

19. OLOWO AJAKA: 1760: A great warrior of no mean order. He invaded Imaga, Imakeke and Imagongo in Kabba area. He built a hall in the palace for his great charms and no Olowo was able to enter it until Olowo Olateru Olagbegi did.

20. OLOWO ELEWUOKUN: 1781: He had many children. After making them chiefs, he constructed streets which he named after them in all the quarters. He was rich and prosperous. He investitured his son, Aghagunhaiye as Idanike (heir apparent) before he died.

21. OLOWO AGHAGUNGHAIYE: 1833: Being an Idanike, his appointment as the Olowo was automatic. During the inter-tribal wars against Ogedengbe of Ilesha, the Idoanis came from Sosen as refugees and were allowed to settle at Owo by Olowo Aghagunghaiye.

22. OLOWO ADARA: 1876: During this time, the ljesha inter-tribal war led by Ogedengbe was successfully resisted. The Oloba from Akure came to settle at Isho.

23. OLOWO ALADETOHUN: 1870: He predicted the coming of Colonialists.

24. OLOWO ATANLEYE: 1889: During the period, one Captain Rowpal and late Mr. Herbert Macaulay came to survey Owo and District. This, precisely was in 1897. About 250 slaves were set free from the palace (Afin) on the advice of government.

25. OLOWO OGUNOYE 1: 1902: In 1903, the Owo Government School was established. The post office was first built at the Oju-Ogwa from where it was moved to ljebu Quarters in 1913 and again moved to the present site at Ogbon Ogwata where a modern building was built by Olowo, Sir Olateru in 1948.

26. OLOWO OLAGBEGI I: 1913: Father of Sir Olateru Olagbegi. He was powerful, trusted and revered both within and outside Owo.

Some treated him like a divine being. In 1925, Olagbegi I made an official visit to lbadan to welcome the then Prince of Wales (Edwards III). He was amongst the five recognized African Rulers who shook hands with His Royal Highness. Akoko and Oka were granted a separate Native Administration. Before now, they were paying a mandatory and regular fee of Twenty pounds (about forty Naira) to the Olowo.

27. OLOWO ADEOYE AJIKE ATANLEYE II: 1938: The Ute road was constructed from Owo by him.

28. OLOWO OLATERU OLAGBEGI II: I941-1968 and November 1993 to 1998: The subject of this biography. His credo, lifestyle, achievements and problems are discussed at length in subsequent chapters.

29. OLOWO OGUNOYE II: 1968 to 1993: He ascended the throne when Olagbegi II was deposed. During his tenure, Chief Michael Adekunle Ajasin, an Owo indigene, became the first Executive Governor of Ondo State. Also, Ondo State Polytechnic, Owó, and some industrial enterprises were established. He died on March 29, 1993.

30. OLOWO FOLAGBADE OLATERU-OLAGBEGI III: 1999 to 2019: The first son of Sir Olateru Olagbegi. In 1999, he succeeded his father, who died after his second tenure in 1998. Olowo Folagbade Olateru-Olagbegi, who received his staff of office in 2003, was Chancellor of University of Benin, of Abuja, and of Jos at different times. He also served as Chairman of Ondo State Council of Obas.

31: **OLÓWÓ AJIBADE OGUNOYE III**: 2019 To Date

The history of Owo, as summarized in the lives and times of its Obas above, is clearly a chain of remarkable events, laced occasionally with rebellion. Many Olowos, as traditional representatives of God on earth, maintained a high pedestal of existence. But inevitably, some were dragged into the mud.

For example in 1690, Olowo Alubiolokun after putting in forty-seven years of tempestuous reign, was thrown into River Ogbese on the outskirts of Owo in a rebellion. About 1880, Olowo Adara was beheaded for selling Owo children into slavery and Olowo Olagbegi I was suspended for six months before his reinstatement. Olowo Olagbegi II was also suspended for 25 years and he was reinstated in 1993 after the death of Olowo Ogunoye II.

A commentator once noted that God created the world in six days, but while He was resting on the seventh day, Nigerians invented NOISE. But in the case of Owo, its people on the seventh day, invented the act of rebellion! **"Oghoimoro Ilu yo boma yebomaeru"**.

How else could the crisis which enveloped Owo during Sir Olateru's reign be explained?

ATTRIBUTES OF OWO KINGSHIP.

Oluwa Agbaye or "Lord of the Whole universe" is more than a passing phrase on the lips of the Owo people. It is an apt expression of the eminence-social, spiritual, political and military– of the Olowo of Owo among his subjects.

It was no flattery at all because the people regarded the Olowo as an elect of God and they worship him as such. All through the Yoruba Empire of old Obas were regarded as Lords, while other people in the town were no more than loyal subjects. In the past, one could hardly see an Oba in public. The crown was treated with utmost respect and awe, unlike in these modern times when the crown means little more than a decorated cap.

The ordinary way to greet the Olowo is to kneel down and bow the head to touch the ground with prayers wishing him long life and prosperity.

The chiefs salute the Olowo quite differently. After kneeling down, and before touching the ground with his head, the Chief would raise his hands parallel to the ground towards the Oba and say,

Oluwa mi, le ji (My Lord - In your majesty)
Wagbo (May you be strong in health)
Wa to (May you reign long)

Some chiefs have fascinating ways of saying these things and it is usually a delight to witness such greeting sessions.

It is not an exaggeration to say that the Olowo does not just rule, he reigns.

In the past, the Olowo alone had the power to declare war and make peace. He had the power to create or abolish chieftaincies. As the sole authority in Owo, he had the power to allocate land under his jurisdiction. Infact, he had the power to enact, repeal, withdraw or abrogate any law, to pardon any prisoner, or nullity any judgment.

The Olowo was not allowed to see human corpses and should any one carry a corpse across the Olowo's quarters, the person was liable to heavy fine of goats, kolanuts and palm wine.

The use of umbrella when passing through Olowo's palace was forbidden. The offender was liable to some heavy fines or even imprisonment.

The Olowo usually declared the time for the eating of the new yam (Ogunro). It was an offence therefore to carry new yam tubers across or into the town before such a stipulated time.

The Olowo was not allowed to eat in the public. Likewise, he was forbidden to drink or smoke in public. And to say anything provocative before His Majesty, the Olowo, was punishable by death.

The Olowo does not eat, he merely slipped the meal. That, at least was the belief. Afterall, nobody saw him eating in the public.

The Olowo never sleeps. One can only say his eyes are closed during resting (Won re oju). To say that the Olowo is asleep is to declare him dead.

And when the king dies, one can only say (Ekunmuru bale) meaning the lion has lowered its tail. The Olowo never dies! (Ogwaku). This has its antecedents in the general Yoruba tradition. For instance, in the Oba Koso (Oba did not hang himself) play, what actually happened in old Oyo Empire was exactly the opposite of what the title meant, but nobody dared to say Oba so (or Oba hanged).

As in the English tradition, the Olowo was regarded as next to God who must always be obeyed. He must acquire supernatural powers to maintain his command over his people whom he could not let down. Until the establishment of a Local Government at about 1952, nobody could go against the orders of the Olowo in his domain. The Olowo could never do any wrong. (O pi ibaoma, o pi iyeoma o se yegbe soma ose hi doma ko jo orepese).

The Olowo and his Chiefs were the custodians of Owo Customs and traditions. Without the Olowo's consent and approval, nothing could bear the authentic seal of tradition.

THE IGOGO FESTIVAL

The famous Igogo Festival started during the reign of Olowo Rerengenjen at about 1340. Throughout Yorubaland, and in Africa as a whole, people are noted for one kind of festival or the other and Owo was fortunate in having the Igogo which was elevated in glamour by Sir OlateruOlagbegi.

Igogo was also known as the Orosen Festival. This is its Origins: Oronsen was believed to be one of the most beautiful women who had ever lived. She was born at More. After she had matured for marriage, Olowo Rerengenjen was informed about her beauty and he soon fell in love with her. But she explained certain things that should not be done in her presence, among which was the stirring of Okro. The Oba gave instructions to the other Oloris to preserve all the prohibitions in the palace.

But after sometime, one of the Oloris one day caused (as often is the case with rivals) these forbidden things to be done in Oronsen's presence. As a result, she left the palace and entered the bush at Ugbo-Ogwata (where the Post Office is at present). She was pursued but she refused to come back and the people did not come back. The hunters who went to look for her later met her at (Ugho-Uluoja) in a big forest near Isuada. She stopped to eat there and forgot her head-tie.

She refused to come with the hunters and when Rerengenjen heard about all these things, he went out himself to persuade her to return. She still refused, but instead, promised to save all Olowos from future troubles if some sacrifices were made in her honour every year. These included the killing of cows, goats, fish, dogs, hen and such others. Additionally, the following incarnations were to be said on such occasions:

> *Olilie he hun, Olilielehun, Oluwa agarajigholeji (thrice) Oronsen More, odon jo, osunsu o sun. A ghorofohunodun, Ologhoomo re, otese, osogho, on isala, onisare, A so erenla, OdoaguntanOge-obuko, Ogun-Aja, A ke-Odegbe, UgbaEku, UghaEja, Ugha-Ogbigbo. UgbaEgbenrenene, omuyaghen (Oronsen) ma durun se Ologho o A se.*

> *Olileleghun o (twice) Oluwa agarajigbodeji (thrice) Urunajari, ejafoju; Urunaguntanti, aguntangbegbee; keseri, oduduoron for, oronnufe de, Ugbonwe ye jo alagbedeOwo; otakunyu, Otakunwa, Otakunyamuliajen; Ojegeukun bobo male; Orogbodooyan ye poma, Opoma tan tan o kunefun, ipakuntenrenyadiye ran yu Ado, Obelebele ye jinabeirawe, kema se ejoaseagalamtata, Eyin ka erunbaje, Udeliakon moron senga. A ghorofohunodunoronsedeji, oronsen more odon jo, osunsun o sun ologhoomo re. Ughun a sodongheniyigheniyitomi, oni sale, on sare, Ugbaeku, Ugbaeja, UgbaOgbigbo, Ugbaegen re nene. Ogun aja. A kekeodeghe, Odoaguntan, oogeobuko, asoerenlaomuyagbe (Oronsen) Ma du run se Ologbo o A se.*

The above incantations were repeated in the evenings of the first and second days of Igogo Festival by the Olowo and the Uru respectively, and it is believed that any mistake made by the Oba or the Officiating Minister might cause the death of the offending party before the next festival.

During the festival, the Chief and the people are always in a joyful mood. The young ladies would dress in special traditional attires with beads. Many traditional chiefs and the Iloro Quarters people have different roles to play from time immemorial.

Recognizing it as a veritable part of his people's cultural heritage, Sir Olateru Olagbegi elevated Igogo Festival to an enviable pedestal. His personality and charm also made the Igogo celebrations a headline item in newspapers, several of which normally gave the event an unfettered publicity.

LANDMARK IN OWO: HISTORY OJOMO CHIEFTANCY DISPUTE

Here is one sore point: The Ojomo of Owo Chieftaincy. Though it was created to advance the course of the community, it turned out to be a dark spot on Owo's historical slate.

It is on record that out of the eight Olowos who have reigned since the creation of the title, only two were on friendly terms with the Ojomos. Even the Olowo who created the stool had one cause or the other to disagree violently with the Ojomos. And especially during the reign of Sir Olateru, the Olowo-Ojomo dispute permeated the entire fabric of Owo community.

When Sir Olateru was installed as Olowo, the level of peace, co-operation and tranquility in the town was so high that anyone who talked about the possibility of dispute between Olowo and the Ojomo would have been accused of heresy.

But as things would turn out, the Ojomo chieftaincy came up in the news again and next to the self-exile of the first Ojomo, the dispute brought on that family the unpleasant eighteen years of suspense, trials and tribulations.

BACKGROUND TO THE DISPUTE:

Olowo Ajaka, Olowo Elewuoku and Oludipe (who later became Chief Ojomo) were children of Olowo Ajagbusi- Ekun.

Elewuoku and Oludipe were full brothers, but Elewuoku was the eldest of the three. Elewuoku could become the Olowo immediately after their father's death but Ajaka was crafty enough to gain the upper hand. During Ajaka's reign, it was alleged that he tried without success to kill Elewuoku. Oludipe was with Ajaka and he did a lot to save his brother Elewuoku from being killed by Ajaka.

Although Ajaka had sworn Oludipe on an oath not to reveal any secret plans (including the one to kill Oludipe's brother) to Elewuoku, Oludipe used all the tact at his command to save his brother from being killed. Oludipe would speak indirectly to the walls where Elewuoku lived. When Ajaka died, Elewuoku became the Olowo.

To express gratitude to his brother, Elewuoku investitured Oludipe as Chief Ojomo with Ajegbere and ten wives. (Ajegbere means the beaded mini-cap worn by the High Chiefs but with two opposite lines of beads crossing themselves at the top). But later Ojomo started to wear a real full beaded crown and this culminated in one of the major disputes between the Olowo and Ojomo till today.

The sporting of a crown in Yoruba tradition is restricted to those in whom the cultural powers of an Oba have been conferred and this was far from intention of the initiator of the Ojomo Chieftaincy. The possible argument that Oludipe was a prince just as his brothers (Ajaka and Elewuoku) who also reigned as Olowo is untenable and questionable since no Olowo could install another Oba in the same town. Beyond Owo, such a practice is against Yoruba traditions and norms because two Obas cannot live in the same town.

During the reign of Olowo Elewuoku, disputes arose between Oludipe's son and Elewuoku's heir apparent. When the dispute escalated beyond control, Oludipe had to leave Owo for UgboUsughe. While there, the following Ojomos were appointed: Ojomo Odudu, Ojomo Nwagwe and OjomoAgunloye who returned to Owo during the reign of Olowo Adara. After Ojomo Agunloye, Ojomo Olotu Oyigun was appointed. Ojomo Amaka came next to Oyigun before the title was abolished in 1949.

BEFORE ABOLITION:

The disputes between the Olowo Sir Olateru and Ojomo Amaka from about 1944 mainly centered on the antagonistic attitude of the Ojomo and some inhabitants of the Ijebu quarters, as well as secession proposals to separate Ijebu quarters from the rest of Owo. To antagonize the Olówó, who is the Obaluaye, was naturally a serious offence. The government of Owo was synonymous with the throne and anybody who disagreed with the Olowo in those days was automatically against the Owo administration.

For instance, in 1944, when the Imade College was being planned by the Olowo, powerful elements opted to establish the Owo Commercial College at Ijebu quarters and refused to contribute voluntarily to building Imade College.

Several attempts were made to warn the section by (1) the Inner Council (2) the Native Administrative Council. (3) Owo Development Committee (at the time) and (4) by both the Chief Commissioner (Mr. Whitely) and the Resident J.B. Bovel Jones. When it came to a climax, the government set-up a commission of inquiry in 1948 comprising of the Ooni of Ife, Sir Adesoji

Aderemi (Chairman), the Osemawe of Ondo and the Ewi of Ado-Ekiti.

COMMISSION OF INQUIRY AND ITS REPORT:

The Ooni's Commission of Inquiry sat at Owo for four days. The members moved around Owo and took evidence from the Olowo and his Chiefs, and from Ojomo Amaka and his followers. Contributing to the commission's report, the Obas described the creation of Ojomo title as a "political blunder" and condemned, in unmistakable terms, any attempt to separate ljebu quarters from the rest of Owo, because according to their findings, Owo was an indivisible whole. Ultimately the commission recommended that:

(1) The Ojomo should lay down his beaded crown (which was the main source of conflict in the town) and remain as the local Chief of the ljebu quarters as in the case of Ojummu (Igboroko quarters), Ajanna (Isaipe Quarters), Osere (Ehin-Ogbe quarters) and Akowa (lloro quarters).

OR

(2) The abolition of the Ojomo Chieftaincy title while all Ojomos should remain as Omolowos.

OR

(3) The re-location of the Ojomo and his followers anywhere outside Owo (but not within a radius of 45 kilometers to Owo).

When the report was conveyed to Ojomo Amaka and his followers, they tentatively decided on Omojomo instead of Omolowos on the condition that Omojomos would be given a ruling House in Owo Chieftaincy. Following this, a lot of correspondence was exchanged on the actual meaning of

Omolowos. The Olowo and his Chiefs affirmed the traditional role of all the descendants of all Olowos as members of the Olowo family with the powers to elect an Olowo. They contended that nobody was qualified to be appointed an Olowo except his father had once reigned as an Olowo. And Since Ojomo Oludipe did not reign as an Olowo, all his descendants were not qualified to mount the Owo throne, let alone have a ruling house.

No conclusive decisions were made on the finding of the Ooni Commission before Ojomo Amaka died in 1949. Neither could leaders of the Ojomo family and ljebu quarters decide on who was to become the next Ojomo without proper consideration of the recommendations of the Ooni commission. But immediately it was heard that the leading elements in ljebu quarters had chosen the second recommendation above, arrangements were engineered to abolish the title and to have the Omojomos and Omolowos. Many traditional rituals were performed towards this end including the Apagbe Moduare Songs

ABOLITION OF OJOMO CHIEFTANCY:

In 1952, Mr. S.K. Amaka, the son of late Ojomo Amaka was unilaterally installed the Ojomo by some ljebu people without reference to the Olowo and his Chiefs. This was contrary to a section of the law and the matter was taken up with the government. Immediately there were uproars, demonstrations and several actions by the town's people against the unapproved installation of the Ojomo, which confirmed their secessionist plans.

Within the very week the incident took place, a bye-law was passed by the Owo Native Authority which forbade anybody from parading himself as a Chief without being duly installed on the orders of the Olowo. Mr. S.K. Amaka was later arrested, tried and fined for violating this law. On appeal, however, he was set free. But to preserve peace in Owo, Regional government took a quick administrative action of abolishing the title in 1952. Since then, the Ojomo Chieftaincy dispute had been turned into a subject of political controversy.

The resuscitation of the chieftaincy was reopened by Dr. Nnamdi Azikiwe and late Rev. Ogunbiyi who sought to re-echo the matter in the old Legislative Council, but all to no avail.

THE RESUSCITATION:

Evidently, the Ojomo family is big and influential. It embraces eminent personalities, resident in and outside Owo. Several attempts were made to reverse the abolition which lasted eighteen years. It should, however, be noted that the divisions in Ijebu quarters in favour and against the resuscitation of the title was partly responsible for this impasse. It was a case of a house which was divided against itself. Majority of those in support of the Ojomo Chieftaincy joined political parties different from the one to which Sir Olateru, as the Olowo was sympathetic. And when the crisis against Sir Olateru erupted in 1966, one of the accusations raised against him was that he (Sir Olateru) was responsible for the abolition of the Ojomo title.

The accusation was the first on the list given by Sir Olateru's former bosom friends and advisers. The inference was that it was he alone, who abolished the title. In response to accusation, Sir Olateru quickly consented to the government that the title should be revived and the Ojomo family was requested to present a candidate for the vacant stool. It was a time to act with military precision and Sir Olateru's opponents were embarrassed by his fast moves and political masterstroke.

But Sir Olateru's final deposition was rooted more in the national political scene of the time than what his opponent at home believed. His detractors had wanted to make a big issue out of the abolition and make Sir Olateru alone the scapegoat.

The Ojomo Chieftaincy title was reinstated in 1972 during the reign of Oba Ogunoye. The two opposing camps in Owo (those for and against Sir Olateru) were consulted by the government before the final resuscitation. It must be mentioned that inspite of the political differences surrounding the Ojomo's title, Owo people still preserved inter-marriage and observed many social engagements together.

And happily, this particular intrigue was not allowed to degenerate to fatricide as in the ancient times. For example, Late Magistrate Ojomo attended and chaired the engagement of Prince Folagbade Olateru-Olagbegi to his wife in Lagos in 1968, and the two families exchanged correspondence afterwards. This proved, without any iota of doubt, that despite all these differences and disagreements, the families wanted to remain as one. The common aspiration today is that whatever remains of Owo people's cultural heritage will be exploited to nurture the spirit of unity among various sections of Owo, especially since political power is no longer vested in natural rulers.

OLOWO OLAGBEGI 1

His Highness Oba Olagbegi 1, the Olowo of Owo had the distinction of being the first literate Olowo. He was also very known for his dynamism. But a brief insight into his ancestory will explain it all. He had a very charismatic father.

Some people hold the view that if it was in the days of Olagbegi I, the Owo crisis as it concerned Sir Olateru (with his Christian attitude), could not have taken seconds for the late Oba to quell with his supernatural powers.

When his father died in 1902, Olagbegi I was too young to be appointed Olowo. After some time, the District Officer sent him to Calabar to acquire some Western education. But when he came to Owo on holidays, Olagbegi I refused to go back ostensibly because Calabar was too far from home. He was then taken to Benin City where he was trained for six months.

So on the 8th August 1913, Olagbegi I was installed the Olowo of Owo after the death of Olowo Ogunoye. He was a favourite of Owo after the death of Olowo Ogunoye and he had enough goodwill to start his reign in grand style. Oba Olagbegi I believed strongly in the divine right of Kings like his fore-fathers. He was bold, courageous and strong-hearted.

In 1919, the Owo Native Administration was inaugurated under his regime. Consequently, the payment of tax was introduced. But in 1924, a political crisis broke out and culminated in suspension of Oba Olagbegi 1 from royal office for six month at Akure. Among the causes of the strife was tax rates which were considered extortionate. Another source of the crisis was the dispute between him and Chief Ojomo. The latter was wearing the crown, in violation of traditional norms.

After his reinstatement, Oba Olagbegi I continued with his good works and the political intrigues was soon forgotten. In 1925, he made an official visit to Ibadan to welcome the then Prince of Wales (Edward III). He had the honour of being among the five recognized rulers who shook hands with the Prince.

On the 20th February 1938, Olagbegi I passed on and his death was greatly mourned by Owo people at home and abroad. He was fondly remembered by his people for his gallantry, Supernatural powers and nobility.

OWO CHIEFS:

Like what obtains in other towns, the Obas appoint their Chiefs according to their historical and political circumstances from time to time. Individuals were appointed chiefs based on their past services to the Obas or to the towns generally, others for their bravery, especially during civil wars, while some were appointed based on political and administrative considerations.

The traditional chiefs in turn have crucial roles to play in their cultural millieu.

As representatives of the Obas, chiefs were always frontrunners in their societies and they were expected to display exemplary leadership. Their responsibilities are heavy and people look up to them for one thing or the other. In the olden days, the chiefs served as the protectors and defenders of the people, just like the Obas. They were also appointed Court Presidents and Judges who decided cases on the basis of customary rules and practices.

Owo chiefs were no exceptions to this broad mandate. The Olowo, as the sole Native Authority in his domain, appointed his chiefs to assist him in discharging the responsibilities of his office. Their importance depended very largely on their traditional positions and customary influence. There were the High (Traditional) Chiefs and Minor Chiefs. A minor chief is one without a traditional role to play and could be a wealthy person and an important personality in the society. Nowadays, many chieftaincy titles of honourary nature are classified specially for dignitaries.

Owo chiefs were appointed to head villages and hamlets in the past. The Olowo gave them large acres of land on which to farm with their families. Evidence of these abound around us up till today. Many villages were named after the chiefs that ruled them. The chiefs had their different chieftaincy paraphernali-beads, drums and traditional names and special praise names (Oriki) which distinguished them from one another. Traditionally, the chiefs could marry as many wives as possible depending on their levels of endowment. This enabled them to form strong family ties, and extended families from ages. Today, the ancient edifices of some traditional chiefs are evidence of their importance and age.

Talking about masquerades, there were chiefs who were connected with (egungun) masquerades and their annual celebrations. Many of the chiefs had important functions to perform with the Olowo during important celebrations like the Igogo Annual festival.

The appointments of chiefs are marked by ceremonial practices and whenever any of them died, special burial ceremonies are also performed. But if a chief has not performed the Ero festival (performed after about fifty years of age) he could not be given a full traditional burial.

The honour and privileges attached to Owo chieftaincy were so strong that they were synonymous with the customs and traditions of the people.

PARENTAGE, BIRTH AND EARLY LIFE

"Some are born great, some achieve greatness and greatness are thrusted on others" Williams Shakespare.

NOBLE PARENTAGE:

Sir Olateru Olagbegi was born great. And by dint of hard work, perseverance and sheer efforts, he expanded the base of his greatness.

No doubt he is a force to be reckoned with and he remains a formidable pillar worthy of positive mention in any true historical literature about Owo, and indeed Nigeria.

It is not unusual in any human society for great things to be predicted before they ever happened.

Even "Heavens," as the saying goes, "proclaim the birth of princes." Sir Olateru's father, who was then a well-known Prince, had been told that a child would be born to him and because of this, he (the father) would one day be an Olowo (which actually came to pass). Sir Olateru's mother also had the same prediction that she would deliver a powerful son who would reign as the Olowo with his fame spreading across the seas: She was still a spinster then, and like the biblical Mary, she kept the predictions in her heart, pondering how and when they would come to pass.

Prince Olateru's father, Olagbegi I, was one of the children of Olowo Atanleye who reigned from 1889-1902. He was a bold man who ascended the throne with a touch of distinction.

As a Prince he had married Ameri, Sir Olateru's mother, who was born into the family of Chief and Mrs. Osuporo. Mrs. Osuporo hailed from Chief Aribo's family in Ijebu Quarters in Owo. The mother, Chief Ameri Olashubude Osuporo was a granddaughter of Madam Ajirenike, granddaughter of Ojomo Oludipe (1st Ojomo to be created). From their photographs (in the subsequent pages in this book), it is obvious that Sir Olateru's personality emanated from equally admirable parents. Chief Ameri unfortunately died in 1940, aged 60, a year before her son ascended the throne in 1941. She was a quiet and loving mother. She laboured, suffered and was humiliated for the sake of Olateru, her son. Although she had many children, Sir Olateru's only full sister is Mrs. Racheal Ogunrinde, mother of about seven children. Olowo Olagbegi I was 65 (sixty-five) years old when he died in 1939 or thereabout, and whie Ameri, his mother, lived for 60 years before she died in 1940.

A WONDEROUS BIRTH

At Sir Olateru's birth, it was a taboo to allow a pregnant woman to deliver in the palace, where, as it was believed, the baby could be killed through witchcraft or any other family intrigue. The oracle usually decided a safe place, village or town where the princes or princesses would be born.

To be born a prince is to be endowed with greatness, but like all good things, greatness has its own prize. Before Sir Olateru was born on 21st August 1910, a Sunday, certain rituals were performed for his sake, especially to ensure his future greatness which had been foretold.

Before a large family gathering on his eight day, Sir Olateru was christened "OLADETERU" meaning "The Owner of the Crown is capable of shouldering great responsibilities." He was given all possible spiritual protection the traditional way and he enjoyed the best that native medicine could offer.

As usual, his father the king assigned slaves and many wives to Prince Olateru even when he was under one year old.

Sir Olateru was christened James Titus at a later age of about eleven in the church. By and large, Prince James Titus was popularly called J.T. by all and sundry. At times they called him Alade. After his installation as Olowo, people ceased from calling him any of these names, and like other Yoruba Kings, he came to be addressed as "Kabiyesi" which literally translates as 'We cannot query him."

As Alade advanced in age, he was beloved by the people not only for his winsome appearance, but also for his general behavior. He was humble especially before elders who in return, bestowed many traditional blessings on him.

From about one year to seven years old, people of insight could read greatness in him. And whenever he played with his peers, they gave him special regard not because they knew he was a man of noble birth, but because of the aura of great powers and charisma that surrounded him.

Chief Aribo, with whom he grew up, recounted that when the children played together he, (Alade) was either made their head without them knowing that he would become an Oba one day, or while others were gathering leaves and sticks (in the absence of modern toys), Alade would not be bothered to do anything. There were always ready hands to serve him.

What many people read as one's characteristics in life may be attributed to when, how, and under what circumstances one was born. To be born as a prince presupposes greatness, honour and prestige, and if the stars were favourable, one's future was assured especially if one was as hard-working as Sir Olateru Olagbegi.

Traditional Africans are often interested in the stars because they believe astrology gives adequate answers to virtually all occurrences. Sir Olateru, who was born on Sunday August 21, 1910, came under the Zodiac Sign of Leo, symbolizing a lion. According to a book of Zodiac signs: "Leos are said to have all sorts of possibilities, for they are large-hearted, far-sighted and idealistic. They dislike details, preferring to deal with big schemes in which their organizing ability may have full sway. They are sincere, staunch and loyal, sticking to their friends. They have the ability to inspire others and to be the main-aspirant of a new cause or venture. They have a sense of responsibility but dislike routine. "This was also written about them:

"Out of the night that covers me

Black as the pit from pole to pole

I thank whatever gods there be

For my unconquerable soul".

"Moreover, Leos, led by the heart, have strong likes and dislikes, and this causes them to make faulty judgments occasionally, which they might find difficult to correct, owing to their pride.

The consciousness that they have superior intellect may develop into an unbridled love of power and the exploitation of less brilliant and more impressionable people. After laying his hands on the plough, a Leo does not look back. Like what somebody said critically of him. "He likes people to do his bidding. Such power and drive must be seen as a specimen of African ancestors, who a flamboyant Nigerian politicians would describe as men of "timber and calibre."

CHILDREN:

He (Sir Olateru) is perhaps the only living Nigerian who has more than 120 children. In the language of a politician, the man who has many wives and children does more for the society than a man with one wife and one child who talks about increase in population.

Not only did he have so many children, but all the children are very successful in their chosen fields of education, business, and sports, among others.

Sir Olateru is blessed with many beautiful and handsome children and a commentator has noted that all his children, though born of different mothers, look alike, resembling only their father, another great proof of Sir Olateru Midas touch.

An interesting thing about him is that he names his children to reflect events that play significant role in his life. Examples are

Olamoju:	Mine is the greatest
Oladaiye:	Multiplied wealth
Folagbade:	Taking the crown with grace/victory
Bowofade:	Respect the crown
Olabanwaye:	I came to the world with wealth (Born with silverspoon)
Olabamarajo:	Wealth/good things sooth me

Oladutemu: No one can sink my wealth, grace, etc.

Ayoade: There is joy in crown

Olafobe: Wealth predicts

Adedugba: No one can take my crown

Adegbayi: Crown is prestigious

Adero/Adegbenro: Children born during Ero festival.

Afindayo: In those days, it was a taboo to have children in the palace and when the mother of Afindayo was in labour (within the palace), the child was to be forced back to the mother's womb. When Papa Sir Olagbegi heard of the incident, he ordered that the woman should be allowed to have the child. She thus became the first child to be given birth to in the Palace. Hence Afindayo means Palace, a source of joy.

Another feature of the children is the belief of Sir Olagbegi inequality of the children among their peers.

There was this story about one of his children who got engaged in an argument with a fellow student. The prince cursed the other boy's father and the boy cursed the Kabiyesi in retaliation. When the boy's father heard of it, he almost killed the boy.

But when Sir Olagbegi heard of it, he scolded the boy's father, saying that the boy did the right thing and he gave his son 10 strokes of cane for cursing another boy's father.

Another major feature of the children is the unity that subsists among them. Most of them attended the same school, Government Primary School, Owo. Whenever any student abused an Olagbegi, such Olagbegi would quickly pass the message around that there was a student to be disciplined at the end of the school hours. The message would be quickly circulated like wildfire and all the Olagbegis would meet at the foot of the mango tree in order to mete necessary disciplinary action on the erring student. And such a student might be confronted by between 25 to 30 Olagbegis.

Also, if an Olagbegi is sick, within 24 hours, the message must have gone round and you would see most Olagbegis at the sick bed of their offspring.

Finally, in the family, there are some children who are senior to others by few hours. For examples, Adebo, now Mrs. Adeola, was seven hours older than Adejare, while Titilade, now Mrs. Akinibobosu, was 48 hours older than Ayoade (Mrs. Omoyeni).

Two people within the family (now deceased) that were too dear to Sir Olateru Olagbegi and the entire family were late Olori Florence Adoti Olagbegi and Prince Adegboyega Olateru Olagbegi.

Late Olori F.A. Olagbegi was like a mother to all children of Sir Olagbegi. She took special interest in the welfare and educational growth and development of all Olagbegi's offsprings.

Outsiders could hardly differentiate the children of Olórí Florence from others. She bought uniforms, sandals, books, etc., for all the kids. She was more or less "Minister of Education" within the family, and she was adored and respected by all and sundry. To say the least, she was people-centered.

Prince Adegboyega was an easy going, sociable, bold, charismatic, hardworking and flamboyant gentleman. He was loved by all and sundry both within the family and Owo town.

He was a good sportsman (footballer) and was nicknamed KROBO. He was an epitome of Olagbegi.

A ROYAL PHOTO ALBUM:

If all Sir Olateru's glamorous pictures could be published, they would have, in themselves, told his story in full, even without writing a word. But the few that could be accommodated in this book are apt illustrations of what the rest are. Sir Olateru is a favourite of many because of his consuming generosity.

He is tall, robust and elegant, with a radiant skin. He is said to be as handsome as a Greek god, prosperous and kind, as well.

But he does not allow wealth or the many good things of life to make a vegetable of him. Sir Olateru played tennis regularly to firm up his bones. Many wonder how at an advanced age with so many children and responsibilities he could still play the game of tennis so well.

OF CHARACTER: The Strong and the Weak Points:

It is not an exaggeration to say that our subject is far-sighted, convincing, trusting, progressive, and courageous. But like other human beings, he has his own faults. Under the pressure of an important task, he could be over-bearing, yet gullible.

Yet he has all great attributes of a Leo. This is so much that after he was installed Olowo, people who did not know anything about astrology nick-named him "Omo-Ekun" (a Lion) simply because of his strength of character.

In effect, Alade was not only born into a royal family, he was naturally born great. Through adequate parental guidance, he built himself a successful career.

Had Sir Olateru not been a natural ruler, he would have excelled either as a political scientist, a journalist, a clergyman (which he once aspired to be), or a teacher.

FORMAL EDUCATION

The missionaries who brought education to Africa in the seventeenth century did so largely on religious grounds. In most towns and villages, it was optional to send children to school.

Actually, many parents had to be persuaded to educate their children who were more useful on the farm, than learning, which appeared to have no immediate reward. More so, slaves or stubborn children were sent to school where they believed flogging would help discipline such children. In one word, schooling by then was seen as a form of punishment, meant only for the underprivileged.

Alade (Sir Olateru) being a prince who was seriously loved by his father was, at first, not allowed to go to school. But the prince was not pleased with this restriction because he was anxious to learn and was attracted to the poise of the few clerks, teachers and Europeans he saw around. After he was allowed to go to school following much persuasion, his father ensured that he was never flogged no matter the level of his offence. The condition was that if it became necessary for Olateru to be caned, any of his numerous slaves would be sent for to receive the punishment on behalf of the Prince!

Alade's personal interest in education carried him through the elementary classes at the Owo Government School where Chief Pataketo Enahoro, the father of Chief Anthony Enahoro, former Action Group stalwart and Federal Commissioner for Information under Nigeria's military government headed by General Yakubu Gowon, was the headmaster. He was a strict disciplinarian.

In 1956, when Sir Olateru made Chief Enahoro, his former headmaster, Chief Uwala of Owo, he recalled with pride the good behaviour of Alade who did not allow his parents to spoil him.

Sir Olateru had been interested in sports right from an early age. He played football and took part in high jump. As an active wrestler, it was a matter of pride that none of his colleagues at that time could floor him. Wrestling was a popular outdoor African game, and most famous wrestlers found it easier to win the love of women.

MATRIMONY

Marriage never presented itself as a problem for Prince Alade as it did to other men. He had everything! He was handsome, wealthy and powerful. Besides, Prince Olateru was given wives at birth and as time went on, he received more. If he was not ready for marriage with any of them, the lady was required to pay some dowry in the Native Court to free herself. Otherwise anybody who cohabited with such women would be guilty of adultery, an offence which attracted heavy punishment.

Prince Alade did not allow "love for women" to mar his career and he was very selective in these matter. Though pressure were brought on him from all angles, he did not get married until he was eighteen. His first son, Alademeji who died in 1959 was born in November 1929, at the age of 19 (nineteen). He could marry as many wives as possible. In the African context, polygamy was the order of the day. Besides, as a prince, monogamy was ruled out since the number of the King's children in the olden days was a measure of his greatness.

The first daughter, Oladeseju (now Mrs. Okunrinboye, a Nursing sister at the Island Maternity Hospital, Lagos) was born in 1931. Late Adedolapo (Mrs. Yusuf) who died in 1968 was born in 1932; Olajope (Mrs. Fadero), a nursing sister at UCH Ibadan, was born in 1936.

After his ascension as the Olowo in 1941, Sir Olateru gave birth to three sons: Folagbade, Adebamiji and Adeyanju, who were born in that same year.

The first son to be born on the throne i.e. OMO ORI ITE is Folagbade who was born in June.

The second son, Adebamiji, was born in November and the third one, Adeyanju, was born in December.

The first son, Folagbade was a legal practitioner, and a Professor of Law at the Nigerian Law School. He was the Counsel to the Vice-President of the Federal Republic of Nigeria during the second Republic in 1979-1983. He later became Olówó.

The second, Adebamiji, is the Rector of Federal Polytechnic, Ilaro. A Ph.D holder in Urban and Regional Planning and a former National President, Nigerian Institute of Town Planners.

The third, Adeyanju, was the former Chairman of Owena Bank (Nig.) Plc. and is now Chairman/ChieF Executive of Capital Investments & Trust Company Limited, Lagos. He is also the chairman of Owo Community Bank, Owo.

By 1993, Sir Olateru has a total of about 120 children, the youngest being about three years old. Many are in Universities worldwide, while others are in primary and secondary schools in Owo, Ondo State. Numerous others are holding executive positions.

There are so many interesting things about Sir Olateru's children. They all look alike, so that immediately one sees any member of the over 120 strong family, one recognizes him or her at once and none of them is ugly. A friend of the Olowo once asked, "Kabiyesi, how is it possible to have these children born by different mothers and yet they all look alike and like their father only?" When the friend demanded to be taught the secret behind the method, Sir Olateru smiled and replied that it was God's gift.

People continue to wonder how he can recognize all of them. During an interview recently, one of the interviewers digressed a little and asked one of the children, "You are so many but how is it possible for your father to recognize all of you?" He quickly replied; "If it is possible for the Headmaster of a school to know his pupils, it is not difficult for our father who begot us to know us all." When the father heard this, he was at first annoyed as to why his private affairs should be discussed in a public interview, but he was satisfied with the wise reply.

Mention must be made of the unprecedented unity existing among the wives (about forty) on the one hand, and the children on the other. Sir Olateru's willpower is extended into his family and public responsibilities alike. The wives (Oloris), apart from their obedience to their husband, rely passionately on his leadership. Indeed up till now, they have not done anything to betray their royal matrimony. Disputes could arise, often accompanied by tension, but they are quickly ironed out.

The children are a bit different. They are young, agile and progressive and would like to challenge "Dad's authority" over many issues. But their father has always been equal to the task, being a disciplinarian of no mean order. The older ones among them have found to their amazement that hardly can any philosopher beat their father's wisdom, logic and experience. And in many cases they gave up their weaker points of view in the face for wise counsel from their father. Among them exists a unity and love never known among Omo Olowos (the children of Olowo).

In 1969, a family club tagged, "Sir Olateru Olagbegi's family union," was formed to provide a forum not only for family discussions and planning, but also for "letting out steam."

EARLY APPOINTMENTS:

Prince Alade continued to grow by leaps and bounds. His physical power was tremendous. Bicycle riding was one of his hobbies He could beat almost anybody in any race, and the style and dexterity with which he rode the cycle was marvelous.

He could ride back-wards for long distances without any collision. When he left school, his father did not want him to go away from him. So he started work at the Owo C.M.S. School as a teacher before he later joined the then Owo Native Administration under his father, as a tax clerk in 1931.

It was here his knowledge of the area and people of Owo became widened. He is so blessed with retentive memory that up till now, he remembers his age-old association with many people. Indeed, he could trace the history of nearly all the families and people in Owo and districts.

He was transferred to the Treasury in 1936 as a Treasury Clerk where he remained, till 1941 when he became the Olowo.

TENNIS

Prince Alade started to play tennis right from his youth. The early European officers who visited his father were his friends and through them, he developed a keen interest in tennis. Shortly after, a tennis lawn was built near the Owo Native Administration Office where he practiced with others regularly. While other colleagues or princes had interest or indulged in the pleasures of life, Alade was very regular every evening at the local tennis court. At a time, he became a tennis organizer in the town and the surrounding districts. Boys who picked balls for the players were paid from a monthly contribution to which the players subscribed.

HIS COURAGE

Sir Olateru's life is a lesson to all mankind that should be adored while he is still alive, not after his death. To recognize the talent of a genius and press for his continuous stay in a position of responsibility is worthy.

Sir Olateru is a genius who had a lot to offer his society, with his Christian faith, knowledge and great intelligence. And his hard-work which earned him economic security. With all these, Sir Olagbegiwisely built himself a formidable net that, with God's grace, can shield him from all odds.

As a good Christian, his belief in the finality of God's plan for Man is solid. Those who seek his help in respect of personal problems were always fully satisfied that if even their problems were not to be fully solved, they would be given enough advice and solace to face life with renewed courage. He is a great comforter. He always brought his own problems under the light of the Christian doctrine and anyone who wants to sympathize with him in moments of grief will hardly have a new thing to say to him.

There was a story that a sympathizer came to him during a crisis with tear-soaked eyes. But Sir Olateru's striking response was that his travails were common only among extraordinary persons in extraordinary positions in life. He concluded by saying, "Haven't you read about the Kings of England who were beheaded when their people rose against them? We should thank God that we are still alive."

He was also in touch with the lowly. On one occasion he was attentive enough to some beggars praying and he remarked, "Even these people thank God. What a great faith they have!"

Moreover, his strong faith was interwoven with hard work. Apart from the few possessions Sir Olateru inherited from his parents, he worked hard to build an appreciable material base for himself. For without deliberate planning and hardwork, it would not have been possible for him to nurture his numerous children and get them as educated as they are. Sir Olateru's ability to make use of his time gainfully is one of his greatest natural assets for which he glorifies God at all times.

Mention should also be made of his knowledge and high level of intelligence without which most of his plans could all have gone off-course. And in moments of adversity, everything would have collapsed under the heavy weight shrewd scheme of his adversaries. Sir Olateru knew how to arrange his priorities to an advantage. It will be to his eternal credit that in spite of his travails all his supporters had faith in him and all that he represented.

Others in the same position and who face similar troubles would have succumbed and been crushed out of existence.

Sir Olateru, like all respectable persons, has his own will, which is reviewed from time to time.

An important feature of this will is that it demonstrates Sir Olateru's love both for Owo people and his children. Like Ceasars' Will, if Owo people know how Sir Olateru loved them and the town, and how keen he was to let them have an inheritance, they will rise up and ask for the reading of the Will-The-Will-The-Will!

In this context, what was paramount in Sir Olateru's kind mind is the progress of Owo and his utmost desire was to be in a position of power to advance the course of his beloved town, more than he had ever done.

In fact, having been in the wider field of politics, government and economic activity, he was in a unique position to connect so many factors towards the advancement of the people whose problems he was already familiar with.

Some critics may ask that if he was not alive, won't someone else come to the rescue of the town? But the fact of history, as somebody puts it, is that he was alive, and as long as his place was difficult to fill, so long will strong sentiments be expressed over one of the very few who could save Owo town from doom.

Whatever happens, Nigerians are living witnesses to the fact that Sir Olateru took everything that happened to him with courage and with a firm belief that God would guide him throughout his life. If he lived for a hundred years more, men will still say, "This is his finest hour." In the words of Dr. Nnamdi Azikiwe, he would have this to say:

> "My life has been a joy to me
>
> No matter where I go
>
> I've learned to live in harmony
>
> With kindly friend or foe
>
> What though the adder puffs the way
>
> At me to pounce with greed
>
> It frane how beit will decay
>
> To vilify its deed
>
> For life must roll and men must sway
>
> Like atoms of the air
>
> And live we must from day to day
>
> To do age the Devils Loir
>
> But life has been a joy to me
>
> No matter where I go
>
> I've learned to live in harmony
>
> With kindly friend or foe".

HIS ADMINISTRATION AND ACHIEVEMENTS AS THE OLOWO

In those early days, Olowos were the political and cultural leaders of their people. There were no politics and no politicians, no councils and no councilors, no political parties and no parliamentarians. So any Oba, who was literate, intelligent and hard working was free to go ahead with the progress and development of his town.

When Sir Olateru was appointed Olowo of Owo and judging by the rapid progress and events that followed, one might be constrained to believe that the Owo people had, in him, an answer to the reknown saying of Josiah Gilbert Holland (1819-1981):

"God give us Men a time like this demands;

Stout hearts, strong minds, true faith and ready hands,

Men whom the lust of office does not kill,

Men whom the spoils of office cannot buy

Men who possess opinions and a will

Men who have honour, men who will not lie

Men who can stand before a demagogue

And damn his treacherous flatteries without winking

Tall men, sun-crowned, who live above the fog,

In public duty and in private thinking.

Progress and in fact competitors in administrative achievements were between one Oba and the other. And so God gave Owo people Sir Olateru, He was ambitious. During his administrations, he uplifted Owo and its people in very many ways. He started, for instance, by comparing his town with more advanced towns like Ile-Ife and Abeokuta. He aimed at getting those good things of life which Owo lacked. If Sir Olateru had the magical powers to change Owo and its people instantly in 1941, he would have done it. But even without such powers, he made great differences.

HOW HE DID IT

First, the Chiefs gave him their maximum support. This was because they knew how industrious their king was. At other times, or with any other lazy Olowo, the devil might have engaged them and the people in petty jealousies or triffles, or in drinking and wining away their days in pleasurable pursuits. Sir Olateru also made a productive use of the love and loyalty the generality of Owo people had for him. Both the Chiefs and the people thus were prepared to co-operate with him to do anything, just any thing. For instance:

(1) Whatever was wanted as taxes, the people were ready to pay, unlike in the past when they revolted against an Olowo for obnoxious taxation; and

(2) Any communal work or the launching of any development scheme was done unanimously

FINANCE

The problem with every developing society is invariably that of funds. In the case of Owo and Sir Olateru, the financial problems were manifold and progress was slow in the first one or two years. The people were mostly farmers and the few traders in town were strangers. Cocoa, which became a buoyant economic product in later years, was not in great demand in the market then. As a result, Sir Olateru's tasks were to get what he could from the Government, on the one hand, and to harness his people to give cash and materials towards any project that was to be launched.

FROM 1941 TO 1968

For clearer understanding of Sir Olateru's exploits they will be discussed in three parts; namely, 1941-1951, 1951-1966, 1967-1968 and later his second coming 1993-1998. At these different stages, many factors were brought to play in the Owo administrative machinery that one could observe how the changing pattern of Olowo's duties reflected changes in the entire country's political scene. This period can be termed the conservative age. The age when the Olowo was still holding the full reins of power. But the Government had its representative in the District Officer stationed at Owo. In governmental activities, the Olowo acted as a Liaison Officer between the government and the people. The Olowo chose his high chiefs (who were, in turn, representatives of the people) as his advisers and they formed the "Inner Council Chiefs". The Nigerian nation came into existence under a formal government at about 1900- some

41 years before Sir Olateru was appointed the Olowo. So the whole country was just finding its feet within the emerging framework of western civilization.

A TYPICAL DAY IN SIR OLATERU'S LIFE:

As a matter of tradition, an Olowo was not expected to come out to see people as commonly done nowadays. His face was a prized item which could not be seen in public anyhow. Except on ceremonial occasions, the Olowos remained indoors and were worshiped as gods. He could get anything done through his chiefs or his household representatives. But Sir Olateru, on assumption of throne, came out to the people. He was usually outside in the morning as early as 8AM to do the day's work, unlike some Obas who would indulge in or continue with pleasure even in the mornings. In his office which he had built by himself, he attended to official correspondence which, before then, was the monopoly of the Native Administration Treasurer.

He would read all the files and letters himself and make relevant comments on every letter to indicate the action that should be taken. Among his typical day's activities are: the holding of meetings with chiefs on current issues, interviews with complainants, exchange of visits with the Divisional officers on governmental activities, plans for the progress of the town and the Districts with various bodies, and leadership in resolving District and Divisional land matters.

He was expected to be President of the Owo Divisional Appeal Court, but the Oba found it difficult to personally attend its sittings because of his other duties. Sir Olateru therefore delegated his judicial powers to one of his Chiefs. All these things continue till 3p.m. when he would retire for a short rest in the afternoon. But before that, he must have been to his farm for about an hour for inspection.

5.00PM - At 5p.m. he was up for the tennis game which he played every day except on Sundays, and when it was dark (unlike these days when there are floodlit tennis courts) he retired to the house.

9.00PM - At about 9p.m., other state duties continue-these included receiving visitors and many of his close councilors, state meetings where necessary, and planning the duties of the next day.

1.00AM - He would not retire to bed until late in the night at about, - 1a.m. to 2a.m.,

5.00AM - and he would wake up for prayers at 5a.m. before another day's work began.

Usually his breakfast was light, consisting of bread and tea, eggs, or bacon and some oranges or grapes.

In the afternoon, he took heavier meals like pounded yam or rice or amala. And in the evening salad or other light refreshments were his delight. He smoked cigarettes but since 1968, he began to smoke cigar.

He normally took some beer after playing tennis. He often wore white native gowns for which he was famous. In his day-to-day activities, he carried himself as a pleasant and radiant personality who encouraged anyone to work with him.

ENTERTAINMENTS AND GIFTS

An important aspect of Sir Olateru's success was in the lavish ways he usually entertained people. He was so warm and generous that everybody felt at home with him. A stranger once remarked that after Sir Olateru has entertained you, he would also give you money for petrol for your car. Who will not like such an Oba, he asked. And as a way or life, he gave alms to the poor and tips to nearly all his workers in order to encourage them.

Almsgiving was always observed, especially on Sundays in strict obedience to God's commandment. He himself had said that God gave him everything freely and he was duty bound to do likewise.

During the celebrations of Igogo festivals and indeed other anniversaries, lavish spending and entertainment were regularly arranged amongst school children, strangers and Sir Olateru's subjects. He also organized small parties regularly for important visitors on special occasions.

With his education, experience and intelligence, there was no sphere of human life or endeavour that he could not discuss at length with his visitors. There was never a dull moment with him. On the whole, he was very kind and generous, and these sterling qualities more than anything else, accounted for the spread of his glory and fame. Without this basic knowledge, it will be difficult to understand why and how many rallied round him to ensure that he achieved so much for his people and the country as a whole.

IMPORTANT ACHIEVEMENTS FOR THE PERIOD 1941-1951:

The palace is a good starting point. Both to visitors and Owo indigenes, the palace was the synosure of all eyes because Sir Olateru pursued its transformation vigorously. When no fund was forthcoming from the treasury, Sir Olateru committed his private funds to the renovation of the ancient palace he inherited. Mention should be made here about old large walls built around the palace through communal labour. Before this time, there was only a one-story building in the palace complex and this was built by his father, His Highness late Oba Olagbegi I.

After planning the whole compound to conform to modern

tastes, Sir Olateru quickly erected a modern storey building in front of the palace. A road was constructed around the palace and all centres of traditional importance were planned out for easy reach. The old Olowo Ajaka's building which no Olowo could enter or demolish was re-constructed to the greatest surprise of the town's people by Sir Olateru. Many frightening discoveries including awful charms were found in the house. For instance, one white fresh egg was found on a stone at the centre of the house when it was forced open centuries after it had been abandoned.

And by this singular act of bravery, Owo people believed Sir Olateru was a re-incarnation of Olowo Ajaka.

The modernization of the palace was not an easy task. From the furnishing of the sitting rooms with royal decorations and fittings, to the planting of flowers around the open yards, it was evident that new life had actually come to Owo. As far as the whole town was concerned, a new Native Administration Building Bye-Law was made to regulate the building of houses with standard and hygienic conditions. Furthermore, new areas were planned out for expansions.

SCHOOLS:

During this period, Sir Olateru made provisions and increased the number of elementary schools from about four to twelve. The stride was remarkable. The population of children of school age rose from about 1,330 in 1941 to 4.563 in 1951 and it was through his foresight that adequate provision was made for the ever increasing population of school-age children. The Anglican Christian Missionary Society made Owo a centre for training male and female teachers when St. John's College and St. Mary's College were founded. St. John's College started as a Grade III Teachers Training College, while St. Mary's College stood out inspiringly among women training institutions. Sir Olateru's dynamic efforts made it possible for these institutions to be founded at such a time. All were made possible through his liberal nature and his great ability to make friends.

Moreover, he personally founded the Imade College with the support of the whole town. The Oduduwa College at lle-lfe had been founded and in order to emulate Ile-Ife's educational advancement, Sir Olateru named the College historically after the first Olowo who came from Ile-lfe, Olowo Imade. He gave it a large area of land and provided training facilities for Mr. Michael Adekunle Ajasin (later Chief M.A. Ajasin, who was to become the be first civilian Governor of Ondo State) to further his studies and to become the first Principal of the College. With time, Imade College rose to be one of the best Colleges in the country, educating and training eminent Nigerians. Today, Imade College stands as a symbol of the spirit of self-help, determination and co-operation between Sir Olateru and the Owo people.

All these carefully planned projects in turn brought enlightenment to the people. The town started to expand tremendously. Both the new buildings and other attractions brought beauty and splendour to the town.

ROADS

While new buildings were being constructed, care was also taken of roads. Sir Olateru started by reconstructing old streets and tarring the motorable roads. New streets were planned out to make room for future street lighting, supply of pipe borne water, drainages, and other public utilities. Village roads were also constructed and all roads leading to the farms were taken up for rapid expansion. Farmers were happy with Sir Olateru's initiative for improving their lot and for inspiring them to embrace self-help and co-operative pursuits.

HOSPITALS

At this time, the nearest hospital to Owo was the General Hospital at Akure, about forty eight kilometers away. Sir Olateru was not pleased with this situation, so he approached the Roman Catholic Mission and with the help of the Government, the Owo St. Louis Combined Hospital was founded. This was one of the greatest achievements of Sir Olateru and the people were very proud of it. They did not have to travel forty eight kilometers in order to get medical treatment for serious and urgent ailments anymore.

On the other hand, the Owo Native Authority founded the "Maternity Home" using Sir Olateru's personal house which he donated. It was the first building used for expectant mothers. At first, the traditional and closed system of child-birth was very difficult to abandon for fear of the children being killed through witchcraft under the new open system. But as time went on, the Maternity Home enjoyed faithful patronage, with Sir Olateru himself taking the lead. Before then the Oloris (Olowo's wives) were not allowed go give birth to their children in the palace He did not only patronize the Maternity Home, he also decreed that all expectant mothers and ante-natal mothers should remain at the palace and insisted on medical treatments to be applied rather than making cock and goat sacrifices to unknown gods.

RELIGION

Sir Olateru gave unparalleled encouragement to the spread of Christianity and Mohammedanism. He was able to champion religious tolerance and although he was a Christian, he gave moral and financial supports to Moslems to build a new imposing Central Mosque befitting the town.

Thereby, paganism which was rampant among the people before then was discouraged significantly, Christianity progressed in leaps and bounds. New churches were founded and Sir Olateru made sure that he attended all the Churches in the town and district to ensure that his spiritual leadership was not in doubt. His father, Oba Olagbegi I, founded the 'New Church' which pioneered the Methodist Church. But he gave prominence to his mother's Church- Saint. Andrews Church, Owo.

MARKETS AND THE LOCAL ECONOMY:

Think of a village and an undeveloped market and you know exactly what Owo town markets were when Sir Olateru ascended the throne. It was another challenge and he took it up boldly. The main market (Oja Oba) was reconstructed and market stalls were built to accommodate market women who were thus protected from sunshine and rainfall. The sale of food items were done under hygienic conditions, supervised by the Sanitary Inspectors. Other market facilities were provided in all other quarters like Obada at Oke-Ogun Street to meet up the expansions that was going on in the town.

OBAS CONFERENCE (PELUPELU):

Before the setting up of the Western House of Chiefs in 1955, the Obas in the Western Region used to meet yearly on a rotational basis. They were used by the colonial government to run the administration at the early stages of colonial rule known as Indirect Rule.

Government needed the Obas for peace, order and good government. The yearly conferences soon became the venue for the coming together of old dynasties and old empires. In this respect, to attend such meetings involved great preparations as there were lots of cultural fun fare (African powers) and big personalities involved. Those were the days that the bugle was used to announce the coming and exit of Obas who were usually in their big flowing gowns followed by large numbers of their respective chiefs and personal staff.

This opportunity afforded the Obas to be part of the progressive trend of this period. For instance, some Obas as a rule were not allowed to travel out of their domain. The Olowo too could not travel beyond River Ogbese, about twenty four kilometers away. But when it was on the Government's invitations, the old order had to give way to the new. Their geographical knowledge was thus widened, and the Obas became more friendly than in the old days of inter-tribal wars when they treated each other with suspicion and rivalry.

Sir Olateru was in the forefront at this period and it was the beginning of his popularity, fame and reputation. He was not only one of the few literate Obas then, but his winsome personality won him tremendous admiration in and outside the conference hall. He was very bold and while many Obas could not stand up to address the government and their fellow Obas, Sir Olateru was able to demonstrate his intellect, power and dominance.

His wisdom, logic and oratory were soon well known and no one was surprised when he became the Secretary and the spokesman of the Obas when the conference took place in Benin in 1944. The late Sir Ladapo Ademola, the Alake of Abeokuta, Sir Adesoji Aderemi, the Ooni of Ife and others stopped at Owo to see Sir Olateru before proceeding to Benin. The visits elicited great celebrations and funfare being one of the greatest honours accorded Owo.

CREATION OF ARAGWAGBAIYE: CHIEFTAINCIES:

In 1947, only the High Chiefs could come into the Olowo's Council, although there were other eminent sons and daughters of Owo who could help him in his administration. Besides, the appointment of the Chiefs was hereditary and there was no opportunity for intelligent natives to become royal advisers. So he appointed two Aragwagbaiyes (non-hereditary titles) for Igboroko-Quarters, and one for Ehin-Ogbe Quarters. One for Iloro Quarters, one for Isaipaw Quarters and one for Ijebu Quarters to meet the demands of the town's growth.

Those who opposed this idea (which was with the consent of the majority of Owo people especially the youths), did so on the ground that the Aragwagbaiyes were placed on higher ranks than the older chiefs. But since it was the Olowo's prerogative to create chieftaincies, Sir Olateru was said to be in order. The first set of the Aragwagbaiyes so created were:-

(1) Chief Ladenika   - The Aragwagbaiye of Igbokoro
(2) Chief Obaskemipe   -   ”   ”   ”   ”
(3) Chief M.B. Ashare   -   ”   ”   Ijebu Quarters
(4) Chief Alanuma   -   ”   ”   Ehinogbe   ”
(5) Chief Oyegun   -   ”   ”   Isaipe   ”
(6) Chief AdeloyeAboluwodi" ”   ”   Iloro   ”

They were in this manner incorporated into Owo native laws and customs as high chiefs, receiving salaries, sitting as Court members and as Olowo's Inner Council Chiefs and they were allowed to wear or dress as other High Chiefs.

A ROYAL VISIT TO THE UNITED KINGDOM

Sir Olateru's fame continued to rise. In the few national newspapers circulating then, his activities, especially those bothering on his development schemes, were always reported and highlighted. He continued to make many friends in official circles, with other Africans and even Europeans, in the tennis courts, inside and outside Owo. So in September 1950, the British Council in Nigeria decided to sponsor him to the United Kingdom to widen his experience in local government administration for six weeks. The news was received with joy and jubilation. He was the first Olowo to visit the United Kingdom.

Owo indigenes, elected Chief Sasere to go with him while the Yeyesa and Chief Aruwajoye went with him on family and friendly basis respectively. The journey was interesting and it took them to historic places in the United Kingdom.

Among important places visited were the British Parliament, the Buckingham Palace where they met the King of England, playwright William Shakespeare's hometown, and other places of geographical and historical interests.

The reception accorded Sir Olateru and his entourage on their return was, to put it simply, great. They were met in Lagos by traditional dancers from Owo and elaborate receptions were organized for them in Lagos and Ibadan and they got to Owo on the third day.

At Owo the reception was a tumultuous one. They were met several kilometers away from Owo in a car cavalcade along Akure/Owo Road. People were dancing and rejoicing for the safe arrival of their Oba. Gun salutes and many traditional dances made the occasion impressive and indelible.

It was realized eventually that Sir Olateru's experience had been greatly enhanced by this visit and his progressive administration was generally accepted and encouraged by the people. As a matter of fact, changes in his personal characteristics and his administrative wisdom soon became widespread. His spoken English improved significantly enough to prove that he had been to England and Oxford. The idea of having public parks in the town was another experience he brought from his overseas tour. On the whole, Sir Olateru gradually became a great and prominent leader on all fronts. Everybody wanted to know him.

1952-1960

This period can be aptly described as the Modern Age. Party Politics had started. The National Council of Nigerian Citizens (N.C.N.C) conducted a country-wide tour in 1947. Dr. Nnamdi Azikiwe and Prince Adeleke Adedoyin called and paid an official visit to Sir Olateru Olagbegi in the Palace to talk about the on-going independence struggle. They had heard much about the support of the Obas for their struggle for Freedom.

Generally speaking, there was political awakening throughout the country and the youths were not to be left out. Gradually political power was being transferred, not to the Obas and monarchs, but to the "newcomers"- the politicians who could face and challenge the colonial masters.

Many of the changes that were or about to take place were not new to Sir Olateru. The Egbe Omo Oduduwa was inaugurated at this period. And in 1952, the Action Group Party was formed and the Party's launching ceremonies took place in Owo, with Sir Olateru and Owo people playing a significant role. Many observers acknowledged the great honour and political importance bestowed on Owo during Sir Olateru's reign. Also in 1952, the former Native Administrative Council which comprised of the Olowo and his Chiefs was enlarged to embrace representatives from each Quarter in Owo. In 1955, the then Western Regional Government passed into law the famous local government law of 1955 which enabled local councils to have elected members known as Councillors with few of the Traditional Chiefs as permanent members.

Throughout the Region, the Councillors' powers began to take a new turn. Most of them saw the change as the taking over of powers from the traditional Obas and Chiefs, and in some cases, the Councillors were reckless and power drunk. In Owo for instance, where Sir Olateru was the Chairman, many old men could not believe the hot and open exchanges that went on between the Olowo and the Councillors. The Olowo's authority had never been openly challenged or subjected to controversy. Some of the old men got annoyed and requested Sir Olateru not to have anything to do with the councils. But he was more experienced and in reply would tell them that, that was the new order of things, and that the days of the "Divine right of Kings" were changing to give room for young ones to take part. Some of the old men and Chiefs could also not believe their Oba dressing plainly and playing tennis with commoners.

This transitional period in Sir Olateru's life will be long remembered in the history of Owo. It was a case of playing the chess with the older generations and at the same time running the cricket field with the young elements. He was able to understand all the problems and their implication for everybody. Also, he knew in his heart of hearts that what was uppermost was the progress of his town.

He continued to struggle with the different arms of the Government to see that Owo was not left out in the scheme of things. Among his priorities for the town were a good town hall, good roads, a telephone network, pipe-borne water and electricity.

The only public hall at this time was the No. 1 Court Hall near the New Town Hall. When Sir Olateru applied to build it, the Government turned down the request because of lack of funds. He wrote again through the District Officer to say that the cost of the Town Hall should be spread over a number of years and if possible he would ask his subjects to augment any amount approved by the Government with voluntary services. The suggestion was again turned down. He had to travel to Ibadan on several occasions to persuade the authorities to reconsider their stand. When it was becoming apparent that his efforts would fail, he brought the contractor face to face with the Government. The contractor had agreed with Sir Olateru earlier to accept what was in the estimate for that year, and assured him that as the work progressed, he would render both material and financial assistance to them.

When the Government officials realized that Sir Olateru was not prepared to give up on the project, they gave their approval ostensibly thinking that the plan would fail.

But it did not fail. Thus the Owo Town Hall project was launched. And the success of the project was a tribute to the commitment of no other than Sir Olateru whose untiring efforts saw the work through, inspite of government's unwillingness to approve sufficient funds for it.

When the Town Hall was opened, Sir Olateru appeared to be the happiest man on earth because Owo then could boast of a Town Hall befitting its status in the Region.

OWO COUNCIL SECRETARIAT

At this period, the Owo District Council could not boast of any good or modern building for its workers. Sir Olateru thought it necessary to build a Secretariat with modern conveniences for the Council's Executives. He gave out land for the purpose near the Town Hall and when work was started, he contributed a lot in supervising the construction work from beginning to the end. Today, both the Town Hall and the Secretariat on top of the hill overlooking the palace remain worthy contributions to the town's development.

OTHER DEVELOPMENT SCHEMES

The new Post Office and the telephone service were not under the direct control of the Local Council, but Sir Olateru considered them to be part of his priorities. What he needed was to get to the root of where these things were being considered. He was sure of making friends there, and friends in turn would give him enlightenment. Sir Olateru had to travel several times to Lagos and made necessary contacts which eventually resulted in the erection of a new Post Office Building and telephone installations in Owo within a comparatively short time. In no time, Owo became the first town in the whole of Ondo Province to have all these modern amenities, ahead of Akure which was then known as the Headquarters. It was also on record that Owo was amongst the few towns that had pipe-borne water supply which was considered to be an outstanding achievement of Sir Olateru and for which he would always be remembered.

Electricity was installed at this period making Owo complete as a modern town.

Minister Without Portfolio

After the formation of the Action Group Party by Chief Obafemi Awolowo, the party was able to form the government in 1952 and Sir Olateru was appointed a Minister without Portfolio- a post which he held for nine years. His achievements in and outside government circles endeared him to many leading personalities in the Region. He had the great energy to work for his own people and at the same time to shoulder the state's responsibilities creditably.

The more insight he had to the inside workings of government the more Owo progressed, and many problems confronting anybody or institution at home were personally taken up by him, and in a majority of cases, solutions were found to them. Before undertaking any project, he always prepared his case and arguments in advance like a good advocate so that no points could be raised in any arguments to embarrass him.

1961-1968

By 1961, a strictly logical analysis of Sir Olateru as the interpreter and supervisor of his tradition in an abjectly uncivilized society has been one of dominance of power, while the same time observing the growing but slow westernization process. Some natural rulers attempted to resist as a change but they failed while those who succeeded saw the change of possible consolidation of power. In some places the wind of change had left some natural rulers in conflict with the new social order, but it was not so with Sir Olateru who had wonderfully and creditably embraced many of the new ideas as they came.

By 1961, Sir Olateru was already twenty years on the throne. Many of his children who were more than twenty years of age had started to enjoy University Education in Nigeria and Overseas. All round him, his labour was already bearing fruits. All his people who were farmers had started to realize the importance of his sermons on hard work; and those involved in Western Education had started to reap the fruits of their labour. The name of Sir Olagbegi as an Olowo of Owo who was capable of leading his people had been established beyond all reasonable doubts and the Owo people were proud to belong to the big family well known as Owo under his umbrella.

But at the same time, partisan politics was in full swing throughout the country. In a place like Owo, if you were not a member of the N.C.N.C, you must be an Action Grouper, and if not, you should belong to Northern People's Congress (N.P.C) and so on and so forth. To this extent, views were divided on local and national matters, including chieftaincy matters. It is a pity therefore that this "golden age" ended up in chaos for the people of Owo.

WESTERN HOUSES OF CHIEFS AND ASSEMBLY

Sir Olateru was able to impress both the Western House of Chiefs and the House of Assembly with enviable qualities which ranked him high among the leading natural rulers in Nigeria by then. Among other leaders, he was able to lead, guide and enlighten other natural rulers in the House of Chiefs. His ability to lobby among the Western elected representative made him an outstanding figure. When the motion for the State's Independence was to be debated, he was one of those who championed its passage in the House of Chiefs. Hardly was there anybody with whom he did not have additional contact or personal relationship in the 400-strong bicameral legislature. He became the president of the House of Chiefs in 1965, before the 1966 Coup d'etat. He was also among the three Obas chosen to attend Constitutional Conferences held in Nigeria and Overseas.

Besides, Sir Olateru also served in various Committees and Regional Board-notably the Western Region Scholarship Board and the Tenders Board.

Talking about peace, unity and good neighborliness, he has a tall record. On more than one occasion, he toured the whole country to visit natural rulers, notable personalities and see historic places in the North, East and West.

Furthermore, if and when there were disagreements among Obas or their people throughout the Western State, he was always chosen among members of Committees of Obas to settle such cases. His wisdom and influence in such matters were exemplary.

A State Of Emergency

The Nigerian political upheaval which started in the Western State in 1962 leading to the declaration of a state of emergency is not the subject of this chapter, but the glorious part played by Sir Olateru and other Obas, can be discussed. With his versatile knowledge and boldness, he spearheaded and led other Obas to the Late Prime Minister for the resolution of Western Region's political crisis.

The more Sir Olateru was in the front line in the affairs of the Country, the more the support and love he enjoyed among his people and Nigerians generally at home and abroad. As a man of integrity, he had already made an in-road into people's hearts. He was wanted, admired, loved, respected and ever trusted and his integrity is the very core of his essence. It is the sum total of his personality and his being.

NATIONAL POLITICS AND THE OWO CRISIS

In all human gatherings, there always are people of divergent views. In Owo during the twenty-five year reign of Sir Olateru, there existed pockets of dissent. The causes of such disagreements ranged from personal animosity, political quarrels, jealousy, to betrayal. But before disgruntled elements in Owo could successfully rear their heads, they had to wait until the political crisis of 1966 which enveloped the whole country and put Sir Olateru's fate in the balance. It was an opportunity for outside enemies to make use of the minority elements in Owo for their selfish ends. However, Sir Olateru's image and good works had been well established and the Owo crisis only came as an opportunity for his courage and heroism to be tried.

And so after the coup d'etat in 1966, the wave of revenge on political opponents struck at Owo and other places. The people never had it so bad. Although the details of the crisis are dealt with in other chapters, it must be pointed out that there was increasing conflict between the politicians in government and natural rulers. Hence, Sir Olateru, as powerful and as influential as he was, could not resist the inevitable clamp of the powers that were. But the agitation for his reinstatement after the bitter fight, should remind all mankind to appreciate a living hero, rather than wait until they die. In this context, it is noteworthy that Sir Olateru's social, academic, and economic status have enabled him to market his personality and stimulate his subjects to pledge their continued loyalty.

Is He Olowo Elewuokun Or Olowo Ajaka?

Considering the life and times of Sir Olateru as related to the progress and prosperity he brought to Owo, it is now appropriate to examine whether it is Olowo Ajaka or Olowo Elewuokun whose spirit we were beholding. As earlier been pointed out, it is customary in Owo for an Olowo-elect to pick one of many swords belonging to past Olowos. This enabled the people to forecast how the new Olowo's reign would turn out to be. To do this, the Olowo would be blindfolded by the Iloro Chiefs and his hand led to where the swords were assembled. It was always an exciting moment of any installation. People would wait anxiously outside for the announcements, and following this, there were jubilations and rejoicings, especially if the sword chosen represented a former peaceful and prosperous Olowo.

It was said that Sir Olateru first picked that of Ajaka before his final choice of Elewuokun's sword. Whatever it was, the life pattern of Sir Olateru was similar to those of the two late Olowos. But one thing that should not be forgotten is that Sir Olateru might be in a 'Class' of his own. Apart from some similarities or dissimilarities he had with the two late Olowos, the conditions and atmosphere under which he served his people were quite different from those of the former kings. Besides, the whole idea of picking one of the ancestral swords might of course not be wholly indicative of how the Olowo's reign would be. The practice would continue though, but this is an age when superstitious beliefs should always be closely scrutinized.

Comparison:

Elewuokun: - was prosperous and had so many prominent children. He was beloved by his people and his reign was peaceful and he lived long. So is Sir Olateru who had manychildren and a remarkable record of twenty-five years of successful reign behind him and was reinstated in 1993 for another long reign.

Ajaka: - was a warrior noted for numerous conquests. He had only one son and it was alleged that he made a powerful charm out of the boy to enable him win his wars. Sir Olateru was a warrior too in the sense that he fought hard for so many of his achievements for Owo. His fighting spirit was said to be reminiscent of that of Ajaka. But unlike Sir Olatèru who had many children, Ajaka's love for family settlement was nil. However, Sir Olateru's singular boldness to break and reconstruct Ajaka's power-house was seen in traditional circles as a very strong indication that he is Olowo Ajaka reincarnated, pure and simple.

As mentioned earlier, Sir Olateru is by himself, a first Class personality. Whichever way, Sir Olateru's progressive activities will for a long time, represent the turning point for good in the history of Owo.

OBASHIP IN NIGERIA

The institution of Obaship in African society today is witnessing rapid changes brought about by political and economic factors. It is generally agreed that Obas and chiefs have important roles to play in our society at large. Under the present day cultural re-awakening, thanks and glory should go to the institution without which the historic past could have had no meaning

For many centuries, African natural Rulers were the repository and custodians of their people's customs. They were the interpreters and supervisors of traditions. They were the first politicians, who wielded total power until the "Westernization" of thought and life. Thus the wind of change brought the natural rulers to conflict with the social order. It is hard to change, but gradually many natural rulers have succeeded in adjusting themselves to the new age. It is left for governments not to forget them easily and to make provisions for their welfare and economic prospects without which the honour and loyalty attached to their high posts will be diminished. As in England, the position of Obas should be safeguarded against political activities or controversies.

WHAT FUTURE AWAITS OUR OBAS?

There is no better way to end this chapter than to cull a Publication in one of the national newspapers, Morning Post (April 27, 1971) on the above subject. It reads, "Nigeria now has the most opportune time to decide firmly on the future position and role of our natural and traditional rulers, defined here as the kings and chiefs. Since Nigeria came into being, we have been ambivalent regarding what we want to do with our traditional rulers. In many respects, our regards amounted to lip service, a situation which should be rectified during and after the military regime.

"Like many new African states, Nigeria is a plural society in terms of its component diverse institutions and social and cultural systems. The fact that these diversities have been brought together to constitute one country is well known to be the result of accident of colonisation and imperialism. This fact also meant the importation of the Westminister model of parliamentary government, thereby creating two main categories of ruling elite in Nigeria, under a new distribution of power".

"Prior to colonisation and to the incorporation of indigenous politics- the kings and chiefs, that is the Emir (Sultan, Shehu, etc.), Oba (Alafin, Ooni, Olówó, etc.), Obi, Ovie, etc., and their Chiefs occupied the highest positions in their respective societies and wielded great power though hedged about by their constitutions and other forms of checks. Some of these traditional rulers have been shown to have had the power of life and death within their social and cultural milieu. Not much thought has been given to the position of the traditional rulers since their societies have been made to exist under the new state structure, behold the mere mention that no one expects them to perform the same traditional roles as they did prior to the 20th century".

"The traditional rulers have been placed in a weaker, indeed powerless position in the political organisation of the new state. On the other hand, new elite position holders have exploited every advantage contained in the Nigerian Constitution and political system in relation to the traditional rulers. The results have been the domineering attitude, disrespect and blunt insults by the new elite who by tradition are the subjects of the traditional rulers".

"The traditional rulers among the remaining 20 percent that is coinciding roughly with the urban populations function amongst people with divided loyalty… to various traditions and to modernity. The traditional rulers themselves adapt to accord with the demands of such urban heterogeneity. The salient point to note is that in spite of the past disorganising effects of party politisation of the kingship and chieftaincies and of the factionalisation created by party politics, a large part of the Nigerian population is tradition-bound within diverse cultural contexts".

"The vocal few and some of budding elite who claim to be very westernized(conveniently forgetting that the kingship is still held high even in highly industrialised England and other European countries) have pointed and presented our rulers as undesirable and irrelevant to development. It must be pointed out that many of our traditional rulers possess secondary and university education or have passed through formal Islamic education. Most of them make both personal and institutional adaptation to social and economic change".

"Development is a concept often narrowly and erroneously interpreted as coterminous with economic development. Equally important or perhaps a more important type of development is social and cultural development. Economic develop must occur in relation to socio-cultural development, otherwise society will lose itself or have no identity. In this regard, it is generally accepted that traditional rulers, being the trusted keepers of our traditions and cultures, are indispensable in respect of roles necessary to advance the social and cultural development of a people. They are particularly indispensable in matters pertaining to mass communication and mobilization in such traditional cum transitional societies as Nigeria".

"If the foregoing is common knowledge, it is surprising that traditional rulers have only been receiving lip service in the society. It surprising that they have been exploited and manipulated by our politicians and government functionaries. It is a sad verdict on those who by virtue of their legitimate positions in indigenous systems, have contributed greatly to the stability of society".

"This fact has endeared the traditional rulers not only to the British rulers and occasionally to civilian regimes, but also to the current military regime. The military government has animportant duty to create a respectable and functional position for traditional rulers".

"This may have to do with giving them constitutional

recognition and responsibility. The best position is the one that will remove them farthest from party politics and from financial dependence on politicians. It is common knowledge that these two factors - politics and financial resources- created the two major problems which traditional rulers faced before the military regime; numerous cases of depositions and exiles, one-penny-a-year Obas, of government-appointed kings and chiefs, of divided kingdoms and of party-incited subjects were the order of the day".

"Yet it is not easy to suggest solutions. Not in Nigeria where party politics has permeated the fabric of the society. However, one key constitutional step may be taken by the military government in this regard. That is, to give a constitutional position to our kings and chiefs and place them under the state governor's office. Their positions and salaries may thus be part of structures and votes of the governor's office, irrespective of whatever political party controls government either at the National or States levels. However, we cannot continue this act unless we tacitly give it our approval. Indeed, we should act the opposite way. The state governments have made some attempts to help stabilise our kingships. For example, the Western State has done so through a recent compilation and printing of the Chieftaincy Declaration settling our succession rights and procedures in the various administrative divisions of the state".

"To cherish and retain traditions and cultural identities traditional rulers - the custodians of the diverse social and cultural systems – ought to be given constitutional and respectable positions in a post-military Nigeria. But ironically the best decision on the constitutional position of our kings and chiefs can only be taken under a military government!". concluded the write-up.

OWO CRISIS AND DEPOSITION

"Ambition Is so powerful a passion in the human breast that however high we reach, we are never satisfied."

- Nicolo Macbiaveli

Olateru Olagbegi had achieved everything: fame, international and national respect and prominence. He is better respected and held in higher esteem than many Obas or Obis or Emirs in Nigeria despite his tribulations for about a quarter of a century. But in disallowing his ambition to affect his humility and self-respect, he proved Machiaveli wrong.

It is a truism that there can never be a smoke without fire. The events which led to the uprising against the Olowo in 1966 have their roots in the previous administrative structure of Owo Council and the political upheaval throughout the then Western Region, nay the whole country. It is appropriate to classify this upheaval into two categories: Remote and immediate. Sir Olateru Olagbegi had the privilege of reigning during two distinctive periods- the old and the new era.

Remote Cause

Firstly, record shows that Sir Olagbegi's natural dominant position in Owo political and administrative organisation was a threat to new power seekers under the new Local Government.

Secondly, the Local Government reforms of 1955 gave the local councillors virtually all major powers over the Traditional Rulers. Thirdly, the allocation of land and Chieftaincy reforms were widespread and were used by opponents to kick against the Native Authority. All these matters were used maliciously by political opponents for their smearing campaigns.

Besides, the intra-party crises within the Action Group greatly affected the politics of Owo. Loyalties for the leadership of the two opposing factions were sharply divided to the extent that political victimisation was the order of the day. Also responsible was the controversial Western State Election of 1965 which resulted into chaos and the breakdown of law and order throughout the state. Another factor was the coup d'etat of 15th January, 1966 in which Chief S. L. Akintola, the Premier of the Western Nigeria, was killed. Sir Olateru's opponents seized these happenings as opportunities to wage total war against him. The coup particularly gave the wrong idea that the military government was out to crush political opponents.

Petitions

There and then, some indigenes of Owo took advantage of the fear which the Military Government had instilled in everybody to petition the Government for Sir Olagbegi's removal as the Olowo of Owo. The Late Lt. Col. Adekunle Fajuyi who visited Owo after the coup was greeted with placards requesting the government to depose the Olowo.

On February 28, 1966, the Owo community led by the late

Chief G. Ade Sasere wrote a letter to the then Permanent Secretary, Ministry of Local Government in Ibadan, and made the following allegations, amongst others, against Sir Olateru Olagbegi:-

(1) (a)   Chieftaincy Matters: That the Abolition of Ojomo Chieftancy title was unconstitutional and was prompted by high-handedness of the Olowo who used his influence and misled the Government to abolish the title.

(b)   Creation of Aragwagbaiye Chieftaincy:

This innovation gave privileges to commoners to have a say in the administration of the town because before it, only the traditional chiefs were running the affairs of the town. Aragwagbaiye was expected to be a representative of the town and therefore to be elected by the adult males in each quarter. It was also alleged that the Olowo did not allow the system to work.

(c)   Idaniken: It was also alleged that he introduced Idaniken- the heir apparent post which only his children could occupy.

(d)   Prostitution of Chieftaincy:

(i)   Chieftaincy, which was a sacred and honourable institution in Owo, was alleged to have now been a thing of derision, because the Olowo by his greed for money cheapened the institution. Chieftaincy in Owo was no more a reward for meritorious service to the community but an easily purchasable article.

(ii)   The tradition of Owo permits the members of each chieftancy house called "EBI" to present a candidate to fill any vacant post of a Chief in the family, but Olagbegi violated this tradition with impunity.

(iii) In 1959, the Olowo Olagbegi II made 40 of his children both boys and girls chiefs in different quarters in Owo and districts without the prior approval of the quarter chiefs.

(2) Sale of Communal Land:

(a) Lease of Communal Land: It was alleged that he seized the power of allocating and leasing of communal land in Owo from the District Council- the body vested with this authority.

(b) Sale of Afin Land: That the Olowo violated the collective decision of Owo people that the vast land that surrounded the palace should be given out freely to the people of Owo and instead he sold same to some people.

(c) Illegal Acquisition of Land and Fund: That he illegally acquired the town's land without consulting others, and that he also misappropriated Owo District Council land, property and fund. He was also accused of involvement in other shady deals which were unbecoming of an Oba.

(d) Active Participation in Politics: The Owo people said that as an Oba, he was expected not to be partisan and involved in politics of the day. But instead, the Olowo was actively in support of one of the political parties. That he campaigned actively for this party against the wishes and norms of his people, and compelled his subjects to join this party of his choice.

It was alleged that he was one of the Chief Advisers to the late leader of Nigeria National Democratic Party, Chief S.L. Akintola.

They claimed that if Chief Akintola could be charged with atrocious crimes, the Olowo should not escape the same or even greater charge because he misled the government in committing so much atrocity.

The letter containing the above allegations was signed or thumb printed by 50 people, including 29 Chiefs.

Counter-allegations were made by another group in the town who described the above petitioners as political confusionists, urging the government to dismiss the allegations.

Sir Olateru Olagbegi also defended himself against all the allegations.

A commission of inquiry was ultimately set-up by the then Western State government to ascertain the authenticity of the allegations. The commission met and discussed at length with concerned parties and it latter submitted its findings to the government, Surprisingly, Government did not issue a white paper on this report, yet the Oba was suspended for six months.

Investigation:

In March of the same year, the Government requested the council of Obas and Chiefs to examine the matter again. Among the charges levied against the Olowo were that Sir Olateru:

(1). Took active part in partisan politics.

(2). Encouraged abolition of Ojomo Chieftancy title by the ````Government.

(3). Engineered the creation of the (six) Aragwagbaiye chieftaincy positions in 1947.

(4). Had an intention to create the Idaniken (heir apparent title).

In his wisdom, Sir Olateru studied the above allegations and replied thus:

(1) He was merely supporting the government of the day for the welfare and progress of Owo people and not that he was-involved in partisan politics as such.

(2) He was not the one who abolished the Ojomo Chieftaincy title (which he said he was prepared to reinstate immediately). The title, he explained, was abolished by the government for the peace of the town.

(3) The creation of six chieftancies was by Owo people and if their creation was not popular, he was prepared to drop the idea.

(4) He was not planning to create any Idaniken at that time. Sir Olateru finally explained that these charges brought against him were politically motivated and that he was being persecuted for serving as the President of the House of Chiefs under the banned N.N.D.P. He said he had served under seven different governments meritoriously. He complained, however, that his accusers were not brought face-to-face before him, a step which he maintained, was against the principle of natural justice.

Suspension

After all the investigations conducted by the Council of Obas and Chiefs, a letter was sent by the Military Governor suspending Sir Olagbegi from office for six months on the 6th June, 1966 as against his removal which his opponents were asking for. In a covering letter the Permanent Secretary to Ministry of Local Government explained:

(1) That His Excellency, the Military Governor, having considered the advice of the Council of Obas and Chiefs with respect to the accusations levelled against you by members of the Owo Community, had decided to suspend you from the office of the Olowo of Owo for six months starting from Wednesday the

15th June, 1966.

(2) That the implications are that you will cease to perform any statutory, customary or traditional functions and rites pertaining to the office of the Olowo of Owo for a period of six months. You will also cease to enjoy for the period specified all salaries, allowances and other perquisites attached to the office of the Olowo of Owo.

(3) That His Excellency has also decided that during the period of your suspension, you and your family will vacate the Afin and that the Afin will be cared for in the traditional way by which this is done when there is no Olowo in office. He ended by saying;

(4) That it is the ardent hope of His Excellency that this period of suspension will be utilised by you and the Owo people to restore mutual trust and confidence which will bring about real affection towards you from your subjects.

Appointments of Co-Regents

The Governor further appointed the following Chiefs as co-regents for the suspension period:

Chief OjumuFadeyi (Chairman),
Chief SasereAdetula (Deputy Chairman),
Chief OsereOlakunori,
Chief Akowa Daramola,
Chief Ajana Sule,
Chief Elerewe Olakunori,
Chief Aragwagbaiye Aboludi,
Chief Aralepo,
Chief Eminowa.

PACKING FROM THE PALACE (AFIN)

On June 15th, 1966 many Oloris (Olowo's wives), who had stayed for more than twenty-five years in the Palace (Afin), packed away solemnly to their respective places. Sir Olagbegi was in lbadan when the announcement was made over the radio and the national dailies. There he remained until after the suspension. The children, led by Mrs. Oladeseju Okunrinboye, took charge of personal properties and their removal to other houses in the town. And Chiefs Osuporu, Aribo and Olubola took charge of state properties which were handed over to the co-regents with the keys to the palace. Among the properties handed over were 16 (sixteen) Beaded Crowns, 2 (two) Beaded Gowns, 5 (five) State Swords, 10 (ten) Patako Akun, 1 (one) Seseki Gown, 17 (seventeen) State Umbrellas, I (one) Iyun Sword, and other 50 (fifty) items of royal properties listed out, signed for and received by the co-regents.

Peace Committees:

History recorded that it was a pathetic scene and people wept bitterly when the Olowo was leaving the town. The suspension came to many people as a surprise. But the families and friends courageously organised peace groups to appease the section of Owo people opposing Sir Olagbegi. Before the suspension, Sir Olateru had himself gone round the people and made concrete efforts at the Town Hall to appeal to the youths who were aggrieved. The Peace Committee led by Chief S. B. Aruwajoye and the members of the Egbe Otun Oluwa on the one hand and another led by Chiefs Aribo and Osuporu families on the other, went round the different sections of Owo Community and the Obas and other leaders in the Western State to bring lasting peace at Owo.

The then Permanent Secretary in the Ministry of Local Government stated that the governor had remarked that "it is gratifying to note that your Highness has been making continued efforts to reconcile yourself with those of your people who still show open hostility towards you. It is hoped that with the renewed efforts on your part, you will succeed in placating them."

Thus the original intention of the Government was presumably to allow tension to die down, but the political extremists were bent on having their pound of flesh. Two incidents happened to indicate these tendencies (1) The marketplace was changed to another place (Ogwata) used only during the interregnum of an Olowo. (2) Trees near the palace were cut (as if traditionally there was no Olowo). The then Military Governor of Western State, late Lieutenant-Colonel Adekunle Fajuyi, called the co-regents to order, and warned them against any further provocative actions, because, as he said, Sir Olateru was merely suspended and not deposed. It was understood that some of the boys who carried out the cutting of the trees near the palace died few hours after, a case where the tradition was apparently defending itself!

It is to be noted that, a month after the suspension in July 1966, late Lt. Col. Fajuyi was killed in the second coup. It then fell on Colonel Adeyinka Adebayo (who later became a Major-General), as Military Governor to witness the other aspects of this political crisis at Owo.

Incidents During Suspension

In spite of all efforts to resolve these matters at home and abroad, political fanatics continued to wage war both within villages and hamlets. Sir Olagbegi's large acres of cocoa, rubber, coffee and palm trees in different places were laid waste. Some were set on fire by the people. It was alleged that many of the cases were reported to the police but nothing was done.

Moreover, some chiefs and known supporters of Olateru were

allegedly flogged in the nights, and illegal courts were set up to try supporters of rival political party who were branded as "Olowo" people with the hand - the hand was the election symbol of the N.N.D.P.

A majority of Owo people greatly wondered what the Military Government was up to. Many people decided therefore to watch and pray since nobody appeared to be doing anything about the breakdown of law and order.

Reinstatement

The Permanent Secretary, Western State Ministry of Chieftaincy Affairs in a letter dated 14th December, 1966 wrote to reinstate Sir Olateru as the Olowo of Owo after the expiration of six months of the suspension thus: "Your Highness would have observed that the suspension order notified in Gazette No. W.P.L.N. No. 47 1966 ends at mid-night today 14th December1966. I am to inform you that the Council of Obas and Chiefs has advised His Excellency, the Military Governor, to the effect that you should be allowed to resume your office as soon as the order lapses."

The Permanent Secretary (Late Mr. O. Bateye) went to Owo to read the letter to the co-regents and some other people the next day. But that very night, two of Sir Olateru's houses were burnt by some unknown people and this matter was reported to the police. Surprisingly, no concrete action was taken by thegovernment.

One Year Self-Exile

After the reinstatement and judging by what was happening, Sir Olagbegi did not resume duty immediately as the Olowo. So, voluntarily, he stayed at Ibadan for more than one year to allow more time "to recultivate the affection and loyalty" of his people.

The following points might have been responsible for the failure of the reconciliation efforts made by the then power that-be

· The political opposition against Sir Olateru indicated that political vendatta was likely to be at work because none of the cases of arson, assault, and looting that was reported was effectively investigated.

Some official reactions to Sir Olateru's persecutions were unfavourable.

The political opponents at Owo, apart from the encouragement received from their political godfathers, have done many things to a point of no return and did not know what Sir Olagbegi's reaction would be on assumption of duty as the Olowo. Many feared his vengeance which he (Sir Olateru) had indicated in the press and radio was non-existent.

Some princes have been tipped as likely successors during the suspension and a lot of behind the-scene action had taken place to the extent that losing the battle against Sir Olateru meant total ruins financially and otherwise to them and their families.

Some local political leaders also saw their doom if Sir Olateru resumed duty as the Olowo

Sir Olagbegi's trial was also on the national level and his success or failure was a challenge to one of the political parties, and hence in the press and underground a particular political party aided and abetted anything that would adversely affect Sir Olateru's official post.

Although Sir Olateru was reinstated, no salary was paid him. This was another aspect of official highhandedness.

Press War

The Nigerian Press played a prominent role in Sir Olateru's affair during the crisis. The issue was important enough to catch newspaper headlines. Sir Olateru before this time had both consciously and unconsciously built such a powerful reputation for himself that very few natural rulers could contest with him in any propaganda scheme or mission, so he was always in the news. In addition, either through error of ommision or commission, both his supporters and opponents, rightly or wrongly, selected the news media to press home their points up to a state that none of the parties would like to loose the battle. Some of the sections of the press too were divided politically and so they also joined in championing the causes of their supporters. The Government too realizing its actions or inactions on this issue, particularly as it affected one of the leading traditional rulers in Nigeria found itself in a state of dilemma.

On the whole, during his trials. The press contributed one thing to Sir Olateru's popularity. That is, his ego and fortitude were nationalised and he nearly became an international figure.

With further reference to press publications in 1967, there was a full-length historic publication in the Woman's World about Sir Olateru's merits as the Olowo and many photographs about his activities. This annoyed some of his opponents at home apparently because publicity was still being given to somebody they wanted to 'crush'. In some newspapers where Sir Olateru was attacked there were captions such as the "Olowo's Affairs," containing adverse comments on his administration, "The case against the Olówó," and so on. And in some newspapers supporting him, one could read such things as, "Owo; we want Olagbegi II,"and so on.

Obas' Visit To Owo

As a result of this impasse, an arrangement was made for some prominent Obas to visit and meet the faction against Sir Olateru at Owo and to appeal to them. In February 1967, the Obas, led by late Sir Adesoji Aderemi, the Ooni of lfe, arrived Owo and held a meeting in the Town Hall with the faction opposing Sir Olateru. In the evening of that day, few of them were called to Akure where another meeting was held, but it was impossible to effect any settlement. A letter addressed to Sir Olagbegi by the Permanent Secretary, Ministry of Local Government read thus... "Kabiyesi, I am directed by His Excellency, the Military Governor, to inform you that he has received the report of the Council of Obas and Chiefs on their unsuccessful attempt at effecting reconciliations between you and your people during their recent visit to Owo. His Excellency has noted in particular that your brother Obas have advised you to take necessary steps to pacify your people in the traditional way and to report to the Council of Obas and Chiefs the result of your efforts by the end of May 1967.

"It is His Excellency's hope that your fresh efforts will achieve full reconciliation with your people by the end of May. If by that time, however, no agreement has been reached between you and your people, steps will be taken towards a final determination of the matter, in the public interest and the general welfare of the people of Owo."

Either by design or accident, the intervention of other Obas was alleged to have been organised to further certain political aspirations rather than reconciliation, and perhaps that was why it failed. The Owo meeting was assembled along the lines of political rally and it was not easy to talk to people in such a forum. A more rational and traditional way was adopted by the Obas when they called their leaders to Akure for heart-to-heart discussions, but this was not followed up beyond this point. For it is inconceivable for any group of people not to hearken to the voice of such highly-placed natural rulers.

Security Sought To Go To Owo

With all these happenings, Sir Olateru decided to go home so as to enable him continue the reconciliation efforts. He wanted to be there himself to be able to handle the problems himself. He knew the participants and the problems. Although, he might not be able to profer solutions to all the problems once and for all, he would be able to put heads together with the elders to find some amicable solution.

It was a state of emergency throughout the country. In spite of this, it was rumoured that some people in the opposition were determined to shoot him whenever he visited OWO. This was reported to the Government and the police. In order to avert any chaos during his proposed visit to Owo, Sir Olateru decided to seek full police protection for himself and his family during his visit from Ibadan.

But he was surprised when the Military Governor said he would only give him one unarmed orderly. Because of the State of Emergency, he was constrained to ask for police security from the Federal Government. Part of the letter to the inspector General of Police, Alhaji Kam Salem, read as follows:-

"It is with a deep sense of maintaining public order and security in Owo in the Western State that I am putting this urgent request before you to provide full security measures to convey me from Ibadan where I am residing temporarily now to Owo, my domain. At this period of our national crisis, it is appreciated that all efforts are being directed towards solving our national problems and I do pray that God may grant the Federal Government early victory over the enemies of the Republic. In any event, I hope you will give me the indulgence to state here briefly all the relevant facts necessitating this urgent request more so at this period of Emergency."

He enumerated some of the previous points and concluded by saying, "In conclusion therefore, I am earnestly and sympathetically requesting that a security guard of twelve armed personnel (or such number as may be deemed necessary) be assigned to accompany me to Owo and to stay there for a number of days to ensure peace, normalcy and tranquility in Owo. This request, apart from my personal safety, is made in consideration of the situation in the country generally, and the admitted incidence of violent crimes."

It is relevant to add here that the Council of Obas and Chiefs fully supported this idea of security. In reply, the Inspector General of Police provided Sir Olagbegi with 12 (twelve) armed policemen, but when they got to Ibadan, it was alleged that the Government disallowed them from carrying out their duties.

Three Months Ultimatum To Go To Owo

Exactly one year and one day after Sir Olagbegi had been reinstated, but was still in self-exile at Ibadan, the military Governor, Major General Adeyinka Adebayo at a press conference at Ibadan gave him three months to go to Owo to resume his official duties as the Olowo of Owo.

The following is a transcript of a tape-recorded exchange between General Adebayo (then Brigadier) and the Olowo of Owo:

BRIDADIER ADEBAYO: "Kabiyesi and gentlemen, I have come to the conclusion to make the position of the West Military Government clear over the matter of the Olowo of Owo. It appears the position of the West Military Government has been misunderstood in certain quarters despite the fact that I have personally taken it upon myself to see that Olowo returns to Owo. It appears that there is no appreciation for all my efforts and the efforts of the West Military Government.

"The decision to suspend the Olowo for six months was taken by my predecessor and I took over as the Military Governor during that suspension period. And in December last year, when the Six months' suspension expired, I lifted the suspension and I said to the Olowo then that he could go to Owo if he wanted. Before then, he came and saw me twice and I gave him my personal advice as a Yoruba man. And I think I can recollect quite rightly that I said he should use his fellow Obas to go to Owo and appeal to his people.

"And I think, quite rightly too, I said, on the second occasion, that instead of staying at Ibadan, he should move near his people. And infact I said on one of those two occasions that when I was small and when Obas got into trouble with their people, they used to use the darkness in going round to talk to their people.

"I was doing this as a Yoruba man and I was doing it as a military Governor, I was distressed early this year when a lot of publications were made in the newspapers because I thought newspaper wouldn't help the issue. Again, the publications have started, one in the Sunday Star of November this year, the second in the same Sunday Star of December 3, this year. And there was another one in the Morning Post last week. And the latest is in the Morning Post today.

"Well, I am not disproving the popularity of Olowo of Owo in Owo. I am not disputing the support of his Chiefs have for him. Again, some time this year, a lot of petitions were written to the Commander-in-Chief and infact certain authorities had to write to us from Lagos asking us or advising us, that's the way they put it now, that the Olowo should be returned to Owo. I have never said that the Olowo should not go to Owo. But I want to make my position clear today in the presence of Yoruba people, that the government, any government, whether military or civilian, has no right to force any Oba on his people. If the Olowo feels that he had the support of his people or others they call kingmakers, I will like those kingmakers to come to Ibadan and take the Olowo themselves from Ibadan. But I will like an assurance from the Olowo that there will be no trouble from Owo.

"On the other hand, no government whatsoever can impose an Oba on his people. It is the wish of the people to have an Oba and it is the wish of the people not to have an Oba. But categorically today, I will not force the Olowo of Owo to go to Owo. But if he feels he's safe, if he feels he has the majority support at Owo, I am prepared, well I will not force the issue.

"Again I will not use my soldiers to take the Olowo to Owo. But I am prepared to give you a police orderly, as I said before, to escort you to Owo. I think one of the papers quoted the instance of the Orangun of Ila that we sent troops to Ila before we enthroned the Orangun. This was absolutely false. We did not send troops to Ila. The Mobile Police went to Ila because they knew I was going there for my own personal security, not the security of Orangun. My troops and the mobile force went there for my own personal security.

"Again I should remind the audience that certain incidents took place at Owo about one month or six weeks ago in that some of the troops based at Owo were used in surrounding the house of one of the co-regents and the old man came to hospital in Ibadan for a few weeks. I personally saw him there. I am not saying the Olowo himself did all these things, but may be some of his supporters did it. I am not interested in that. I am moving all the soldiers from OWO. I have told the Area Commander to move the soldiers from Owo this week. And you (Olowo) are at liberty, if you feel you have the support of your people to go to Owo any time you like.

"The government will not force you to go to Owo and the government will only maintain law and order if trouble breaks out when you go there.

"Well, gentlemen, I think I should make my position clear. I will only say one thing again, that as from today, I don't want to see any publication in the papers about Olowo of Owo. Whether you (Olowo) tell me that you wrioe the publication or not. I will not like to see anything in the papers because if I do I will take serious action against whoever writes the thing or whoever incites the people to write. Lastly, I will give you, as from today, three months to settle your trouble with your people. If you don't settle within the next three months I will take drastic action about the whole situation."

Sir Olateru Olagbegi's Reply

"Your Excellency, the Honourable Ministers and other gentlemen. I can say that I am absolutely flabbergasted at the action His Excellency has shown here this morning about me. Some time ago, I went to Chief Ajayi (the then Commissioner for Local Government) and said that I would like to see His Excellency with Chief Ajayi himself. Three days ago, I got a call that I should book an appointment with the Private Secretary which I did. And fortunately yesterday, the Private Secretary rang up that I should see His Excellency at around 9 o'clock. And coming here is just to see His Excellency and to beg of him, after a year and a day of revocation of the suspension, to go home. Perhaps when coming I made a note or two but not knowing that His Excellency will be making the speech he had made about me.

"Before going through one or two things I put down I think it will be only better to reply to His Excellency's remarks that he has just made about me, because, as I said earlier, I never knew that he was going to take this form at all. To be frank and as a Christian I haven't seen the Morning Post of this morning. I don't know at the moment what it has spoken about me. I think newspapers in every country can say what they like. But the action is there with those responsible for authority. The Governor of the Western state, as a plenipotentiary, can do what he likes. He is a man with full powers so that if any publication comes out again, according to him, he will deal with any papers of that type. That lies with him. He can do anything because with me, I know that whatever I write, I shall always direct my letters through the Governor to anywhere I like to write. And I think I have the right to do that, I did one at a time through him during which His Excellency thought perhaps I have seen Major General Yakubu Gowon. I told him I've never met him (General Gowon). And up till today, I am saying, I am under his regime with that of the Governor and l am bound as one of the Obas and one of the Nigerian citizens, to uphold and support him in all that he's doing.

"Then a reply came through His Excellency to my petition that the settlement of the matter is within the competence of the government here. In other words, the settlement of the matter is in the hands of the Governor. Well, His Excellency has made mention of police. It was true I've been here. Perhaps this is the second time since His Excellency has been here (in office). He made mention of giving me an orderly. Your Excellency, when so many of my opponents have been here to threaten and to talk ill about me, of shooting at me if they should see me, I told him that what I needed was a full security, which for God's sake he should give to me as your humble servant. At a time, he said a policeman should be given to me and the police constable should be unarmed. I told him, I don't think this is fair to me as a citizen, as one of the responsible people in your State. And when our late father, the late Alake, I shouldn't mention him perhaps, when he was to go home (from exile in Oshogbo), he was given full security. But all these put together, I was thinking what was good for the goose was also good for the gander. If security has been provided for people, why on earth has it not been provided for me, if I am a citizen under you, and if you are not taking any side, and if even I have not wronged you. Each time I come here, he will tell me he has sympathy for me, he hasn't anything against me.

"Well, as a Christian, I take it from him he's exactly like that. He has the power, he should give me security home, regarding me as one of his citizens, regarding me as one of his humble servants. If there should be riot in the place (Owo), it is not an individual that should face it.

"I said inter alia I was to beg it of His Excellency to allow me to go back home. It was a year yesterday, since I have been languishing in a sort of exile in this place. For God's sake and as a citizen, he should help me.

"There is nothing after all that is static in this world. I thought I was going to see him in private with Chief Ajayi. He (Governor Adebayo) was In London and I know how he felt about it before he was made Governor. I had some friends with you then. I know how much you felt for me before you ever came to this place. And why on earth? You are the same man! If you were able to feel for me 4,000 miles away, why no sympathy while you and I are sitting down together?

"Nobody can ask me not to come to Owo provided His Excellency approves of it. My suspension was announced consecutively for three days but when it was lifted, not a word about it on radio. Now he may be younger than I, he's father today to whom God has given the sword. He shouldn't use it for one man and not for another. You can't punish a man twice for anything. For 27 years on the throne, there was no bad report about me. No corruption, no oppression. The Olowo of Owo had misunderstanding with his people, same with the Alake and some Obas."

"I am your son, you are the father. To whom am I going to run?

"Have sympathy for God's sake on me. For almost 27 years on the throne, I had no trouble. Go and see my record and get well your part for there the honour lies. Once an Oba is recognised by government, nobody must molest him or disturb the peace of the town. You said it at Ila. See that nobody disturbs me. Make it workable in my case.

"I was born and bred in Owo. It pleased God to make me their Oba all these years. I remember the Oyo riot. It is wise of that one learns from the misfortune of others. Please, for God's sake, for God's sake, have sympathy with me. Give me protection to go back home, for God's sake. I appeal to His Excellency to let me go to my home, according to the advice of the Council of Obas and Chiefs and their begging on my behalf, Commissioners, leaders of the Yorubas, the Civil Service, for God's sake, give me protection to return home. Chief B.A. Ajayi, I beg you, please."

After a long silence, Governor Adebayo replied to the Olowo.

GOVERNOR ADEBAYO: "I will not allow any of the Commissioners to speak. I am happy I called this meeting and the manner in which I called it, I am happy you (Olowo) are able to speak out. From what you have said, it appears to me now that I am the accuser."

OLOWO OF OWO: "Please, for God's sake you are not."

GOVERNOR ADEBAYO: "It appears, Kabiyesi, you have not appreciated my effort or it appears that I am lying to you. No one advised me when I lifted the suspension order.

"Again, I was the one who forced your brother Obas to go to Owo. Personally, I disgraced people carrying placards in the hall and on the road.

"Again when the Inspector General said you should be given 12 armed men to go back to Owo I sent a Commissioner of Police to visit the place. He reported and I sent the report to Lagos. I was not bound to send the report to Lagos. Chieftaincy affairs is a state matter and not Federal."

OLOWO OF OWO:-"If you kick me out who is going to beg you?"

GOVERNOR ADEBAYO:"It is all right, I am not annoyed with you, I cannot be annoyed with you at all, because you are my father. You said I was taking sides. That's an unfortunate statement to make. But I am not annoyed. Wiith whom should I take sides? You mentioned the case of the Olu. That is the Midwest. This is Yorubaland. If the Governor then in the Midwest felt the Olu was wrongly deposed, he had a right to reinstate the Olu of Warri. I have a duty to you as well as to the people of Owo. How can I impose you on the people at this time when there is a war and when I knew we are going to meet the force of the people there.

"I will not take you to Owo by force. I have done my best to talk to your people. But if you decided to go today, I will not stop you. I will give you an orderly to take you from here, but I will not place you in a Rolls-Royce in a motorcade and bodyguards. But I will make sure police are there to maintain peace. I will tell the Police at Owo that the Olowo is now on his way, make sure there is no trouble there.

"I know the tempo at Owo. But since you said your chiefs have support of the people, well, what is the problem? There is no problem. If you feel I have not done my duty, I know I have satisfied myself that I have done my duty. You have the right as Olowo of Owo to go to Owo. I will advise the police to keep the peace, but if there's any riot at Owo. I will deal ruthlessly with Owo and those that caused it..."

The stage was thus set for what came to be the final battle. The press and the radio carried this news in an elaborated way as if there was going to be war somewhere- it was top of the news on the radio and front page headlines in all the national newspapers. After this, everybody was waiting for what will happen next. Will the Olowo take up the challenge? If so, when will he go to Owo with one unarmed orderly? These and other questions were agitating the minds of the general public. The recorded tape of the discussion was not made public otherwise everybody could have known what exactly transpired at the meeting. All that was reported in the radio and front page stories was that, "The Olowo was given three months ultimatum to go home." For instance, the public was not made aware about the Olowo's humane and sympathetic appeal, the Governor's stand over press statements and the question of security and the fact that the Governor said he would deal ruthlessly with anybody causing trouble on Olowo's arrival. The expectations and tensions among the citizenry were high. People were anxious to know what would follow within the three months.

Arrangements

At first, nothing happened - at least not through the month of January 1968. But all sides must have been preparing hard on what to do, and how to react if certain things happened. At Owo, nobody knew exactly what the Olowo's opponents would do, but there were confirmed rumours that some people would employ thugs to cause trouble, and the Olowo's supporters countered by employing hunters to guard the Olowo's house in the night. Two of his houses had been burnt in the night. But nobody knew that such a large scale violence in broad daylight involving the burning of about 90 (ninety) houses, would ever occur on the ninth of February. Later, it was alleged that thugs from Ibadan were employed, together with some from Owo, to set on fire some marked houses of the Olowo and those of some of his known supporters, along with a plan to eliminate the Olowo.

On the other hand, the Olowo was steadfast in his prayers more often than not at Ibadan and praying that God may guide him all right, but as far as going to Owo was concerned, he had firmly said, "Nobody" can stop me from going to Owo." So he had decided to go, come what may. He kept the date and time of his return firmly to himself alone. Three important happenings must be mentioned at this point- (1) When some of his supporters from Owo reported to him that it was necessary to buy their own guns in case of any revolts on his arrival at Owo, Sir Olateru's reply was that nobody should fight anybody as he did not want his reign to be marred by bloodshed. He added that if the government was on his side as promised by the Governor nothing would happen. (2) After the awful incidents, it was later alleged that paid spies were sent around the Olowo by some big men to know the actual date so that their plan for the violence might not fail, and (3) Realizing that the Olowo's great psychic powers could make him foresee such pending catastrophe, and the possible changing of his plan, they therefore employed some powerful African charms so that he could not alter the date. Whether this was true or not, it happened. And under normal circumstances, some people agreed that he could apprehend such things with his enormous powers and could have change his mind to go at another time. Maybe it was God's wish. Julius Ceaser knew and so did our Lord Jesus Christ. They -the great men- always knew what would happen to them.

Journey To Owo

The expectations amongst the people of Owo was that the Oba would come in his Rolls Royce and this would have made the alleged plan to eliminate him and his supporters as soon as he arrived Owo quite easy. But, the Olowo disguised in a French suit and sat in one of the land rovers used by the OKE-ANU church of Ibadan with the inscription "JESU LONI" There were two cars in front and behind. The journey which should have started as early as 9 o' clock in the morning did not take-off until 2 o'clock in the afternoon because of somebody who volunteered to go with the Olowo. (Later recognized as one of the spies) but who failed to turn-up at 9 o'clock as previously arranged.

The plan was to arrive Owo quietly during the day before people would be aware of his arrival to avoid confusion from anybody who might have wished to take the law into his own hands. Little did anybody know that on the same date, a meeting was arranged to be held in the town hall - and the telephone from Ibadan to Owo was not to be interrupted so that the Olowo's journey stage by stage might be monitored.

At this time, there were road blocks on the way because the Nigerian Civil War was going on. So the Olowo's entourage was thoroughly searched by wild military officers at about 15 road blocks. But the interesting aspect of it was that while about eight men were always asked to alight from the vehicle in which the Olowo was, he alone was left inside without a word to him not even to honour him as the Olowo. This was miraculous. He was not recognised as anybody at all. Anyone in the vehicle that day would have concluded that even if heaven were going to fall at Owo, the Olowo would be safe, and so it was.

At Owo

Immediately the people who had been holding a marathon meeting in the Town Hall saw the van going towards the direction of the palace, somebody was sent to check who it was.

The trouble might have been spontaneous if they had seen the Rolls Royce they were expecting. But somebody who had previously been kept at the palace (Afin) quickly ran to them at the venue of the meeting and assured them that it was the Olowo. There and then all their plans were let loose. The Olowo's van was first set ablaze to prevent his escape from the palace. From about 5 p.m., when Sir Olateru entered Owo on the 9th February, 1968 till 5 a.m. the following morning, about seventy houses (including six of his own) were set on fire. While about thirty were looted. The plan was too perfect to be believed.

As said earlier, the plan was said to be a secret one and not one (repeat not one) of the Olowo's people or supporters knew that he would be arriving that day. It was feared that if they knew, the opponents would get to know and they would have planned to cause trouble. So up till today, some people still denied the story as true. This was so because in the pandemonium that broke up, everybody ran for the safety of his or her life and property since nobody knew the next line of action of the rioters. It was already dark and up till the next morning before the Olowo was taken away by the police, nobody saw him, of both the supporters and the opponents.

It was alleged that the lukewarm attitude of the police and the army towards the rioters escalated the problem. This, inspite of the fact that both Chiefs Elerewe and Osuporu had informed the police and the army in advance without any positive response from both ends. The police and the army later claimed to be waiting for directives from Ibadan.

Later, since they were not prepared to do anything while "Rome was burning" some people drove to Akure about fourty eight kilometres away. But for the safety of those sent, they had to make an Isrealite journey of going through Ikare and Ado-Ekiti, which amounted to about one hundred and thirty two kilometres.

Throughout that night, word went round especially in important circles that the rioters had succeeded. For instance, when some of Olateru's supporters got to Akure that night, the Police Officer inquired from them whether they were sure that the Olowo was still alive at Owo. They told him he was there at the palace. Then the officer got his men ready for Owo to arrest the situation. It was already daybreak and the Olowo was out alone in the whole of the big palace (the thugs had all run away for fear of being discovered). The Olowo walked to his sister's house about three hundred metres away from the palace and sent Chief Ogunrinde (who was surprised to see him) to the Owo police station. Chief Ogunrinde was about to be detained when the police officer from Akure who arrived at the same time invited him to take him (the officer) to where the Olowo was. On getting to the place, he invited the Olowo to come with him to Akure but the Olowo insisted that the police officers should remain in Owo to maintain peace. But the officer insisted that he was acting on orders from the Government. At last Sir Olateru went with them to Akure where he stayed for three nights in a Rest House before he was asked to be brought to Ibadan.

The following points must be mentioned in any accurate account of those wonderful events

(1) The Olowo's safety at the palace was miraculous. There was no help from any security agency, the army nor the police, but God Almighty. He was there throughout the night with a friend, one Mr. Ogunyoye Majekodunmi, who came with him from Ibadan.

When asked how he escaped, the Olowo said he was praying throughout the night. But Mr. Ogunyoye said he witnessed a great spiritual activity, because he saw the Olowo in action in full powers for the first time in his life and that it was a display of God-given African powers. He explained that with prayers and other incantations, the Olowo was able to confound the surging crowd especially two of them who shot at him and fled, leaving their guns in fear (One of them was alleged to have actually confirmed the story: he said that as bold as he was, he did not know what forced him to throw away his gun and flee).

(2).The trouble at Owo was one-sided. If the Olowo's faction had been alerted, there would have been bloodshed which did not occur although sixty houses were set on fire. History will record this as a great credit to Sir Olagbegi's tolerance.

(3). At Akure when the Police Officer phoned to inform the late Deji of Akure to extend greetings to Olowo, he asked the officer whether the police officer knew the Olowo very well and asked him to drop the telephone and come to him. When he came back, the officer told his supporters that the Deji wanted to ascertain whether it was true he actually saw the Olowo (who was presumed dead)

(4) At Owo, the faction against the Olowo summoned a meeting to congratulate themselves after the incident the following day. One particular Chief who presided said he was happy that the Olówó had been fought to a standstill (not knowing that the Olowo was alive and kicking at Akure).

(5) The Press also carried the news in no less frightening ways with headlines such as, "Olowo in hiding..., Where is the Olowo?" and so on. During an interview with pressmen at Akure, it was reported under a Daily Times front page headline that Olagbegi said amongst others, "I have seen death but did not die. I expect the governor to fulfill his promise to deal ruthlessly with the trouble makers."

At the same time, he prayed for his adversaries that "God may forgive them for they knew not what they are doing." A particular press report claimed that the Olowo had been killed and maliciously concluded that it was the Olowo who had given himself to his enemies.

The third day, the Olowo was taken to Ibadan and he stayed in his house with policemen on guard. At this stage, nobody knew what was going on and what was going to happen. No arrest was made at Owo until days after the complaints have been lodged with the police. The following historic events happened during this period:

(a) The Owo people and the Kingmakers still indicated their loyalty for Sir Olateru as the Olowo and dissociated themselves from the lawlessness by some political groups which they condemned for lacking confidence in themselves.

(b) Following this stand, an arrangement was made to amend the Chieftaincy Declaration of 1957 by reducing the kingmakers from twenty to seven so as to appoint a new Olowo.

(c) When the jet-speed action was going on, Owo people in a mass rally, organised a press conference in Lagos and attempted to see the Head of State, General Gowon, on the matter.

(d) In spite of this, on the 18th November, 1968, a new Olowo was appointed.

(e) In March, 1969, Sir Olateru's deportation order was cancelled.

(f) During all these times, Owo people continued to pay Sir Olateru visits and in the peak of confusion and provocation, he always appealed to them to remain calm and that by God's power, everything will be alright. He gave definite instructions that nobody should retaliate or resort to the use of force.

Chapter 6

SIR OLATERU OLAGBEGI'S 80TH BIRTHDAY CELEBRATION

History was made on August 21, 1990 when Sir Olateru Olagbegi (KBE) attained a prime age of 80- a decade more than the recommended Biblical injunction which is 70 years.

The occasion was marked with Pomp and Pegeantry by his family, children, friends and foes alike both at Owo and Lagos.

The event was well reported both in the print and electronic media. Hitherto, the preparation for the great occasion started in earnest in 1989 when it was envisaged by his kids that papa would be 80 in August 1990. A planning committee that would organise a befitting party for him was set up by his family and friends alike.

The celebrant at first felt reluctant to be declared such an old man when he was so "young" at heart and as strong as a lion. Oftentimes, he would jokingly pose such question to his children. "By" how many years am I older than you? His 70th birthday could not be celebrated in 1980 because of the same argument of his fear to be declared an old man.

An elaborate preparation was made so that the occasion would be a huge success. The programme of activities covered a week. The ceremony started with a special dinner on Monday September 24, 1990 at the Lagoon Restaurant in Victoria Island, Lagos. The dinner party was chaired by the Late Rt. Hon. (Sir) Adetokunbo Ademola, the first Chief Justice of the Federation.

A billiard tournament followed on Tuesday September 25, 1990 and almsgiven on Wednesday September 26, 1990. This was followed by a tennis tournament on Thursday September 27 and worship at the Owo Central Mosque on Friday, September 28, 1990. The occasion was rounded off with a church service at Saint Andrews Church, Owo, on September 30 and a night party same day at Owo.

The whole of Owo town wore a new look and the people enjoyed every second of the occasion. Even though Sir Olateru Olagbegi had not been reinstated as the Olowo of Owo, the impression of most people was as if he had once again crowned as the Oba. Feasting of all and sundry was the order of the day and about 30 cows were slaughtered for this joyous occasion, and each family got substantial parts of the cows as their shares as demanded by Yoruba culture.

The Thanksgiving collections both at the Mosque and the church during the occasion were among the highest in the history of the town.

The occasion should have been marred because a political undertone was read into the celebration and efforts were made to stop this joyous occasion.

The late Oba Joseph Adekola Ogunoye II, the then Olowo of Owo, went to court in order to file a motion exparte brought under order 33 (2) of Ondo State Rules of the High Court.

The applicant's prayer (Oba Ogunoye II) was for an interim injunction as shown in the ex parte motion vl 2 restraining the defendant until the determination of a motion on notice from publishing anything which portrays or tends to portray him as Olowo of Owo and (2) restraining him from performing any rites or doing anything capable of portraying him as Olowo of Owo. The second prayer is to restrain the defendant, his servants, privies and agents from wearing, distributing or wearing an African print material (Exhibit A) at the Celebration of his 80th birthday anniversary or at anytime whatsoever until the determination of the motion on notice.

It is heartening to note that the application was dismissed. Hence the programme went on without any hitch. It should also be noted that his children outside the country celebrated the occasion abroad.

This shows one thing: the unity that subsists among the family of Sir Olateru Olagbegi.

His memorable speech at the occasion is hereby reproduced:-

FIRST and foremost, my sincere thanks go to the Almighty God for preserving my life up till the present moment. If I have millions of tongues, I don't feel I can adequately thank the Almighty God for all his mercies on me and my families inspite of all odds and tribulations.

I want to thank the Chairman of this occasion and all other guests for responding to the invitation of my children to honour me for attaining the age of 80. It has given me an opportunity of meeting many of my friends from far and near. I will never forget this ceremony and the sight of you all as long as I live.

On life generally, I think we all here know that life is full of interesting and exciting moments, from the time when one is born to the time one answers the call of God. I would not waste your time here to talk about my own experiences of life, some of them have been public property. There will be a time for all these in future. But I have noticed that one needs a great spiritual drive to do many things, to achieve many ambitions, and to climb great heights. I thank God again here for giving me some of these qualities to work in the past and up till the moment for my great country Nigeria generally and Ondo State and Owo Division in particular.

Moreover, I am overwhelmed with joy at this occasion that I don't think I have room for making speeches on current affairs. Nevertheless I am appealing to the government to provide for the position of Obas and Chiefs in the country at least a consultative body in our constitution. As regards our present transitory period, I seize this opportunity for congratulating the government for a job well done so far, and to congratulate our Head of State, President Badamosi Babangida for all his activities and to wish him everlasting success.

I would like to thank all my children for what they have done. They have spent both time and money to make this Celebration a success. It is my prayer that the God Almighty will continue to help them and that their own children may do similar things for them in future. It has never been my wish to celebrate my Birthday publicly. I am therefore caught unawares when they decided to celebrate it. I am therefore very happy to thank them publicly and my wives, the Oloris, for doing all these things.

Finally I thank Chief Bero for the able way he has proposed my toast and for all the interesting things he said about me. I am deeply touched also by what our former Head of State, General Olusegun Obasanjo, said about me. It has evidently proved to me that a friend in need is a friend indeed.

Once again, I thank you all. God bless.

OLUSEGUN OBASANJO
P. O. Box 2286 Abeokuta Ogun State.

8th September, 1990

Prince Lafo Olateru-Olagbegi,
Honourable Secretary,
Sir Olateru Olagbegi Family Union,
c/o 1, Oke Olagbegi Rest House,
P. O. Box 1,
Owo,, Ondo State.

Dear Prince,

I WRITE to acknowledge the receipt of your letter of 5th September, 1990, and to thank you for your thoughtfulness in inviting me to the Special Dinner in honour of Sir Olateru Olagbegi on the occasion of his 80th Birthday celebration on Monday, 24th September 1990. Unfortunately, I will be in New York for another ceremony from which I cannot be absent.

I came to know Sir Olagbegi only since I served in Ibadan from 1967. Sir Olateru Olagbegi is indeed a remarkable individual, matured and great in wisdom. A man imbued with polished dignity and gentlemanly conduct. His philosophical calmness in the face of adversity is apparently the prime fountain of his strength. An engaging traditional ruler, with an admixture of love, awe and fear from his subjects and hate from his adversaries. His choice to face his fate with a renewed believe and conviction in himself, rather than jeopardise the social equilibrium of his kingdom and subjects, is a pointer to the innate goodness in him.

Sir Olateru Olagbegiis a natural royalty. I believe his unfortunate deposition in those dark days neither detracted from, nor diminished his personal clout. Some are indeed born great. Greatness cannot be bought, although it may be courted. Sir Olagbegi was born great while achieving greatness at the same time.

Siring a large family is an arduous task in itself, but being able to manage and organise such with limited disequilibration and disintegration at the time of adversity must draw the necessary kudos to the man at the head of the family. The fact that Sir Olateru-Olagbegi can enjoy so much goodwill from Members of his family, after all said and done, is an indication of the degree and level of the bond of affection and loving tenderness with which Sir Olagbegi has organised and built his life, his person and his family. I join all of you in saluting the builder and achiever in him and the indomitable courage be bad always exhibited.

Sir Olagbegi is a builder of resource, who laid the first brick in his life on the edifying rock of tolerance and determination to face life with all its vicissitude. Like the wise builder who choose to erect his house on a rock, Sir Olagbegi's life and all that he lived for and symbolized, has withstood the vagaries of an inclement political weather.

Mine is a salute to courage, a salute to resourcefulness and a salute to the grave wisdom, of age and of royalty undiminished and underided by ephemeral negativities.

His contemporaries are unfortunately becoming endangered species due to the fine mortality of humankind. We can only hope, pray and ask the good Lord to spare him long enough for us to drink in sufficient quantum from his weatherbeaten experience and wisdom. May his last days be resplended with fortune, satisfaction, blessings of God and vindication.

Congratulations sir Olagbegi and accept my sincere wishes for many happy returns.

Regards.

Yours sincerely

General Olusegun Obasanjo

OLUSOLA OLOIDI

DR. SOLA SARAKI
M.B.,B.S, (LONDON) L.R.C.P. (LOND) M.R.C.S. (ENG)
THE TURAKI OF ILORIN

N: 661537/664029 21/25 Broad Street, P.O.Box 3798, Lagos, Nigeria

The Hon.Secretary,
Sir Olateru Olagbegi Family Union,   29th June, 1990
c/o 1 Oke Olagbegi Rest House,
P.O. Box 1,
Owo,
Ondo State.

Dear secretary,
SIR OLATERU OLAGBEGI'S 80TH BIRTHDAY ANNIVERSARY

I like to acknowledge the receipt today (29th June, 1990) of your letter of 8th June instance, informing me of the family's joint intention to organize the 80th birthday anniversary of our beloved father, Sir Olateru Olagbegi, which event comes up on August 10, 1990.

I also like to say that I give my fullest support to the deliberations, decisions and ratifications of the Planning Committee in this matter and commit the members of the Committee into God's guidance in the effort.

Please do not hesitate to keep me informed, as soon as possible, of the over-all decision of the Committee and the terms biding on each member of the family in the bid to ascertain the success of the anniversary.

Long live our father, Sir Olateru Olagbegi!

Thank you

Yours sincerely
DR. SOLA SARAKI
TURAKI OF ILORIN

OMO N'OBA EREDIAUWA CFR
OBA OF BENIN

THE PALACE
P.O. BOX 1
BENIN CITY

Our Ref: No. Palace. 98/Vol.V/110   Date: January, 1991

Sir, Olateru - Olagbeji, K. O. E.,
O W O.

Dear Sir Olateru,

    During the preparation for your last birthday Anniversary celebration, I received an invitation for which I was most delighted even though my name was wrongly spelt. Unfortunately however, I actually saw the card after the event. Since the envelope bore no postage stamp, I asked my office how it came. My Secretary informed me that it was brought by your daughter who introduced herself as a lecturer in the University of Benin. It was my intention to invite her to discuss the celebration and how she could lead my Chiefs to give you my greetings but strangely enough, my Secretary has been unable to re-establish contact with her and that has been responsible for the delay in sending this letter. I cannot wait for my Secretary's search any longer. Belated as it is, I hereby offer you my felicitations and wish you many more years in continued good health.

2.   I hope, once this contact has opened, to be able to visit you one of these days, if I may. This was another thing I had wanted to discuss with your daughter if I met her - the possibility of paying a visit.

    Best wishes.

Erediauwa

OMO N'OBA EREDIAUWA,
OBA OF BENIN.

Sir Olateru Olagbegi

Sir Olateru signs the marriage register of his daughter Adedolapo – Mrs Yusuf at the marriage Registry in 1959

Sir Olateru Olagbegi and the audience during the proceedings of the
KUMAPAYI INQUIRY

When Sir Olateru succeeded in getting telephone for Owo in 1948, it was amidst great joy and jubilations

The famous Rolls Royce WQ 1 which the town could not boast of was owned by the Kabiyesi. It was used on important occasions. Sir Olateru allowed his children used it for their weddings
"I will not carry you to Owo in a Rolls Royce" Not this one but that of the Gove rnment"

The director of Prison Mr. Ajomo Adepoji welcomed Sir Olateru to the organization's party in 1974

Adeyanju (B. Litt. Oxford) Folagbade (LLB. London and Adebamiji (M. A. Town Planning) were about to sail to U. K. in 1960 for the golden flees which they won creditably. Here their father and the captain of M.V. Aureolivere wishing them "bon voyage"

What a clever management; A photograph of Princes and Princesses of Sir Olateru in 1956 after a thanksgiving Church Service

In the House of Parliament in London in 1950 – Chief Obafemi Awolowo, Sir Olateru, The Yeyesa and Late Chief Sashere behold for the first time the historical moment of the English System of Parliamentary Democracy

At 65 years Still Strong and Agile

Sir John Rankine the Governor of the Western Region was in attendance during Sir Olateru's Anniversary Celebration on March 13th 1956

Sir Olateru with Chief Aruwajoye and Late Chief Sasere in Cornwell England during their historical visit to U.K in 1950

Sir Olateru at the Ministers' Quarters in 1954 at Ibadan

His Lawyer son, Folagbade, presented his case during one of the sittings of the IKUMAPAYI INQUIRY

Sir Olateru Olagbegi with the Olu of Warri

Sir Olateru Olagbegi with His Olori (Queen) in London

Chapter 7

WHAT PEOPLE SAY ABOUT SIR OLATERU OLAGBEGI

Sir Olateru Olagbegi was one of the sons of Late Olagbegi I - the Olowo of Owo. He was installed the Olowo of Owo in 1941 at the age of 31 years. He was very dynamic and progressive. He enjoyed the co-operation of his High Chiefs whom he used to entertain lavishly at the Palace. He was the favourite of the youths. He was one of the well known Obas in then Western Region. He played a leading-role in the Nigerian politics and he was made a Minister-Without-Portfolio in the old Western House of Assembly.

Immediately he came to the throne, he started with the renovation of the Palace. He urged the Chiefs and the town people to do the same in their respective houses. The development of Owo town was uppermost in his mind.

Sir Olateru Olagbegi gave plots of land freely to people who were prepared to develop them. He was a social figure among his comrades who described him as a courageous and ambitious Oba. This good ambition became clear when he was made the Chairman of the Western State House of Obas in succession to the Ooni of Ife in the early 1960s.

He made education one of his priorities immediately he came to the throne. He urged the youths to go and further their education. This call made many youths to look for Secondary Schools outside Owo that had no Secondary schools by then. He used to visit these grammar schools outside Owo to see the progress of these Owo youths. He wanted same for his children who were then in the Primary Schools and he arranged for lesson teachers to coach them in the Palace. He was instrumental to the founding of Imade College which was followed by many other Secondary Schools at Owo in the late 40s and early 50s.

Sir Olateru Olagbegi wanted the best for his town and people, he saw to it that pipeborne water came to the reach of Owo and environs in the early 50s and was followed by electricity in the late 50s. Whenever Sir Olateru Olagbegi visited Lagos, the love for his subjects used to make him go round the Ministries to seek employments for Owo sons and daughters who might be jobless.

Through the dynamism of Sir Olateru Olagbegi, the Roman Catholic Mission established its hospital at Owo, the Town Hall was built, and most of the bushy places in the centre of the town now have imposing mansions put-up on them; examples are the Fajuyi Road, Uka Road, Ogwaluwa Street. All these places and many others were given out by Sir Olateru-Olagbegi, free of charge.

This period was the peak of Development in the history of Owo when Sir Olateru Olagbegi was the Dynamo and Chief M. A. Ajasin was the Battery.

After the period listed above, I was away from Nigeria and thus cannot say what happened at Owo that brought about the fall of Sir Olateru-Olagbegi.

Why He Fell

Some people, especially the elites, said he was ambitious and vindictive. If there is any retrogression in Owo today, it is due to the disagreement between Sir Olateru Olagbegi and Chief M. A. Ajasin who were the dynamo and battery respectively as far as Owo past development and progress were Concerned.

Sir Olateru Olagbegi is my brother-in-law (He married my sister who had died since 1951)

I want to remain anonymous, please.

Sir Olateru Olagbegi came from a royal family at Owo and became an Oba from 1941 to 1968.

During his tenure as an Oba, he made sure that anytime or anywhere he sees you, the first question that he will ask you is about your work. And if you give a negative answer, that is you don't have job, he will give you notes to various companies, and surely one of them will give you a job.

He is an elder Statesman that will not allow his fellow citizen to suffer.

I don't know him much.

Dayo Adegoke
Chief Executive Officer,
Adedayo Adegoke Enterprises, Lagos.

Sir Olateru Olagbegi is blessed with all good things of life especially the four essentials that human beings crave for; abundant wealth, children, long life and good health. Despite his wealth and popularity, he is humble and eager to learn from others. He is a pride to Ondo State nay Nigeria.

Chief Imam of Owo in a sermon during his 80th Birthday Celebration in 1990

Sir Olateru Olagbegi is blessed with useful and successful children. His children are found in nearly all professions both within and outside the country. No doubt, he is a successful, hardworking and lucky man. He has done well within the 80 years of his life. He is an asset to Owo people.

Officiating Minister at St. Andrew's Church, Owo during his 80th Btrthday Celebration.

7th October, 1968.

Sir.Olateru Olagbegi,
Rest House
c/o Divisional Office,
Okitipupa.

My Dear Cousin,

MANY thanks for your letter of the 30th September. It is God's opportune time that the engagement of your boy to Miss Kuyinu has brought us together again. From time, there was nothing that could have severed our relationship other than the Ojomo Chieftaincy dispute. It was after several years that I sat down and thought over the matter that what did anyone gain by quarelling with one another? Owo is such a God created town that everyone is connected with every family either father or mother side.

I have learnt after some years of serious thought that, if I do not agree with you, why shouldn't I agree with your children who may agree with me. I do not at any time pray for the downfall of any of my town man. What does it profit me? I will never claim to be an Egba, Ijebu or Lagosian. Is it my glory that you or your properties were destroyed? In the eye of an educated man, I am regarded as an element who came from a barbarous part of Nigeria. Why? Because when the people were quarreling with their Oba they proceeded to destroy his houses and property. Very few of our people ever sat down and think about this.

It is a fact that I have been away from home since 1918 but that does not make me to agree with those called civilized men in Owo to encourage the destruction of people's houses and properties. What position I have attained today, I claim I come from Owo. Michael Ojomo will not be called a member of the Alake, the Awujale or Oshemawe family. The children of the Apele, The Oniyere or the Oloba are my children and whatever comes on my way, I will do for any of them.

The matter of Ojomo Chieftaincy has from time immemorial been a thorn in the flesh of the Oke-Owo people and it was an ill wind which blows nobody any good.

I am not in favour or ever supported any element who agitated for your destruction and God forbid I should have hands in such plan. Rest assured that your children are mine and whatever concerns any of them concerns me;

Do not look forward to the changes and chances of this life in fear; rather look to them with full hope that as they arise, God, whose you are, will deliver you out of them. He has kept you hitherto. Do you but hold fast to his dear hand, and He will lead you safely through all things; and, when you cannot stand, He will bear you in His arms. Do not look forward to what may happen tomorrow.

Our Father will either shield you from suffering or He will give you strength to bear it.

Whatever way you think I can be of service to you here, please do not hesitate to send or write.

Believe in God that you will surmount the present difficulties and trials, "that after winter followeth summer, after night the day returneth, and after a tempest a great calm."

Yours sincerely,

M. E. Ojomo.

OLUSOLA OLOIDI

ESTERN STATE LAWN TENNIS ASSOCIATION
(Affiliated to the Nigeria Lawn Tennis)

Secretariat
Western State Sport Council
Liberty Stadium,
P.M.B 5106 Ibadan

9th December, 1974.

DR. A.O. OJOMO
AYO ADEGIKE
2411-3
NO VALTA.3/ VoL.II/50.
Sir Olateru Olagbegi, K.B.B,
1, Sir Kofo Abayomi Avenue,
Papa,

Kabiyesi,

Letter of Appreciation

The chairman and the entire members of the Western State Lawn Tennis Association thank you most sincerely for making it possible to be present at the last Western State Lawn Tennis open championships which took place on the 30 th November, 1974. The Association is also grateful for the cash donation presented to the winner and the runner-up of Sir Olateru Olagbegi Cup.

2. The Association notes with satisfaction and joy, your great interest and contribution to sports and especially L,awn Tennis. It is on record that your contribution to the promotion of sports in this state is unparalleled.

3. We sincerely hope that God will grant you long life and good health for the continuation of the noble role you are playing to promote sports.

4. With warm regards.

Yours faithfully,

(AYO. ADEGOKE)
Honorary Secretary,
Western State Lawn Tennis Association.

Chapter 8

AGITATION FOT THE REINSTATEMENT

Since his deposition in November 1968, Owo people, through different organisations, have been petitioning the Government to conduct a plebiscite to test the popularity of Sir Olateru Olagbegi as the Olowo. In a petition by the majority of Owo Kingmakers in June 1974, the Chiefs pointed out that to have an everlasting peace in Owo, the government must allow the kingmakers to decide who should be their ruler and allow the people to decide through a plebiscite. In either case, they boasted of more than ninety percent support for Sir Olateru Oagbegi.

This issue generated a lot of controversies. A school of thought believes that his dethronement was mere political vendetta, hence the need to revoke the order while another school of thought believes the action was in order.

Various publications on this issue are published so that readers could judge the fairness or otherwise of the dethronement.

MEMORANDUM SUBMITTED BY SIR OLATERU OLAGBEGI (KBE) THE RIGHTFUL OLOWO OF OWO.

DETAILS:

1. This memorandum is submitted by me Sir Olateru Olagbegi (K.B.F). I seek recognition as the rightful Olowo of Owo under part 1 of the Chiefs Edict, 1984.

2. The memorandum comes within Clauses B (i) and (ii) of the Committee on composition of the Ondo State Council of Chiefs and on the Recognition of certain Chieftainces under Part I of the Chiefs Edict, 1984

3. It is a well known fact that the Olowo Obaship Dispute has been a protracted one for about 18 years and the Government has not found an answer to the problems and confusions generated in Owo since then.

4. From on or about March, 1941 till on or about June, 1966. (Twenty-five years) I was the recognised Olowo of Owo under the Owo Native Law and Custom.

5. From the inception of Regional Government there was a necessity for Chieftaincy declarations embracing the whole of old Western Region. The intention was to set out clearly the procedure to be followed in the selection of candidates for recognition under the Chieftaincy law, if an Olowo dies and as such there is a vacancy. Before the incumbent was made the Olowo, there had been 2 conflicting Declarations.

6. (a) One made and approved in 1957 and;

(b) Another allegedly made in 1968 which was later

found to be a forged document. Both are attached Marked (A & B) respectively.

7. The first declaration (A) made in 1957 and referred to in Clause 5 above was made at the Request of the then Western Region Government to regularise Chieftancy Succession throughout the Region. It was then considered by the Chieftaincy Committee (Consisting of the 27 Traditional Members and 101 representatives of the Owo District Council) and submitted for ratification by the Council. After this it was sent to the Government for approval. After successfully passing through all these Channels it was approved and registered by the Government in 1957.

8. The second declaration (B) was said to have been made during an uprising against me as the Olowo of Owo. The action followed immediately after I was unilaterally and wickedly deposed and banished to Okitipupa on the 15th February, 1968. It was not made by any Chieftaincy Committee as there was no record of its origin. On examination it would be seen that it was allegedly made one day at Owo and registered the second day at Ibadan. Nobody knew about the existence of this fictitious declaration until all the declarations in the Region were printed in pamphlets and sold to members of the public in 1971. The horrible thing about the declaration was that it was used in imposing somebody on my people the second month it was allegedly made.

9. The declaration of 1957 was nowhere abrogated legally. Neither was its cancellation gazetted before the use of the fictitious one referred to in Clause 8 above. My contention is that since the 1957 declaration is legally binding, my appointment as the Olowo still stands.

10. I RESPECTFULLY SUBMIT THAT THE 1968 DECLARATION BE REJECTED AND OLOWO OGUNOYE WAS NOT LAWFULLY APPOINTED ON

THE FOLLOWING GROUNDS.

a) It was allegedly made at the peak of the Revolution against me. In other words it was bound to be with bias against me and be in favour of my antagonists during an interregnum as such.

b) The declaration was purportedly signed by a Council Official at a time when the said official had left the service of the Council 4 years before then. It was therefore forged.

The Chairman who was alleged to have signed it was Chief Abolunwodi who is a cousin to one Mr. Ajasin who led the revolt against me. They were and are still my bitterest enemies. How could such amendments be true? The Secretary (Mr. Famakinwa) who was alleged to have signed it had retired from the Council four years earlier before the time. And whereas both Chief Abolunwodi and Mr. Ajasin who was then the Chairman of the Council took part in, and approved of, the first declaration made in 1957. How could anybody take them for their words on their second thoughts and involvement?

11. The 1957 Declaration should be preferred to the 1968 one for the purpose of recognition of who the rightful Olowo of Owo is.

12. Even under the so-called 1968 Declaration of the 7 Chiefs who constituted the Kingmakers, 3 of the Chiefs i.e. Ojomo, Ojumu and Sashere had no incumbents. Four participated, i.e. Chiefs Oshere, Elerewe, Akowa and Ajana.

13. Three out of these four have consistently maintained that the present incumbent became the Olowo by foul means and that he cannot be lawfully appointed the Olowo when I am still alive. This would be contrary to Native Law and Custom of Owo.

14.   Ogunoye demanded the loyalty of these Chiefs as otherwise they would be disciplined.

15.   They refused to be blackmailed and instead, they sent an open petition to the Government asking for my recognition and reinstatement as the Olowo of Owo and asked also for the removal of Ogunoye (*copy of petition is annexed herewith) and marked C.

16.   In consequence of this development, Ogunoye deposed these Chiefs and had them replaced by his own nominees, again contrary to the Native and Custom of Owo. Sc /98/1984 on the 17th of May 1985 judgment delivered and reported in 1985, 5 S.CP. 161.

17.   An eloquent testimony that apart from these Chiefs, the whole Owo Community also refused him recognition in 1985, he i.e. Ogunoye, was warned by the people to cease performing the traditional functions of the Olowo. He refused to heed the warning and performed the Igogo festival to which action the people reacted by stoning him. He has since not performed Igogo festival outside the palace as an Olowo should.

18.   When the Military took over Government in 1966, some disgruntled elements petitioned the Government to have me removed. The Government refused to do so, but instead suspended me for 6 months with effect from 15th June 1966 expiring 15th December, 1966. This was done in consultation and on the advice of the Council of Obas and Chiefs of Western Region.

19.   When the suspension lapsed, I did not return immediately home because there were rumours that some of my antagonists were going to be violent. In fact on 20th December, 1966 (i.e five days after the expiration of the suspension period) some thugs burnt down three of my properties ln Owo in rumoured anticipation of my return, two

of my tenants were seriously injured by gunshot wounds.

20. Because of this, I requested for armed Police protection from the Government in order to go back to Owo. The Government declined and only promised a police orderly

21. On 15th December, 1967 Brigadier Adebayo (the State Governor as he then was) invited me to his office and gave me three months within which to return home as the Olowo and promised only one police orderly. The time limit was to expire on 14th March, 1968. The letter of my reinstatement dated 14th December1966 was duly served and received by me.

22. On 9th February, 1968 I returned to Owo within three months limit. My said return was marked with orchestrated violence by thugs and disgruntled elements and about 60 houses were burnt or damaged in Owo. Six of which belonged to me.

23. On 13 February, 1968 the Government set up Kumapayi Commission of Enquiry to probe the incident. But on 15th February, 1968, i.e. before the commission started sitting, I was deposed. This purported deposition was ultra vires his powers, as he did it without due consultation with the Council of Obas. No meeting was convened between the 9th and 15th of February 1968. The commission of enquiry started public sitting on 5th March 1968. On 15th July, 1968 the Olowo of Owo 1957 Chieftaincy Declaration was hurriedly amended in order to impose Adekola Ogunoye as the Olowo. This was the basis on which the incumbent was imposed on the people of Owo.

24. On 18th Nov. 1968 Ogunoye was forcefully imposed on the Owo people as the Olowo amist public outcry and protestations. The protestations have not abated since then, but the Government has not taken any action to remove Ogunoye and to reinstate me and extend recognition to me as

the Olowo. It is believed that the Kumapayi Inquiry exonerated me.

25. That the Olowo of Owo Chieftaincy be recognised as a permanent member of the Council of Obas and Chiefs of Ondo State since the Olowo is a First Class Oba. Indeed in the defunct Western Region of Nigeria, the Olowo was President of the House of Chiefs just before the Military intervention in 1966.

26. **CONCLUSION**:

Under the Native Law and Custom of Owo, no Olowo can be appointed in the lifetime of the incumbent. This much was established by the Morgan Commission of Enquiry by some witnesses who also asked for my reinstatement (see reports of Morgan Commission).

i. I humbly call on the Government to immediately reinstate me and restore me to the throne of my forefathers and grant me recognition accordingly.

ii. I also humbly apply that the Olowo of Owo be made a permanent member of the Ondo State Council of Obas, as a First Class Oba.

SIR OLATERU OLAGBEGI

APPENDIX A.

DECLARATION MADE UNDER SECTION 4 OF THE CHIEFS LAW 1957 OF THE CUSTOMARY LAW

REGULATING THE SECTION TO THE OLOWO OF OWO CHIEFTANCY

THE OLOWO OF OWO

1. There is only one ruling house and that is the house of the Olowo.

2. Any person being the immediate son of an Olowo shall be eligible to be proposed as a candidate by the ruling house, and if there is no such son, any person being the immediate daughter of an Olowo shall be eligible. Provided that an Olowo who attains the age grade of fifty years and celebrates the Ero festival, may during his lifetime, with the consent and approval of the Kingmakers as defined in Paragraph 3 below and of the elders of the ruling house as defined in paragraph 4 below, select one of his sons (Idaniken) to succeed him, and in such case, such son shall alone be eligible to be proposed as a candidate by the ruling house at the demise of his father.

3. There are twenty Kingmakers, these being the persons holding the following titles:

1. Chief Ojomo of Igboroko Quarter
2. Chief Sashere of Igboroko Quarter
3. Chief Ariyo of Igboroko Quarter
4. Chief Owadogbon of Igboroko Quarter
5. Chief Elerewe of Igboroko Quarter
6. Chief Oshuporu of Igboroko Quarter
7. The two Aragwagbiyes of Igboroko Quarter
8. Chief Akowa of Iloro Quarter
9. The Aragwagbiyes of Igboroko Quarter
10. Chief Oshere of Ehingbe Quarter
11. The Aragwagbiyes of Igboroko Quarter

12. Chief Ajana of Isaipen Igboroko Quarter

13. The Aragwagbiyes of Igboroko Quarter

14. The Aragwagbaiye of Ijebu Quarter

15. Chief Aribo of Igboroko Quarter

16. Chief Iwashokun of Igboroko Quarter

17. The Asuada of Isuada Village: Representing the Village Heads

18. The Alale of Idashen Village: Representing the Village Heads

19. The Oliyere of Iyere Village: Representing the Village Heads

4. The method of nomination by the ruling house is as follows:-

1. Chief Elewere of Igboroko Quarter Omo-Olowo

2. Chief Aralepo of Igboroko Quarter Omo-Olowo

3. Chief Oludasa of Igboroko Quarter Omo-Olowo

4. Chief Oludaiye of Igboroko Quarter Omo-Olowo

5. Chief Owabumaiye of Igboroko Quarter Omo-Olowo

6. Chief Adafen Ajogbo of Iloro Quarter Omo-Olowo

7. Chief Adefen Ewu of Iloro Quarter - Omo-Olowo

8. Chief Osula of Ehinogbe of Iloro quarters – Omo Olowo

9. Chief Olarogbo - Ọmọ Olowo

10. Chief Imaran of Isaipen of Iloro quarters – Omo Olowo

11. Chief Modonrogho of Iloro quarters – Omo olowo

12. Chief lwashikun of ljebu of Iloro quarters – Omo Olowo

13. Chiel Arashokun of of Iloro quarters – Omo Olowo,

Those acting for the ruling house shall meet together to nominate a candidate for the title and the Senior Elder from Igboroko Quarter (Olori- Ebi) shall present the candidate so nominated to the kingmakers who will if they are satisfied that the candidate has been properly selected according to custom signify approval and present him to the Iloro Igbahares (lloro Quarter Chiefs) and perform all necessary traditional installation ceremonies made by the Chieftaincy Committee of the Owo Divisional Council which has been designated as the competent Council by Western Region Legal Notice No. 352 of 1955 and signed by the Chairman and Secretary of the Committee this 11th day of December. 1957.

(Sgd)   Olagbegi II, Olowo of Owo.

Chairman, Chieftaincy Committee

Owo Divisional Council.

(Sgd)

Secretary, Chieftaincy Committee

Owo Divisional Council.

APPROVED this 23rd day of March, 1959.

(Sgd) D. S. ADEGBENRO

Minister of Local Government.

REGISTERED this 25th day of March, 1959.

(Sgn)   F.A OGWUDE

For Permanent Secretary,

Ministry of Local Government

Certified True Copy.

....

A. O. AYILEKA

APPENDIX B

DECLARATION MADE UNDER SECTION 9A OF THE CHIEFS LAW, 1957, OF THE CUSTOMARY LAW REGULATING THE SELECTION OF THE OLOWO OF OWO CHIEFTAINCY

THE OLOWO OF OWO

1.   There is only one ruling house for the Olowo of Owo Chieftaincy

2.   The Ruling House is AJAGBUSI-EKUN.

3. Only direct sons of an Olowo are eligible to be proposed as a candidate. There is no specific order of the 23rd Senior Omo-Olowos to consider all the candidates who have submitted their applications to him.

4. The kingmakers shall consist of the following senior chiefs:

   1. Chief Ojumu
   2. Chief Oshere
   3. Chief Ajana
   4. Chief Akowa
   5. Chief Ojomo
   6. Chief Sashere
   7. Chief Elerewe

5. The method of nomination by the ruling house is for the Ojomo to convene a meeting of the 23 Senior Omo-Olowos to consider all the candidates who have submitted their application to him. The following are the Omo-Olowos

   1. Chief Ojomo-Ijebu Quarters
   2. Chief Aralepo-Igboroko Quarter
   3. Chief Oludasa-Igboroko Quarter
   4. Chief Owabunaiye-Igboroko Quarter
   5. Chief Oludaiye-Igboroko Quarter
   6. Chief Ojigbo-Igboroko Quarter
   7. Chief Ojigbo-Igboroko Quarter
   8. Chief Ekungba-Igboroko Quarter

9. Chief Ero-Igboroko Quarter

10. Chief Usikaiye-Igboroko Quarter

11. Chief Obaila-Igboroko Quarter

12. Chief Owogboriaye-Igboroko Quarter

13. Chief Osula-Ehinogbe Quarter

14. Chief Olurogho--Ehinogbe Quarter

15. Chief Solo-Ehinogbe Quarter

16. Chief Saporu-Ehinogbe Quarter

17. Chief Arajuwa-Ehinogbe Quarter

18. Chief Adafin Ajogbo-Iloro Quarter

19. Chief Adafin Ewu-Iloro Quarter

20. Chief Alajawo Asobe-Iloro Quarter

21. Chief Alajawo Alaneyin-Iloro Quarter

22. Chief Adafin Onomagbe-Iloro Quarter

23. Chief Adamigbo Akarakiri-Iloro Quarter

If only one candidate is unanimously nominated the candidate is presented to the kingmakers by Chief Ojomo. If more than one candidate is nominated, a vote shall be taken and Chief Ojomo shall present to the kingmakers the candidate who has the majority vote of the Omo-Olowo present and voting in the meeting. The kingmakers, if satisfied that the candidate has been properly selected according to the custom, will signify approval and present the successful candidate to the Iloro chiefs who will perform all necessary traditional installation ceremonies:

Provided that if Chief Ojomo is not for any reason available to perform the above functions, such functions will be transferred to Chief Arelepo.

Made by the Chieftaincy Committee of the Owo District Council which has been designated as the competent council by W.P.L.N. 127 of 1966 and signed by the Chairman and Secretary of the Committee this 7th of August 1968.

L. A. ABOLUWODI

Chairman, Chieftaincy Committee, Owo District Council

M. L. FAMAKINWA

Secretary, Chieftaincy Committee, Owo District Council

APPROVED this 22nd of August, 1968.

O. AKINYEMI

Permanent Secretary, Ministry of Local Government and Chieftaincy Affairs
REGISTERED THIS 23rd day of August, 1968.

O. AKINYEMI

Permanent Secretary, Ministry of Local Government and Chieftaincy Affairs

PRAYERS:

A. THAT this honourable Committee considers as a matter of urgency my reinstatement as the Olowo of Owo.

B. THAT the position of the Olowo of Owo be recognized

as one of the Paramount Rulers of this State and be made a First Class Oba and one of the permanent (not by rotation) members of the Ondo State Council of Obas and Chiefs.

There was a change of government and Brigadier Rotimi took over as the new Governor, Sir Olateru petitioned the Governor to review his case and to see that justice was done. In his petition, Sir Olateru enumerated his administrative career and how he had been maliciously victimised and chased out of his throne.

PETITION BY INDIVIDUALS

Many Owo citizens and groups of people also sent their petitions spotlighting how Sir Olateru had been wrongly deposed through wrong advice given the Western State government. In a pettion by Mr. S.R.B. Okoro, he said- "I might even go further to add that whilst I believe that Sir Olateru Olagbegi's original suspension as the Olowo of Owo early in 1966 by the first Military Governor of the Western State, Late Lt. Col. Adekunle Fajuyi, as a result of the enquiry he caused to be conducted into the allegations made against Sir Olateru Olagbegi was justified, yet his subsequent dethronement and banishment from Owo by Major-General Adebayo's administration was harsh, unfair and not in the best interest of the majority of the people of Owo. If the opponents of Sir Olateru had allowed an atmosphere of peace and calm to prevail at Owo at that time, I am confident that Sir Olateru himself would have found a way to warm himself back into the good books of his people. I never believe, in any case, in a fight to finish. This attitude invariably creates more problems than it solves."

The press too joined in the agitation to have lasting, solution to Owo problems. Strong editorials were written on the subject.

For example, Sunday Star April 1964 read thus:

"Our research confirmed that within the last twenty-four months (1967), four traditional rulers have been deposed in the western State. They are Oba Green Adebo of Ilisan, Oba Adepoju of Otan Aiyegbaju, The Aseyin, and Sir Olateru, the Olowo of Owo. Of the four, the Olowo of Owo had received a unique and we think harsh treatment. Sir Olateru's properties were extensively destroyed and he lost his throne; he was restricted for months at Okitipupa and he is now barred from going to Owo".

"Sir Olateru was on the throne for some twenty-five years before his throne was taken away from him. We are not aware of any other Oba in the history of Yorubaland who has suffered so much for so long after being in honour and glory as the natural ruler of his people for about a quarter of a century. He is not old enough to retire entirely from public life but he is too old to start a new career".

"Yet, he must live, he must pay the school fees of his children who are reported to be over hundred; he must care for his wives and dependants. But how? Virtually all his means of livelihood are in Owo. Owo is his root. Owo is his life. Yet he must not go there!"

"In another editorial in one of the major newspapers of the time, it was also stated inter-alia: In our previous editorial on this subject, we made it manifestly clear that the peace at Owo vis-a-vis peace in western State was uppermost in our minds and not necessarily who is right or wrong in the Chieftaincy wranglings in Owo".

"It will be unrealistic to pretend that all is well at Owo if the people have not had the opportunity to demonstrate and not be tear-gassed, an action which keeps on recurring every time there, especially during government representative visits and during public celebrations which cannot be carried out without police contigent".

"Most certainly, the government is aware of troubles at Owo and that was why this newspaper honestly called on the present State Government to take an early action about Olowo chieftaincy controversy once and for all".

"Remarkable enough, the Commissioner for Chieftancy Affairs, Cannon Akinyemi, made so many statements when giving his ultimatum that one cannot but be puzzled over government's knowledge about Olowo's Chieftaincy dispute. It is as if the agitators have no decent reasons that could be glossed over".

"The Commissioner had said among other things that chieftaincy law and the Owo Native law and customs required the two chiefs to reconcile with the Olowo and that it was the present Olowo the government recognized".

"Questions arising from these are: where were these chieftaincy laws and the native law and customs when some chiefs previously disagreed with the Ex-Olowo, Sir Olagbegi?

"Secondly, the Chiefs who decamped now in Ogunoye's camp were not given a similar ultimatum, why?"

"Moreover, was it not Sir Olagbegi who was first appointed and recognised by the Owo people and approved by the government as the Olowo for many years? And why was he removed?"

"Why are the people who are agitating plebiscite at Owo still demanding Sir Olagbegi's reinstatement as opposed to the only one allegedly recognised by the government? We feel that these and other burning questions should be given attention by the government".

"It is felt that a case of public irregularity has been established by the deposition and imposition carried out at

Owo, until the contrary is proved".

"The Western State Government should with grace and magnamity rectify its error where it feels it was misled".

"Under the circumstances, observers believe that the mere fact that those in possession of Owo administration since all these years are against Sir Olagbegi who is miles away are alleged to be losing support of their erstwhile followers, goes to show that both the 'imposition' and the 'ultimatum' needed to be carefully looked into."

"For several years, the Olowo stool was a hotbed of crisis. It all started with the agitation for the removal of Oba Olateru Olagbegi from the throne. That was immediately after the army took over power in 1966. Whether the ex-Olowo was rightly or wrongly dethroned has become the subject of heated debate in and outside Owo since 1968".

"One point was clear and will forever remain incontrovertible– lots of events in the shape of political vendatta pervaded the West in the first few months of the Military regime in the West. People who felt cheated one way or the other saw the army takeover as an opportunity to destroy their enemies. This is why doubts will continue to exist in independent minds as to whether the treatment meted to Sir Olateru was deserved or was motivated by the forces which felt cheated during the heights of his glory under the civilian regime immediately preceding the army take-over".

"But a lot has happened since then. Another Olowo is on the throne. Some of the kingmakers recognise him as such while others have refused to do so".

"There was an enquiry into the situation at Owo some years ago. To the best of our knowledge, the report is resting in peace somewhere. The ultimatum recently given two Owo Chiefs to pay homage to the present Olowo has attracted much, but well deserved, publicity within the last few years. The chiefs were said to have refused to comply with this instruction".

"Again, certain things must be made clear. The present Government of Ondo State is not responsible for the dethronement of Sir Olateru. The present Olowo did not put himself on the throne. Whatever action taken by the present government of Ondo state will certainly be seen in this light- that it is making efforts to ensure law and order in that part of the country which has not known peace for many years. The duty of the government is clear- a commission of inquiry should be appointed to go into the claims and counter-claims of the dramatis personae in Owo. The commission of course should be made up of men who are known not to have been involved in the Owo affairs one way or the other".

"It must be recalled that the Olu of Warri was dethroned by a party which felt he had acted against its interests at one time or the other. Another Olu was enthroned. The situation which now arises at Owo arose in Warri and an enquiry was set-up. The result is well-known. There is no reason why this cannot be done in Owo and if it is found that some wrongs had been committed, the situation should be revised. And if found otherwise, the position should remain as it is. Forcing Chiefs to go and pay homage against their conviction is not the answer to the problem at Owo. The present Government of Ondo state has clamoured so much for peace and every effort must be made to help the government achieve its objectives of peace and tranquility. The situation at work must not be allowed to go on indefinitely. It has to be settled once and for all."

OLOWO OBASHIP DISPUTE

OPEN PLEA TO HIS EXCELLENCY, THE WESTERN STATE MILITARY GOVERNOR, COLONEL DAVID JEMIBEWON FOR THE RE-INSTATEMENT OF SIR OLATERU OLAGBEGI AS THE OLOWO OF OWO BY THE OWO PEOPLE:

Published full page of Daily Times of 13/2/76

Your Excellency,

Demand Brief:

Owing to procedural irregularities whereby the past Military Government of the State installed another Olowo on the Owo people, we the majority of Owo Kingmakers, Omolowos and the ninety percent strong people of Owo, acting in concert hereby demand the removal of installed Olowo Ogunoye from office with immediate effect.

We also severally and collectively demand the reinstatement of our rightful Oba, Sir Olateru Olagbegi

Owo people are respectfully appealing to your Excellency openly to institute an Inquiry into the Olowo Chieftaincy dispute in the interest of peace and order and good government in the State. The following legitimate reasons are agitating the minds of all right thinking sons and daughters of Owo since the wrongful deposition of Sir Olateru Olagbegi as the Olowo of Owo. The present corrective Military Administration will, we are sure, correct what the past Military Governments of this State have regretfully done, having regard to the excesses and maladministrations of some former military administration as are now being revealed in the newspapers throughout the country. It is hoped, therefore, that the following grievances will be looked into.

1. HEAD OF STATES STATEMENT ON OBAS

When the present ruler took over power in July 1975, one of the most important and popular statements of the new corrective Regime was that there had been desecration of traditional institution and public humiliation of highly respected natural rulers in the country. In this connection Your Excellency, Owo is Second to none in the handling of our natural rulers in such an irresponsible manner. So far, the Military Rulers have been active on most of their assignments and original pledges. We would not like them to be passive on our own issue. The Military Government and indeed the people of this country are aware about what had happened in Owo, and should please reinstate Sir Olagbegi as our Oba.

2. PROGRESSIVE OBA:

It is well-known fact that nearly all the present developments, culturally and administratively, brought to Owo so far, were energetically spearheaded by Sir Olateru Olagbegi during his twenty-five years as the Olowo of Owo through the influence and goodwill which he commanded when he was in office. He is still very active and can still help Owo and the people, moreso, since he is still willing to carry on his good work if and when called upon to his rightful office.

3. YOUR EXCELLENCY'S RECENT VISIT TO OWO:

When, in September 1975, Your Excellency visited Owo, we presented a Welcome Address which was passed through the Divisional Officer asking for the reinstatement of Sir Olateru Olagbegi as the Olowo. As a matter of fact, Your Excellency saw the groups of Sir Olagbegi's supporters who were not allowed to carry placards by the police. It was a further proof of Owo People's popular demand for Sir

Olagbegi's reinstatement. It is not a new demand simply because there is a change of government. In fact, in February 1975, we had a meeting with ex-military Governor Rotimi on the subject. Before then, we had also had audience with past administrations on the matter.

4. PUBLIC INQUIRY WANTED:

If a Public Inquiry is instituted in the Olowo's Chieftaincy dispute, there will be many interesting revelations about Sir Olagbegi's removal from Office. It is up to the present Military Rulers to inquire into the circumstances leading to his removal before taking a final decision on the matter. This is time to know the truth if the government wants to, we shall be satisfied with the government's final decision

5. USE OF VIOLENCE:

It is not Owo people's policy to resort to violence on this issue, hence this publication so that our grievances might be made known openly. Sir Olagbegi himself has time without number warned against the use of violence. Although it is foolish to raise arms against a military government, it is to the eternal credit of Sir Olagbegi for his condemnation of the use of force at Owo, even though wicked violence was used on him and some of his well wishers by persons unknown before his removal. Thanks to his maturity, experience and his confidence in his people.

6. DEJI OF AKURE INQUIRY:

By all consideration, Olowo's dispute is more serious than that of Akure because Olowo Ogunoye has not the majority of the Kingmakers and the townspeople. When an inquiry was set into Akure dispute, and Owo has not been treated, many people felt that it was because there was no violence at Owo. But none of our leaders felt that way as has been explained above. If, therefore, the Government decides to set up an inquiry into Olowo's dispute the whole country will be made aware of the real truth of the whole dispute.

7. VAST MAJORITY OF OWO CHIEFS AND PEOPLE'S SUPPORT:

Our claim for the vast majority of the Kingmakers, traditional Chiefs and Owo people can be checked physically at any time. Three-quarters of the Kingmakers, to our knowledge, are still solidly supporting Sir Olagbegi together with more than ninety per cent of Owo people.

8. NEW MILITARY GOVERNMENT'S PRESENT STANDARD:

Judging by those who have been removed from office so far, there should be no difficulties in removing Olowo Ogunoye who has been there for only seven years immediately. He is neither enjoying the support of the majority of the kingmakers nor that of the townspeople. We challenge him to an open plebiscite, if he gets a majority vote of the townspeople, we would withdraw from this contest. After all, it was Sir Olagbegi who was first appointed by the Government as the Olowo of Owo and who has reigned meritoriously for twenty-five years and we do not see why the Government cannot re-instate him as the rightful and popular acceptable leader.

9. CHIEFTAINCY DECLARATION:

It will be recalled that when Ogunoye was installed as the Olowo in 1968, the Chieftaincy Declaration of 1957 was amended in 1968. It will be in the interest of justice to enquire into the reasons for the amendments. It will be necessary also to call the then members of the Chieftaincy Committee especially one Mr. Famakinwa to give evidence during such an inquiry.

10. CELEBRATION OF IGOGO AND THE

QUESTION OF PEACE AT OWO:

The celebration of Igogo by a small faction does not mean that there is peace (a relative term) at Owo. An individual can arrange to celebrate any festival in his compound but the present incumbent's celebration of Igogo on the pages of newspapers is quite different from the popular one in which important traditional chieftaincies in Owo take part during Sir Olagbegi's reign. There is no violence because Sir Olagbegi and his people want it to be so.

11. LIFE-APPOINTMENT NATURE OF OBAS:

An Oba is appointed for life. In the old days they were God's anointed and could not be removed just for the asking. It is even against Owo tradition to apppoint another person when one Olowo is still living. Your Excellency will be doing Nigerians a world of good by maintaining justice and fair play at Owo by allowing Sir Olateru Olagbegi, who has not committed any offence, to continue with his own span of life as the Olowo before the Military imposition of any kind. If this is not done, Owo and its people will painfully continue to suffer in silence.

12. SIR OLAGBEGI'S WRONGFUL DEPOSTTION:

Sir Olagbegi went to Owo from Ibadan on the 9th of February 1968 as the Olowo after his reinstatement. Some thugs caused trouble in the town looting properties and committing the basest treacherous arsons ever recorded in the history of Owo and its environs in the whole exercise. On the 13th of February 1968, the Kumapayi Inquiry was set up to investigate the disturbances. Before the Inquiry commenced its sittings, Sir Olagbegi was deposed on the third day, the 15th of February 1968. This, we believe was one of the injustices in the whole exercise.

The action of the then Government was obviously a rape

on the cardinal rules of natural justice which provides that both sides to a quarrel be heard before a decision is taken thereon. When Your Excellency set up the Ademola Inquiry at Akure, the Deji was not immediately deposed, or any action taken until the outcome of the inquiry. The findings of the Kumapayi inquiry has since not been made known to the public.

13. KUMAPAYI COMMISSION OF INQUIRY:

The Kumapayi Inquiry was held in public and why the findings have not still been released since 1968 beats one's imagination. Chief Kumapayi is still alive and in one of the Ministries. Your Excellency should call for his report and publish it as a matter of urgency if the past Government has nothing to hide.

14. THE COUNCIL OF OBAS AND CHIEFS NOT CONSULTED:

We humbly feel that before any drastic step is taken against a first class Oba like the Olowo of Owo, the Western State Council of Obas and Chiefs should have been consulted before deposition. Moreover, as at the 15th February 1968, on the day Sir Olagbegi was deposed as the Olowo of Owo, the action was not supported by the Owo Kingmakers. The two important bodies were not consulted.

15. CONCLUSION:

Finally, Your Excellency owes it a duty to your subjects and tax payers of this state according to your oath of office to right such wrong. We don't need any demonstration or acts of violence to force the hands of your present incorruptible and popular Government to tell the whole world the truth.

Furthermore, our demand is supported by history. In the case of his Highness, the Olu of Warri, now the Chancellor of the Ife University, the impostor was removed when the truth was out after an inquiry. In the case of Aseyin of Iseyin in the Western State, a similar exercise was performed. A public inquiry into Olowo Chieftaincy, no doubt, will help finalise issues once and for all. With respects.

Your loyal subjects

(Sgd) CHIEF ABRAHAM OJO OLAKUNORO

The Elerewe of Owo: KINGMAKER

On behalf of the Majority Kingmakers

AN OPEN LETTER

CONCERNING THE WRONGFUL DETHRONEMENT OF SIR OLATERU-OLAGBEG II

I REFER to your widely read monthly publication, "Headlines," of July 1984 carrying past stories that made headlines on Sir Olateru Olagbegi's dethronement. I hasten to make these Public corrections in the interest of present and future of our generation and also to correct certain wrong impressions which the said publications might have created.

1.   HISTORY OF THE PAST OLOWOS

(a)   Many Owo people will not agree with the impressions created that all the past Olowos encountered one type of rebellion or the other. Apart from about five out of twenty-eight Olowos the rest were progressive, including

Olowo Elewuokun, whose ancestral sword was taken by Sir Olateru Olagbegi II at his installation in 1941.

(b) I don't want to dispute the details of what actually happened about Olowos Alubiolokun, Adara and Aladetokun here for lack of space. But many of the facts have been distorted and Owo historians know the details and will accord them their rightful places when the time comes. But to cite them along with Sir Olateru Olagbegi's episode is grossly misleading. In this modern age of political parties, as rightly stated by you in page 2, "when the army struck in January 15, 1966, the victimized supporters of other political parties who refused to go with him into the N.N.D.P. organised what was known as "Olagbegi must go,"campaign which reached such magnitude that on June 15, 1966, the Military Government of the West under Col. Fajuyi issued a suspension order on Sir Olagbegi. The order was to last for six months after which the nerves could be allowed to cool down enough for him to return to the throne.

(c) Evidently Sir Olateru Olagbegi II is the most progressive Olowo we have ever had and it is on record that he was able with his dynamism and hard work to place Owo on the map in Nigeria and throughout the whole world. Space do not permit the enumeration of what he has achieved for Owo but it is generally felt that since 1966 little or nothing have been achieved. So rebellion of all other Olowo's apart, Sir Olagbegi's episode would not have been so without well known outside political influences. Hence Sir Olateru Olagbegi had requested for a plebiscite to be adjudged by the very Owo people he had relentlessly and efficiently served for more than twenty-five years (vide his evidence before Morgan Inquiry in 1978). He has since been living peacefully with his people to the shame of outside enemies of Owo people's welfare.

2. POLITICAL PARTIES AND OATH TAKING:

(a)   It was not correct that Sir Olateru Olagbegi swore everybody to secret oath in his palace. He was very popular and question of taking oaths was unthinkable. It was the first time that political parties were formed and incidentally the banned Action Group was established at Owo. Chief Ajasin who was trained as the Principal of Owo Imade College, established by Sir Olateru Olagbegi was one of the leaders in the Action Group. So the support given to the Action Group was obvious.

(b)   Sir Olateru Olagbegi was not a "Political party" Politician. And as an Oba he was bound to support the Government, "So that amenities might be offered his domain." It is common knowledge that if he were a party politician as of the day as stated before the Morgan enquiry, the people wish the public to know he would have played the role better than Chief Ajasin and others. If l may ask, who is the Oba that could come out openly to campaign against the present Government however committed he was with the past regime.

3.   RETIRED MAJOR GENERAL ADEBAYO'S POLICY:

(a)   You spoke about "Adebayo's Policy that if the subjects wanted him, the Olowo should return and be received enthusiastically. But if trouble erupted it followed that he was unwanted by his subjects." It is difficult to explain in full here the role played by the General in Owo Crisis. After reinstating Sir Olagbegi, he gave him three months to go to Owo from lbadan and said he would deal ruthlessly with anybody that caused trouble. He had been intimated about outside influence or those planning to cause trouble in Owo as I have earlier indicated. And when some people burnt innocent people's houses, General Adebayo set up an inquiry-the Kumapayi Commission of Inquiry. But before the Inquiry sat he deposed and banished Sir Olagbegi to Okitipupa. The findings of the

Inquiry which later sat have not seen the light of the day. So talking about Adebayo's policy, it is better to leave the rest to God Almighty and history. However for the moment, we are grateful to God that Sir Olateru Olagbegi was saved from the evil machinations of his outside enemies of February 1968.

(b) Sir Olateru Olagbegi was suspended for six months for whatever reasons. He was later reinstated. What offence had he committed to warrant deposition immediately after reinstatement? Did he go to Owo to burn his houses and those of his supporters to justify his deposition? OR why was he reinstated when you know that he was unwanted by the people? We leave all these to God and history.

IMPOSITION OF A NEW OLOWO

(a) Your publication dealt extensively with the irregularities surrounding the imposition of the present incumbent Olowo Ogunoye. Since 1968 nobody has bothered to investigate the alleged forged chieftaincy declaration of 1968 with which he was imposed, the abrogation of the earlier Chieftaincy Declaration of 1957 (of eleven years standing), and the reduction of the Kingmakers from twenty to seven while Omolowos were increased from thirteen to twenty-three. The bitter memories of reducing Chieftaincy holders according to the whims and caprice of the ex-politicians have been dumped on all Owo people since then. Recently we are now witnessing the duplication of Chieftaincies, viz two Elerewes, two Oseres, two Akowas, Two Aragwagbaiyes in some quarters and so on in the midst of two Olowos - Olowo Ogunoye and the Olowo Olagbegi II.

(b) Even if Owo tradition does not say so, to what extent is any government justified in installing an Oba while the present holder is still alive? The institution of Obaship is a life-time appointment. Hence Owo people keep on reminding the Government that it is a rape on Owo tradition if a new Olowo was installed while the incumbent was still alive, a very powerful one at that.

C) What do we have in Owo today? No right thinking persons can say that Owo progress has not been retarded by this imbroglio. The rights of the majority of traditional Chiefs and Kingmakers were denied then. And that of Omolowos. And that of Owo peeople generally when they refused a plebiscite and decided on thuggery.

5. COURT ACTIONS:

(a) Before some Chiefs and Sir Olateru Olagbegi went to court, they were driven to the wall. Moreover, to seek redress under the ex-governor Chief Ajasin who took part at all the stages of crisis was easier than for a camel to pass through the eyes of the needle. The very Chiefs who appealed to Chief Ajasin, himself an Owo man, to settle Owo cases once and for all were deposed.

(b) It is necessary to correct at length the irregularities in your reporting these cases which have not been taken to the Supreme Court. (i) The new regime should be equal to the tasks (ii) The recently promulgated Edict about the Chiefs Law has nullified all court actions. But it is sufficient to say that the details about Olowo's crisis have not been tendered in court. It was only legal tussles about the entertainment of the case. The New Military Rulers are impartial enough to have abandoned court action, and all the matters are before them at the moment.

6. KUMAPAYI COMMISSION OF INQUIRY:

(a) The findings of this Inquiry have not been published up till date. It is not true that the deposition of Sir Olateru-Olagbegi was based on the recommendation of Chief Kumapayi's Commission. He is still alive and the present regime should be able to make use of his services. The deposition was not particularly in the terms of reference of

Morgan Commission of Inquiry for the purpose of plesbicite should settle the dispute once and for all.

(b) Olowo Ogunoye for instance demonstrated his defeatist attitude by not coming out to give evidence in an all important Olowo Chieftancy during the fifteen days the Morgan Inquiry sat at Owo, only Sir Olateru Olagbegi attended throughout.

7. APPEAL TO THE PRESENT MILITARY GOVERNMENT

With operation of WAI, I hope peace will be made to reign in Owo by appointing a Special Inquiry on Owo Crisis about the alleged deposition of Olowo Olagbegi II and the imposition of Olowo Ogunoye II on Owo people or conduct a plebiscite on which Owo people prefers.

OLATERU ARMAIJI

The Owo Kingmakers
(13-4 majority)
c/o Chief Abraham Ojo Elerewe,
No. 1 Elerewe Street,
Owo.

7th June, 1974.

His Excellency Brigadier Oluwole Rotimi,
The Military Governor,
Western State,
Ibadan.

Copy - Through His Excellency.
Brigadier Oluwole Rotimi.

To:- The Head of State,
His Excellency General Yakubu Gowon,
Federal Government State House.
Lagos.

Your Excellency.

OLOWO'S CONTROVERSY

PETITION FOR THE REINSTATEMENT OF SIR OLATERU OLAGBEGI

AS THE OLOWO OF OWO BY THE MAJORITY OF OWO KING MAKERS

On behalf of ourselves, Chiefs and people of Owo, we the undersigned Owo Kingmakers who have been the majority are respectfully requesting that in the interest of peace, justice and good government in Owo, it is high time Your Excellency investigates Olowo's matter and reinstate Sir Olateru Olagbegi as the Olowo of Owo in accordance with the people's choice. In this connection, we beg to recall an open plea published in the Daily Times of the 5th October 1973, which summarises our stand on this vital subjects, and to which no reply has been made.

With your Excellency's permission, Sir, a copy of the publication is attached for your advantage. We are the officially recognised Chiefs and Kingmakers in Owo. We strongly feel that as it is done throughout the length and breadth of the Federation we would decide who should be our Oba. To back up our support for Sir Olateru Olagbegi's popularity we have publicly boasted of more than (90%) ninety percent of the people in Owo in any plebiscite at any time. This principle of majority rule is the only safeguard and guarantee for the peace and good government in Owo.

In our publication referred to above, we submitted that a sufficient case about the past dishonest manoevures in deposing our Oba Sir Olagbegi and the suspiciously accelerated imposition of Ogunoye has been made against the Western State Government under your predecessor and such brazen allegations call for your highly-respected-administration to inquire into - not privately - but publicly.

Furthermore, we respectfully wish to put across to His Excellency the following points so as to assist in the final findings in the interest of the inhabitants and the people of Owo Division.

(a) Sir Olateru Olagbegi has reigned peacefully and meritoriously for more than twenty-five years as the Olowo of Owo, and for His Excellency's information, he also held office as a Minister of Western State Government for more than nine years. He was President of the last civilian Western State House of Chiefs which, as Your Excellency might have known, supported the Government which also supported the Federal and constitutional Government of the day. As your Excellency is aware all traditional rulers are fathers of all irrespective of their private political leanings. And by this virtue as Olowo of Owo, Sir Olagbegi was traditionally made the President of the last House of Chiefs. It all happened before the 1966 Coup that as father of the party in power as well as its opposition, Sir Olagbegi, because of his office as President of House of Chiefs mentioned above under the leadership of late Chief Akintola was asked to resign. And as your Excellency is aware it led to the suspension of the Western House of Chiefs.

It was on account of this that his removal as the Olowo

was planned as a political vendetta. Any other frivolous allegations or accusations levelled against him which can be investigated publicly were an after thought, and mere excuses to carry out the revenge.

(b) After the Coup of 1966, a team of the banned Action Group supporters decided to wage a revenge and this led to false allegations or accusations to the then Governor of Western State, late Lt. Col. Fajuyi. In his Excellency's findings, Sir Olagbegi was cleared of all the charges but was suspended for six months only to allow tension to die down. After months of persuasion he decided to return to Owo but there was another coup, and that delayed his returning back to Owo for another year.

(c) At the later part of 1966 a new Governor was appointed to the Western State- Major General Adeyinka Adebayo. After Sir Olagbegi's reinstatement as the Olowo of Owo he told Sir Olateru at a press Conference that he should return to Owo from Ibadan with three months' ultimatum. Although there were strong information about some Owo disgruntled elements with some ex-politicians outside Owo to cause trouble at Owo on Sir Olagbegi's arrival, mentioned to Governor Adebayo, he (the Governor) replied sharply that he would deal ruthlessly with any trouble maker on his arrival from Ibadan to Owo:(We have the recorded speech for your Excellency's inspection)

(d) On His Excellency's (Major General Adebayo's) advice Olagbegi set out on the 9th of February, 1968 to return to his throne as the Olówó, only to find that his houses and his supporters' houses and properties were destroyed by fire. But there was not a single person who died in the incident, a fact which is contained in Kumapayi's Commission of Inquiry. And for the love he has for the town and the people he then decided to stay out of Owo pending an investigation. But to our greatest surprise, few days after the setting up of Kumapayi's Inquiry, he was deposed and banished to Okitipupa by same group of party supporters before the Inquiry ever sat. After the finding of the

Commission of Inquiry, the reports have not been made known to Sir Olagbegi up till today, and as such we are pleading with His Excellency Brigadier Rotimi to please reopen the Inquiry or if possible make it an open Inquiry.

(e) To show further that the Owo troubles were having the backing of some government functionaries under the direction of some people from Ibadan, on the day of the incident the police and the Army at Owo did not do anything to prevent the people burning houses and there were no arrests made until policemen came all the way from Lagos. All these facts are contained in the Kumupayi's Commission of Inquiry which has not been published since then because the findings might be against the Adebayo Government. The troublemakers were not dealt with ruthlessly as promised by the Governor, and the fact that Sir Olagbegi was deposed before the sitting of the Inquiry into the incident, showed that the then Government was partial on the side of lawlessness.

(f) His Excellency, the Head of State, General Yakubu Gowon, has once said times without number that nobody will be treated as second class citizen in this Country. Perhaps His Excellency would like to treat this place more honourably, and our main concern is Sir Olagbegi's national pride, prestige, and status.

We are not clamouring for the houses and properties which have been burnt but for the heritage left for his royal Highness by the forefathers- the Obaship of Owo. As we have mentioned above we shall welcome any type of Public Inquiry under your Excellency's instructions. And so we want His Excellency to treat this matter more honourable as your Excellency knows what a public figure Sir Olateru Olagbegi is.

(g) With us as their accredited leaders, the vast majority of Owo people representing more than ninety percent (90) of the population, have been co-operating with your Excellency's administration in maintaining peace in the full hope that the matter will be investigated and settled.

We are very anxious that nothing should disturb the peace under which a reasonable Government can justifiably work. With 13 (thirteen) Kingmakers in favour of Sir Olagbegi and 4 (four) against, the administration of Owo has been paralysed in the hands of the minority elements there, and peace has eluded the town ever since Ogunoye was inposed on Owo people. As an impartial Governor we can assure your Excellency that there will be peace in Owo if Sir Olagbegi is reinstated as the Olowo of Owo. The question of peace maintenance is that of the Government which was blatantly denied us during Governor Adebayo's regime. We have instances in history where Obas who were wrongly deposed were reinstated afterwards. The Aseyin of Iseyin was similarly reinstated in 1967 by the Western State Government and there was no trouble. Many examples also abound in the Federation, the Olu of Warri was one. If the truth about Olowo Ogunoye's imposition on Owo people exposed by the publication of the Kumapayi's Report, and the dishonest amendment of our chieftaincy Declaration, it will not be difficult to remove him or tell him where he should go as in the case of the usurpers at Iseyin and Warri.

(h) Your Excellency's principles of administration are based on justice, honesty and fair play. We are respectfully calling on the Western State Government under your impartial leadership not to deny Owo people these fine and godly principles. At the present moment the sad and unpeaceful situation in which the imposed Olowo Ogunoye stays at Owo without the support of Owo people is known generally by the Western State Government and the whole country.

Indeed until Sir Olagbegi is reinstated as our Oba, Owo will not regard any usurper as their monarch. Finally, Your Excellency, it is hoped that the Government will not continue to allow our taxes to be paid to an unpopular Oba who has been imposed on us through the backdoor, and that the appointment of our Oba will be left in the hands of the majority kingmakers or with the people through a plebiscite if possible. It is our prayer that peace and tranquility will continue to reign through the Federation.

We are, Your Excellency,

Your loyal subjects,

Signed by Owo Traditional King makers

1. The Osere of Ebinogbo Quarter, Owo
2. The Akowa of Iloro Quarter, Owo
3. The Elerewe of Igboroko Qtr, Owo
4. The Ogwadogbon of Igboroko Qtr, Owo
5. The Ariyo of Igboroko Qtr. Owo
6. The Osuporu of Igboroko Qtr, Owo
7. The Aragwagbaiye of Igboroko Qtr, Owo
8. The Aragwagbaiye of Igboroko Qtr.
9. The Ariyo of Ijebu Qtr, Owo
10. The Uwashokun of Ijebu Owo
11. The Aragwagbaiye of Ehinogbe Owo
12. The Aragwagbaiye of Ijebu Qtr, Owo
13. The Asuada of Isuada

Vacant:- 1. The Sashere of Igboroko Qtr. Owo.
2. The Aragwagbaiye of Isaipe Qtr. Owo.

AGAINST:- 1. The Aboluwodi of Iloro Owo
2. The Ajanna of Isaipe Owo
3. The Ojumu of Igboroko Qtr Owo
4. The Ojomo of Ijebu Qtr, Owo

BABATUNDE & SONS
Public Relations Consultants
16th Floor, Cocoa HouseIbadan

23rd June, 1972.

His Excellency Brigadier Oluwole Rotimi,
The Military Governor,
Western State of Nigeria,
IBADAN

Thro' The Commissioner for Local Govt.
and Chieftaincy Affairs,
Western State of Nigeria,
IBADAN.

Your Excellency,

TOWARDS ENSURING PERMANENT PEACE AND TRANQUILITY IN OWO DISTRICT.

I VENTURE to address you on a subject dearest to my heart as a patriotic son of Owo, viz, the necessity for creating an atmosphere at the earliest possible moment whereby permanent peace, tranquility and progress can be guaranteed in Owo District Council Area. I have held several meetings both formally and informally with Your Commissioner for Local Government and Chieftaincy Affairs, Dr. Lateef Adegbite, and I have been gratified by his sympathetic understanding of the many problems that beset my unhappy home. Ever since the agitation for the removal of Sir Olateru Olagbegi as the Olowo of Owo started early in 1966, there has been neither peace nor progress in Owo and I venture to assert to Your Excellency that until this vexatious problem is resolved, once and for all, there cannot be any happiness or harmony in that area.

2. Let me hasten to make the point here that even though I am a friend and supporter of the ex-Olowo of Owo, Sir Olateru Olagbegi, I am not so unreasonable as to maintain that his opponents in Owo are entirely unjustified in their strong criticisms of his conduct of affairs in Owo when he was the Olowo.

I might even go further to add that whilst I believe that Sir Olateru Olagbegi's original suspension as the Olowo of Owo early in 1966 by the first Military Governor of the Western State, Late Lt. Col. Adekunle Fajuyi, as a result of the enquiry he caused to be conducted into the allegations made against Sir Olateru Olagbegi was justified, yet his subsequent dethronement and banishment from Owo by Major-General Adebayo's administration was harsh, unfair and not in the best interest of the majority of the people of

Owo. If the opponents of Sir Olateru had allowed an atmosphere of peace and calm to prevail at Owo at that material time, I am confident that Sir Olateru himself would have found a way to warm himself back into the good books of his people. I never believe, in any case, in a fight to finish.

This attitude invariably creates more problems than it solves.

3. The immediate cause of my addressing this petition to you, however, is on the occasion of the release of Chief Olubunmi Thomas Report of Enquiry into the Chieftaincy Declaration of Owo Traditional Chiefs. I am positive that Chief Olubunmi Thomas in his Report would have recommended the reduction of the number of Kingmakers from their traditional 20 to 7 as was done in the discredited amended Olowo Chieftaincy Declaration of 1968, so as to ensure that the number of traditional Kingmakers for all the Owo traditional Chiefs in the districts is the same as that for the Olowo of Owo.

This reduction in the number of traditional Kingmakers is unfair, unjust and not supported by tradition. I am therefore appealing to His Excellency to leave the number of traditional King makers for all the Owo Chiefs, the Olowo included, at 20 as before.

4. There is abundant evidence to show that representation of traditional chiefs as kingmakers has always been related to the various sections into which the town is traditionally divided. This was embodied in the 1957 Declaration which showed the number of kingmakers to be 20. This was widely acclaimed throughout the length and breadth of Owo District Council because it truly represents the custom and tradition of the people. Between 1958 and 1968, when this declaration was said to have been amended, there was no open or secret protest by the people of Owo against the number of traditional kingmakers but in 1968, during the agitation for the removal of Sir Olateru Olagbegi, it was discovered to their chagrin by his enemies that Sir Olagbegi had a majority following among the traditional Kingmakers. They, therefore, resorted to reducing the number to seven to ensure that the majority which Sir Olagbegi had was thus nullified. As a matter of fact, of the seven who were retained as traditional kingmakers in that spurious chieftaincy declaration, only four were present at the meeting where approval was given to the nomination by the Omo Olowos of the present Olowo of Owo. One is constrained to ask what faults, if any, have been committed by the other traditional kingmakers who have been so abruptly and

vindictively denied the opportunity of performing their duties to the Owo people. If they have committed no fault, then it is gross injustice to have removed them as traditional kingmakers, thereby preventing them from performing their age old functions.

5. I wish to point out at this stage that there is very strong reason to believe that the Olowo Chieftaincy Declaration of 1968 is a barefaced forgery. In the first instance, many of the traditional chiefs who were supposed to have attended the fictitiuos meeting purported to have been held on Monday 26th February, 1968 did not attend such a meeting.

Secondly, Mr. M. K. Famakinwa who was purported to have signed as Secretary at that meeting was no longer in the service of the Owo Divisional Council at the time. He had retired since 1963.

I should be grateful if Your Excellency will cause an enquiry to be conducted into this allegation and I can assure you that on our part, we can prove conclusively that the meeting at which this atrocious declaration was said to have been made, never took place in fact and therefore, the said Olowo Chieftaincy Declaration should be declared null and void.

6. In view of the above, therefore, I am praying Your Excellency to agree that the Olowo Chieftaincy Declaration should be included with the other Chieftaincy Declaration of Owo Traditional Chiefs to be discussed at the next meeting which the Commissioner for Chieftaincy Affairs has promised to convene at Owo. Since it is clearly evident that it is only right and fair that the number of traditional kingmakers should remain as before at 20, it is therefore obvious that the number of traditional kingmakers should be same for the High Chiefs as well as for the Olowo of Owo. Besides, I stoutly maintain that the notorious Olowo Chieftaincy Declaration of 1968 is manifestly unpopular and a barefaced forgery.

7. I will not like to bore Your Excellency with too many details in this memorandum but I do hope you will be kind enough to give me an interview at the earliest possible moment so that I can expatiate fully to Your Excellency on my recipe for creating an atmosphere for permanent peace, progress and harmony in Owo. Your Excellency, during the short space of time that you have been in the Western State,

a majority of the people of Western State are convinced that you are honest, well meaning and sincerely dedicated to the principles of justice and fair play. I assure you that l and my people at Owo are prepared to co-operate with you to ensure that your regime will mean a turning point for good in the affairs of Owo. It is my fervent hope that after I have had the opportunity of discussing fully with you and under your brilliant initiative, hearts in Owo District Council area ruled by antagonism will melt to love, minds now intolerant and vindictive will become generous and broad, people in Owo will learn to live and let live. Your Excellency, I am positive that in spite of the many conflicting problems that confront the warring factions in my town today, if all of us rulers as well as those who are ruled respond with vigour to the urgent call of destiny, though the night may be dark and troubled, the dawn will find us triumphant.

Your Excellency, I beseech you, let us have faith that right makes might and in that faith, let us to the end dare to do our duty as we understand it.

8. In conclusion, I commend this short poem by an American Poet - Josiah Gilbert Holland - to Your Excellency:

> "God give us men, a time like this demands
> Strong minds, great hearts, true faith and ready hands
> Men whom the lust of office does not kill;
> Men whom the spoils of office cannot buy;
> Men who possess opinions and a-will:
> Men who have honour, men who will not lie.
> Men who can stand before a demagogue.
> And damn his treacherous flatteries without thinking.
> Tall men sun-crowned, who live above the fog;
> In public duty and in private thinking."

Yours faithfully

S. R. B. Okoro

Owo Leaders Including Traditional Chiefs & Kingmakers.
c/o Chief Elerewe,
1 Elerewe Street,
Owo.
1/9/73.

His Excellency Brigadier Oluwole Rotimi,
The Military Governor,
Western State
Ibadan:

Your Excellency,

CALL BY OWO PEOPLE FOR THE RE-INSTATEMENT OF SIR OLATERU OLAGBEGI AS THE OLOWO OF OWO

We the undersigned on behalf of ourselves, Traditional Chiefs, & Kingmakers, Chiefs and the entire people of Owo hereby solemnly call on your Excellency's Government to urgently review the case of Olowo's affairs in which the ex-Olowo of Owo Sir Olateru Olagbegi was wrongfully deposed and an unpopular person imposed on Owo people.

We feel very strongly that the government cannot and should not continue to close its dutiful eyes on the present events taking place in Owo. It is not necessary to recall the confusion, disorder, and chaos that have been attendant on your Government's imposition of an Olowo since 1968 on Owo people.

Your Commissioners and a good number of Government Officials have acknowledged publicly that there is no peace in Owo.

We are not tired and will never tired of repeating our grievances each time a petition of this nature is put up. We feel very strongly that a solution should be found to this critical issue and no Government worth its salt will gloss over its responsibility for the defence of its people's politiical rights and liberty which are denied Owo people mercilessly.

Briefly your Excellency, what we are saying is that the Olowo

Chieftaincy is part and parcel of our political life, and apart from the fact that the post is being maintained from the taxpayers money, the people should be given adequate opportunity in electing who should be their ruler in the interest of peace, tranquility and good government. Before we draw up our conclusion Sir, the following points are worth emphasising on the matter.

(a) That Sir Olateru Olagbegi has reigned as the Olowo of Owo for about a quarter of a century meritoriously and the power and influence he had established for himself and Owo people during those years are such that to think that he could simply be deposed without many reverses in our progressive march (which are happening right now) is to deceive oneself. Yet he was unilaterally deposed in a questionable way by the Western State Government.

(b) That when he was tried by the Council of Obas & Chiefs, he was not deposed but suspended for six months at the end of which he was reinstated by the Government in 1966. He was asked to resume duty by the Government when some thugs caused trouble by burning six of his houses and about ninety belonging to others who are his supporters. He was forced to come to Ibadan after the incident. The second day the Government set up the Kumapayi Commission of Inquiry, but within twenty-four hours Sir Olateru was deposed and banished to Okitipupa without waiting for the Inquiry to sit. This is the crux of the matter because we feel Justice has not been done at all.

(c) While Sir Olateru was at Okitipupa the Government proceeded to amend the Chieftaincy Declaration whereby Owo twenty Kingmakers were deliberately reduced to seven for reasons which are not obvious to the people. This exercise is still yet to convince the people that the Western State Government has taken the right and impartial steps in the affairs of Olowo Chieftaincy. It is not clear therefore whether the rights of the people have not been taken from them.

(d) The Kumapayi Commission of Inquiry sat publicly but up till now its findings which are very vital to our cause have not been made public for reasons which only the Government could explain. For as long as the Western State Government keeps away the truth about this Inquiry so long the people will continue to expose the ugly features. The whole world would like to know the Government's White Paper on the inquiry. We believe that the Government should not act on speculations instead on cogent reasons.

(e) When once a political injustice of this nature has been established beyond all reasonable doubts it will be very difficult for any Government to disregard the people's demand for rectification. Examples of this matter abound in history. The Western State Government has once reinstated the Aseyin of Iseyin when similar injustices were committed by the same Government. Other States in the Federation have done similar things by correcting themselves, e.g. The Erejuwa, the Olu of Warri.

(f) We commend the dynamism of Your Excellency in seeing to it that every wrong in the West is righted and we are confident that in the present issue of Olowo of Owo chieftaincy tangle you will see to it that justice triumphed.

Although it is not during your time that Sir Olateru was banished in this way, but since Government is government, all the records relating to the issues are within your reach for close study and see that justice is done without fear or favour.

(g) It is in our interest to see that peace prevails in every part of the Western State, Owo not being an exception; but peace can only prevail where the wishes and the rights of the people are not unilaterally trampled upon. It is no use making life difficult for thousands of Owo people in the interest of one man. If the Government is not sure of the wishes of Owo people it should make it a more democratic issue by ordering a plebiscite immediately.

In view of all these glaring and blazing imposition, series of demonstrations have been witnessed by your Excellency, your Commissioners and other government officials against such action. In fact all of them have admitted publicly that Owo is not peaceful. We as leaders have been restraining at great pains some of the agitators against violent acts in retaliation for what they have suffered at the hands of the few usurpers being backed now. We are therefore praying that Your Excellency should appoint, as a matter of urgency and in the interest of justice and fair play, which are the cardinal principles of your administration, a high-powered Inquiry into the circumstances leading to the wrongful deposition of Sir Olateru Olagbegi as the Olowo of Owo and the imposition of an unpopular person on Owo people.

In this connection we beg to point out that it is not fair to continue to pay salaries from the taxpayers' funds to an unpopular person imposed on the people as the Olowo. It is high time this was stopped.

We wish your Excellency a very successful tenure of office

We are,

Your loyal subjects.

Chief Elerewe of Owo Traditional Chiefs & Kingmaker

Chief Ogunleye

Leader

The Olateru Olagbegi Family,
81 Kofo Abayomi Avenue,
Apapa, Lagos.
October, 1973.

His Excellency,
General Yakubu Gowon,
c/o Vice Admiral Wey,
Dodan Barracks, Ikoyi,
Lagos

Your Excellency.

AN APPEAL: THE EX-OLOWO OF OWO'S CASE.

We realise how reluctant you will be to interfere in what might be regarded as the internal problem of the Western State and a matter for the State's Governor.

We are equally reluctant to bother you with our problems realising how extremely busy Your Excellency is in your numerous roles, and, in performing your duties to the Nation, the O.A.U and the world in general. We are fully aware of your heavy commitments but we cannot but appeal to you, as the highest Authority in the land and for humanitarian reasons to use your good offices to look into the present deadlock involving the Ex-Olowo Sir Olateru Olagbegi's case.

Since he was deposed in 1968, there have been endless petitions to the WesternState Military Governors and Chieftaincy Commissioners for his reinstatement by a large majority of Owo people. These entreaties are based on rational thinking and concrete facts rather than on sentiments. Some of these facts are:-

1.   Sir Olateru Olagbegi's deposition was politicaly motivated and all but one of the Kingmakers in Owo are loyal to him.

2.   The result of Kumapayi Inquiry set up to look into his case was never published.

3. Since his deposition the town has not progressed an inch, rather it has deteriorated so much so that it now looks more like a village than a flourishing town it used to be.

4. A large number of the people are very unhappy and ill feelings against the trouble-making minority clique are running very high.

5. There are now endless petitions and demonstrations beseeching the Western State Governor to return him to his people as the Olowo of Owo.

Those of us his children writing this letter have been approached by the King makers to appeal to your Excellency both on theirs and our behalf to use your good offices to look into the matter.

A few of the petitions written by the Owo Kingmakers, the Market Women, the Youth Associations and some Press cuttings on the matter are enclosed to enable Your Excellency see how important the matter is to a very large majority of the Owo population.

We are most concerned that we should not waste Your Excellency's time unnecessarily, but as this problem is uppermost on our minds we are convinced that what involves a very big town in the Western State is also a National problem. Of course we appreciate the fact that your Excellency holds the nation, the people, their happiness and property very dearly.

We are,

Very Sincerely yours

Loyal Subjects.

Adegbite Olateru-Olagbegi

For the Olateru-Olagbegi Family

Chapter 9

THE RETURN OF THE LEGEND

The agitation by supporters of Sir Olateru continued unabated till 1991. However these agitations seemed to have received little attention from successive governments of Western State. It was carried forward to 1976 when Ondo State was created. The Military Administration in the state in 1977 set up a Chieftaincy Review Commission headed by Justice Adeyinka Morgan to undertake a review of all recognized chieftaincies in the state.

Sir Olateru Olagbegi seized the opportunity offered by this commission to plead for his reinstatement. In its record of daily proceedings, No 69, page 30, the Morgan Commission recalled that Chief Owasoyin Ariyo, a high Chief and kingmaker, said, "We are appealing to the Commission to reinstate the ex-Olowo." While Sir Olateru Olagbegi himself appeared before the commission and in his memo 1, paragragh 47, urged the commission to "declare my deposition as Olowo of Owo improper, mischievous and contrary to custom and further that my deposition is null and void and should be reinstated as Olowo of Owo."

However the Commission refrained from making any pronouncement on the issue, while the government, in its White Paper which incidentally was released by the time Chief M.A. Ajasin, one of the supporters of Olagbegi's deposition, had become Governor, said nothing on the issue. Sir Olagbegi's plea for reinstatement did not receive sympathetic hearing due to interplay of forces. Firstly, Military governors who held power most of the time betwee 1968-78 and after 1984 were not in any mood to review actions taken by their ilk, owing possibly to esprit-de-corps consideration. No doubt the enthronement of a new king had complicated issues and Government was already compromised. The Governors thus glossed over the issue which had become too hot to handle. It would be foolhardy to stir the hornets' nest. They must have their reasons.

The Civilian Administration of Chief Ajasin between 1979 - 1983 obviously could not have resolved the matter in Olagbegi's favour for obvious reasons. Ajasin was alleged to be a principal character in the deposition episode of Sir Olagbegi.

Meanwhile, both Sir Olagbegi and the reigning Olowo Oba Ogunoye are advanced in age. Both were in their Eighties by 1991 when the Third Republic came on stream in the states.

It was a matter of conjecture that the final arbiter in the case of the two Olowos would be the immortal God. Oftentimes, there were speculations that Sir Olagbegi planned to use the occasion of the popular festival of Igogo when an Olowo is expected to dance outside the palace, to seize the throne.

Such was the prevalence of the speculations that security was always tightened at Owo during the festival, or at any time alarm was raised by the Olowo that he felt unsafe from the activities of Sir Olagbegi. However the speculations were unfounded going by the peaceful way the man had carried on his protest since 1968.

It was however not in doubt that Sir Olateru Olagbegi desperately wished to get his throne back. It was an ambition that was pursued with all vigour and resources. This obsession was driven not solely as a personal wish but more in consideration for his numerous children, who would be excluded from the throne in future according to Owo tradition if he died outside the throne. It was his wish that even on his deathbed, he should be allowed to sit on the throne and give up the ghost to allow his children to have access to the throne. Thus the common prayer by Sir Olagbegi and his people was for long life.

In the meantime, with the advent of civil rule, Sir Olagbegi, his children and his supporters, were prepared to fight on. All his children were well positioned in the two parties and they made their impact well felt. Also, Sir Olagbegi continued his silent peaceful manouvers towards all those who were against him in Owo and thus began another grand but silent offensive to return to the throne. The long sought opportunity presented itself in 1993. Olowo of Owo was rarely seen in public on account of old age and prolonged illness. At last, he joined his ancestors on March 29, 1993.

The situation was dicey because Ogunoye is now dead. The throne was vacant to be filled and Sir Olateru is alive and ready to occupy the exalted office. The existence of Olateru made the case more technical and unique. According to an article in the Tribune of May 11th, 1993, it raises the question, 'should he be invited back to the throne or should another person be appointed as the new Olowo of Owo?' The question rages. In answering the question, the paper opined that "the people of Owo are divided into two ideological groups, the Pro-Olagbegi -those who want him back at all cost- and anti-Olagbegi, those who would not like to see even his waste products in the palace loo."

The pro-Olagbegi movement or group is headed by Chief A. Adetula, the Sasere of Owo, who is also the Prime Minister to the Oba, a member of the Kingmakers who is adored, loved and feared by the people. With him are Chief Osun, among others. Chief Osun, who was among those people who chased out Sir

Olateru from the palace in 1968, has now turned a new leaf and a repentant man. He described Sir Olateru as a great man of vision who was misunderstood and misrepresented when he was an Oba.

Among the camp of anti-Olowo was Chief Aralepo who in an interview with a Tribune Reporter said that "Sir Olateru's time has gone forever. All the ceremonies that accompanied a dead Oba had been performed for him. We need a new king in the interest of peace, progress and order. There is no going back on his matter. Even I have received up to eight letters from those who are interested in the throne. We need à new Oba and a new Oba will certainly reign in Owo. Sir. Olateru would never see the throne again! Not again."

Another high Chief, Chief Olusola Bayode, in the same interview opined that "no amount of pressure or intimidation from anybody, no matter how highly influential, can force the Iloro to perform all the traditional ceremonies once again, since it is against Owo culture. Even if they bomb them, they would not do it. As far As I am concerned, this man was deposed about 25 years ago. How on earth would anybody, bring or force him on the people without courting trouble? You know. He would avenge all what they have done to him. If he does not want to do it, his followers will encourage him into doing it. Infact, his followers' verbal pronouncements are capable of igniting the town, but since we know what we are doing and where we are heading for we allow them to have free days. But nonetheless, we the senior Omolowos would select a new Oba by the special grace of God. Any attempt to impose him on us would forment trouble and ruin us. One thing is sure, there could be a town without an Oba, but there could not be an Oba without a town," he concluded.

In view of the dicey situation in the town, coupled with previous experience of the Government in the past, the State Government summoned a meeting of the concerned groups on

May 3rd, 1993. According to a news story in the Tribune, "The Report of their deliberations was brought to the hearing of everybody in the state. The government needs to be very tactful in wading into the matter. There are a lot of grounds to be dug, holes to be filled and rivers to be crossed before things could be put right in Owo."

The first sign that Sir Olateru could regain his throne was an appeal made by Dr. Adewunmi Abitoye, the then Chairman of Owo Local Government, in the Sunday Times of April 18th 1993, that the Ondo State Government should revoke the order banishing the former Olowo of Owo, Sir Olateru Olagbegi, since 1968 (25 years ago), to enable him return to the throne. According to him, majority of the people of Owo wanted him back on the throne since the demise of the late Olowo of Owo, Oba Adekola Ogunoye.

To say that the town was divided into two camps on whom to become the Olowo of Owo was stating the obvious. The tension was high and people were eager to know the stand of the State Government on this issue.

One of the ruling houses, the Ajikes, had nominated some candidates as the next possible Olowo of Owo. The situation was becoming dicey, cloudy and gloomy. Both the pro- and anti-Olagbegi seem convinced of their actions and they believed that the aftermath holds serious consequences for the town and the people. It was in this state of near anarchy that the State Government, under the leadership of Evangelist Bámidele Olumilua, remembered the words of Edmund Burke that,"the only thing necessary for triumph of evil is for good men to do nothing." Hence, he promulgated an edict through an order made and signed on the 15th October, 1993 and published as OD S.L.N. 2 of 1993 in the Ondo State of Nigeria, Gazette No. 19 Vol. 18 dated October 27th, 1993 revoking the Olowo of Owo (Deposition) order No. 17 of 1968 wherein the defunct Western State Government deposed Sir Olateru Olagbegi, the Olowo of

Owo. Consequently and by the same order of the Governor, dated 15th October, 1993, the kingship of Olowo of owo has also been restored to Sir Olateru Olagbegi. The order is titled; 'The Olowo of Owo (Revocation of Deposition and Restoration) Order 1993'

According to a release from Mr. Osewole Modupe, Deputy Press Secretary to the then Governor, "the Governor's action was premised on the agitation by an appeal from the majority of Owo people to the State Governor for the reinstatement of Sir Olateru Olagbegi as the Olowo of Owo so that peace and order which had continued to elude the town since the deposition of Sir Olateru Olagbegi as the Olowo of Owo since 1968, could reign. Before the order was made, Sir Olateru Olagbegi was made to enter into a bond with the State Government, promising amongst others: -

(I) Not to prosecute or pursue further any suit subsisting or pending before any court in respect of any chieftancy matter or any matter at all against any Owo indigene;

(ii) To devote the rest of his life towards the attainment and enthronement of peace, order, good government and progress of Owo and Ondo State in particular and that of Nigeria in general.

(iii) To bring all factions of Owo people together under one big family.

(iv) To work assiduously towards the settlement of all outstanding chieftaincy and other disputes in Owo and also recognise and respect the rights, duties and privileges of all chiefs presently in Owo.

(v) To recognise and give respect to the tenure of the Late Adekola Ogunoye and not to exhume his remains or do anything that will negatively affect his interest or that of his family as being feared by some people;

(vi) To support every noble cause or mission of the State Government and avoid anything or taking or precipitating any action that may bring me on collusion course with the State Government or in conflict either directly or indirectly with its goals, objectives, focus, yearnings and aspirations.

Sir Olateru Olagbegi also accepted that in the event of any failure to observe the conditions of the bond, he stands the risk of being deposed and banished by the State Government. The Governor enjoined every indigene of Owo in particular and Ondo State in general to cultivate the culture and habit of forgiveness, as it is only in doing so that we can live together in friendliness and brotherliness and bail out our state from the yoke of poverty and backwardness. He also appealed to any person or group of persons who feels aggrieved by the decision of the State Government to put the past behind them and bear in mind at all times that to err is human but to forgive is divine.

The Governor hereby appeals to all Owo indigenes, wherever they may be, to co-operate with Sir Olateru Olagbegi and eschew violence and chaos in order to restore the lost of Owo town.

Initially when the announcement was made, many people thought was another 'April fool', but when it dawned on many that it was a reality most homes of the Olagbegi's were like carnival and in a frenzied mood.

The town was also in a festive mood. To the Olagbégis, an emergency meeting of the family was convened where it was resolved that Sir Olateru should return to Owo on November 2nd, 1993. He was to be accompanied by his children and close associates. Elaborate arrangements were made to ensure peaceful arrival of Sir Olateru into Owo in order to avoid a re-occurrence of what happened in 1968.

On November 2nd, 1993 the date fixed for his arrival, as early as 7:00 a.m. the town's people-adults, children, both men and women thronged the palace to await the arrival of Sir Olateru Olagbegi. Commercial drivers, motorcylists, bicycle riders constituted themselves into escorts and dignitaries were at Emure-lle, about nine kilometers from Owo in order to give him a rousing welcome and escorted him to the palace.

He rode majestically into Emure-Ile in his golden colour 230 Mercedes Benz, with Reg. No, LA 9947 AH, and he was accompanied by the Ojomo of Ijebu-Owo, Oluda John Agboola, the head of Omolowos. From Emure-Ile, the convoy drove to his residence. At the new Olowo's residence, it was jubilation galore among the Oloris and his children. There was a seven gun salute called the Oteru in Owo tradition which investigation revealed was done last in 1968.

In his speech at the occasion which was titled, "The dawn of a New era," Sir Olateru Olagbegi opined that it was with great sense of humility and appreciation that he stood before his people and that it was historical that he was ascending the throne he lost about 25 years ago. According to him, the tumultous crowd that came to welcome him was a testimony to the yearning of his people for a return to normalcy and a deviation from acrimony, and that the event that culminated to his dethronement had now become part of the history of Owo and it should remain so forever. He pledged to ensure peace and that any act of omission or commission in the administration of Owo in the last 25 years would not be revisited. He noted with nostalgia his feelings of the past years when Owo was the cynosure of all eyes with its rich cultural heritage, torch bearer of Western Education, centre of social-cultural activities, meeting point for giants in politics. All these attributes, according to him had been withered away due to avoidable chieftaincy wranglings.

Sir Olateru stated that he derived his joy from the fact that all is not lost and he took solace in the popular parlance, "When there is life, there is hope." He finally thanked the State Governor, State Commissioners, Special Advisers, Chairman of Owo Local Government, the people of Owo and his children for their supports during the period of his travails and counted on their cooperation in all his future undertakings.

In his welcome address, Dr. Adewunmi Ibitoye, the then Chairman Owo Local Government, was grateful to the Almighty Father for the grace and privilege offered him to be a living witness to the great occasion. According to him, he and his people were happy for having learnt to forgive and forget. To fall and rise, and in fact, to face the ups and downs of life in happiness and sorrow is a clear pointer that Owo Community is one step higher at the moment in the conscious knowledge of the will of the Creator.

He finally thanked the State Governor and his Executives for deeming it necessary to reinstate Sir Olateru and similarly thanked the people of Owo for their resolute and unflinching support for the course of unity which they wisely enough think could be brought about by dousing the last vestiges of divisive and separatist tendencies in Owo.

With the return of Kabiyesi Sir Olateru Olagbegi to the Olowo throne, we have simply told our children and their children that we are done with enmity, hatred and intolerance.

In an interview conducted by African Drum Magazine among the indigenes of the town after the ceremony, it was unanimously agreed that, it was the best thing that could happen to the town at that material time. According to Mr. Olu Ogunmodede, a one-time correspondent of the British Broadcasting Corporation (BBC), he recalled that the only celebration that had pulled such crowd was when the Oba marked his Coronation anniversary in 1964, which according to him, he covered for BBC. In his opinion, the then Chairman of Owo Local Government Dr. Adewunmi Abitoye told journalists that the Oba's coming would change a lot of things in the town. There would be no more acrimony and the people are now very resolute. To those who might be aggrieved, he pledged that enough is enough, our beauty has been eroded, now it has been regained.

Equally elated, Chief John Agboola, the Ojomo of Ijebu-Owo said that everybody has accepted and they are rejoicing. According to the then State Commissioner for Chieftaincy Affairs, Prince Kola Ademeso when contacted, he told African Drum that there was no pressure from some individuals as being insinuated in certain quarters and the Government decision was based on majority support. Prince Ademeso also debunked the claim that Government was only out to gain political supports.

Sir Olateru is now back on the throne. Certain thorny issues need to be ironed out. Will he victimise those who masterminded his dethronement? Will he reinstate the seven High Chiefs who were stripped of their titles by the late Oba Ogunoye (who took over from Olagbegi) for their loyalty to Sir Olateru?

Questions! Questions!! And Questions!!! What the Olowo needs now is the Wisdom of Solomon so that he would reign successfully and carry his subjects along without any acrimony during his second coming.

The event was well reported both in the print and electronic media. It was also a common discussion among the people both within and outside Owo. For example, in the book of Revelation for Today and Tomorrow (1993) edition, Archbishop T. Oluwasanu Olabayo (J.P.), predicted thus: "Last year, I predicted that the Ex-Olowo of Owo, Oba Olateru Olagbegi, will receive the glory of God. It has come to pass and efforts are being made to reinstate him. The Owo people should be magnanimous and forgive the ex-Olowo.

"Those who are against the reinstatement of the Ex-Olowo must remember that no human being is perfect. The ex-Olowo is God-ordained and anyone opposing his reinstatement is opposing God's will".

"For peace to reign in the Community, Chief Michael Ajasin should play a fatherly role so that his name will be written as a man who brought unity to Owo Community. The Olowo should be re-instated. It is then that God's glory will come back to Owo. The Olowo too should not sack those who were against him. If he is re-instated, he should pray against bereavement." - May 18, 1993.

The event was also widely reported in the major newspapers thus:

THE RETURN OF OBA OLAGBEGI

It is good news to hear about the reinstatement of Sir Olateru Olagbegi, the deposed Olowo of Owo. His reinstatement order was contained in an edict signed by the Ondo State Governor, Bamidele Olumilua. According to the Governor, the gesture was necessitated by the readiness of Oba Olagbegi to work in harmony with his subjects. Government also recognised that the circumstances that led to the Oba's deposition no longer exist. Above all, no doubt, is the urgency on the part of the State Executive to restore peace, order and unity to the fractious chieftaincy houses on the one hand, and the Owo people on the other. Olagbegi was deposed in February 1968 by the then Western State government of Major General (Rtd) Adeyinka Adebayo. The deposition was linked to the fractious troubles that engulfed party partisans during the 1962-66 turmoil in Western Nigeria.

We also recall that with the deposition of Olagbegi, his successor, Oba Adekola Ogunoye II, tried unsuccesslully to reconcile the different interest groups in the town. Shortly after his death in March this year, calls for Olagbegi's reinstatement were renewed and intensified by Owo people. Therefore, it is good politics on the part of Governor Olumilua to have listened to the people's agitation and aspirations.

A quarter of a century is really a long time in the life of a monarch. And in the interval, a great deal has happened to monarchical institution in Nigeria through democratic reforms. But the surviving royalties have managed to adjust their perspective and become key players in the politics and economic development of their various areas. It is our hope that the triumphant return of Oba Olagbegi is an auspicious signal for the people of Owo to assume their solution of the palace from tempestuous politics of the moment and co-operation of all Owo citizens arc needed to make the restoration truly beneficial.

Daily times Editorial of November 6, 1995

CELEBRATIONS AS OLAGBEGI ASCENDS THRONE AGAIN

Two things were noticeable in Owo, Ondo State, last Tuesday. The first was the fuel scarcity that left many vehicles on queues in every filling station in the town. The second and the more historic, was the official ceremony for the reinstatement of Oba Olateru Olagbegi as Olowo of Owo, who, but for his dethronement 25 years ago, should have by now been on the throne for 52 solid years!

As his Highness, the Ojomo of Ijebu-Owo told Vanguard "the official ceremony was impromptu because the Olowo of Owo was in Lagos when his reinstatement was officially made public by the Ondo State Government." And, he said further, we in Owo really did not publicise this ceremony, but I think many people will not believe because of the multitude that witnessed the occasion."

It is a fact that nobody will believe that the ceremony for the return of Sir Olagbegi to the Palace, was either impromptu nor unpublicised. As a matter of fact social activities throughout the length and breadth of the ancient Owo town last Tuesday presuposed that the Owo people have for a long time been yawning for the return of Oba Olagbegi to the throne.

Thus, it is not an exaggeration that while men and women, housewives and other feminine inhabitants, invaded the town in expensive assorted attire to celebrate the record-breaking event, the ancestral spirits must have felt proud for the new turn of events in Owo.

One noticeable thing around the Palace, which is centrally located in the town, last Tuesday was the commencement of the Oba Market which has been shifted from the place since the demise of the late Oba Ogunoye early in the year.

The significance of the commencement of this market, after the demise of any Oba traditionally, is that a new Oba or another Oba has been enthroned.

Thus, the fact that business started at the market last Tuesday heralded the reinstatement of Sir Olagbegi. Even, those who still doubted the announcement of his restoration because of conflicting rumours began in earnest to prepare for the celebrations that were to follow later that day.

Apart from the Oba Market the Palace itself shook off the cyst of cemetery-like tranquility that has been hovering on the place since Oba Ogunoye died more than six months ago. The place wore a brighter look as cleaning activities were going on there early into the morning that day.

Although Vanguard learnt that Sir Olagbegi would not immediately move into his Palace because reconstruction and renovation work to the tune of ten million Naira (#10,000.000.00) would soon be undertaken to give the place a modern touch, traditional ablutions were made round the palace, most especially in preparation for the big event that later took place at the spacious pitch in front of the place.

Apart from joyous and merry movements by Owo people round the town last Tuesday, the people, later in the day, displayed their support and solidarity for their reinstated traditional ruler. Their representatives in their thousands went in different vehicles to meet Sir Olagbegi at Ogbese, a satellite town to Owo which is about 15kilometres away.

Elder Emmanuel Afolabi, one of the thousands of people that went to meet Sir Olagbegi at Ogbese, told Vanguard that it was not just Owo people alone that came to meet the Olowo of Owo.

According to him, representatives of other communities in Owoland, as well as communities from Akoko, Akure and other places came to grace the occasion.

Speaking further with Afolabi who is an officer of the drivers' Association in Owo Local Government, said that, "we, in all the drivers' unions from Owo to Ikare Akoko came to Ogbese because we have been praying that he (Sir Olagbegi) should return to his throne."

There is no doubt that the thousands of people that literarily "invaded" Ogbese last Tuesday to meet Sir Olagbegi were very committed to whatever the reinstated Olowo of Owo represents in Owo's chequered history. The hostile tropical sun of the day notwithstanding, they waited patiently for more than three hours, singing and chanting hilariously in Owo dialect until the convoy in which the Olowo came from Lagos through Akure appeared in the western horizon of the town.

To say that Sir Olateru Olagbegi felt greatly honoured by his subjects that have come to welcome him home at Ogbese is to say the obvious. Beaming with smile and waving as his car filed past hundreds of other vehicles parked at the side of the trunk-A that leads to Owo from Akure thunderous shout of "Kabiyesi" rent the air and his convoy from Akure was soon boosted by the parked vehicles in which thousands of Owo sons and daughters have come to welcome him.

As the two-kilometre-long convoy entered Owo at about 3 O'clock in the evening, the atmosphere in the town became highly charged and people in the streets went into a frenzy. Both old and young followed the long convoy round the town. Everyone was practically struggling to catch a glimpse of the beloved king who was setting a record that might soon find its way into Guinness Book of Records.

For the period the convoy went round Owo, most shops were put under lock. And, in spite of lack of taxi cabs people walked from Odo-Ogun, the most western part of the town to Odo-Ijebu on the way to Ifon. As a matter of fact, as the Olowo temporarily branched at his residence near the erstwhile popular St. John/Mary College, the numerous law enforcement agents had to contend with checking the incredible multitude that had already gathered at the venue of the official reception for the Oba.

Still talking about the big crowd that came to witness the occasion, His Highness, Sasere of Owo, Chief J.O. Adetula told Vanguard that the crowd was the biggest in the history of Owo. He said, "I believe that this occasion will remain the happiest for Sir Olateru Olagbegi, the Olowo of Owo. I was not a young boy when he was enthroned in March 1941. The mammoth crowd that has come to witness today's event is ten times greater than the one that came to his installation in 1941."

There is no any exaggeration in Chief Adetula's description, because, if not for the aggressive role of the law enforcement agents, the Press wouldn't have been able to properly cover the occasion. The crowd was such that if anyone had ventured to drop a pin, it wouldn't have found its way to the ground!

Meanwhile, at about 4.45p.m. on that day the occasion kicked off after the Olowo had seated together with his most eminent

Chiefs, which included the Ojomo of Ijebu-Owo as well as the Sasere and other important Omo Olowos (the Kingsmakers), the Owo Local Government Chairman, Chief (Dr) Adewumi Abitoye, and many other important dignitaries.

The occasion was definitely a mini-interdenominational service. Both the Arch-Bishop and the Chief Imam that prayed at the occasion said special prayers for the Oba, his chiefs, Owo town and the entire nation.

In one of his remarks, Arch-Bishop S. A. Fadeyi, who said the opening prayer compared the life and experience of Sir Olagbegi with that of Dr. Nelson Mandela and challenged all Owo sons and daughters to cooperate with the Oba in his pledge and effort at rebuilding the beleaguered town.

And Chief Imam Aladesawe reminded the happy crowd that unalloyed support for the ruler or leader is an important aspect of the Quranic injunction.

In his own speech, Dr. Abitoye, Owo L.G. Chairman said that the occasion was being used to seal the parcel of unity and progress of Owo. Referring to Sir Olagbegi as the father to all Owo idigenes both home and abroad, he further said that, "the time has come for us (Owo people) to put Owo in its rightful position among Yoruba towns."

In his own address, Oba Olagbegi remarked that "My reinstatement as announced by the Government of Ondo State on Friday, 30th October 1993 has been an act of God and the strong determination of the State Government to ensure lasting peace in Owo. It is on this note that I register my thanks to Almighty God for making it possible for me to address you as Olowo of Owo."

He further said that, "History is being made today as I am privilege to ascend to the throne which I lost twenty five (25) years ago. The tumultuous crowd here is a testimony to the yearnings of the people of Owo for a return to normalcy and a deviation from acrimony. The events that culminated in my dethronement had become part of history of Owo and it should remain so forever."

In another development, Sir Olagbegi showed the quality that earned him the post of Minister-Without-Portfolio in the hey days of the Action Group in the old Western Region.

Informally addressing the cheering crowd in Owo dialect, he mixed the facts of the reality of Owo development with some wisecrack that kept the crowd hypnotised until he dropped the microphone to signify the end of the occasion at about 6.30p.m. that day.

The celebrations did not end with the reception of Oba Olagbegi. One important event after the occasion was the group dance round the town by about 60 daughters of Sir Olagbegi. One of them, Mrs. Biola Alonge, told Vanguard that they were excited because,"the words of God has come to pass." Mrs Alonge said that she was at St. Louis in Ondo when her father was dethroned and as she added,"it wasn't a pleasant experience to go through. The whole uproar and uncertainty was too hard to bear,"she said.

Another one of the children, Mrs. Okin, a superintendent with the Department of Customs and Excise, also philosophically told Vanguard that, "God has a purpose for everything. She also maintained that the dethronement of her father was a "hectic situation", and added that, words cannot express her joy for the reinstatement of her father as the Olowo of Owo.

In similar vein, one of the daughters, Miss Adenireti Olagbegi, a student of Federal Polytechnic, llaro, who was never born at the dethronement of her father said that the prophesy in her name has come true. As she said, "I am Adenireti meaning that crown has hope. It is the hope we are all witnessing today."

Whatever is the hope, two youths, Olasupo Abulatan (based in Ibadan) and Miss ldowu Olawole told Vanguard that the celebrations have just begun for the dawn of a new era in Owo.

Culled from the Vanguard November 8, 1993

The Second Coming Of The People's Olowo

AFTER wallowing for 25 years in the dolorous waters, of forced irrelevance, Sir Olateru Olagbegi, the Olowo of Owo, early this month, bounced back to the centre stage of Owo politics. As the traditional head of Owo between 1941 and 1968, Sir Olateru left remarkable imprints on the sands of time. A charismatic leader of note, he bestrode his kingdom like a colosus. The agility with which he carried on was one that could not be wished away. Even the most virulent of his critics acknowledged that he was forward-looking.

Enamoured of his immense proportions the Queen of England, Elizabeth II placed the Olowo in the pantheon of a leader ahead of his time. It was in this regard that she, sometime in the 1950's, conferred on him the title of Knight of British Empire (KBE). He was then the Chairman of Western Nigeria Council of Chiefs. He was so influential and powerful in government circles that he earned for himself the rare privilege of a Minister-Without-Portfolio at that time.

Under Sir Olateru, Owo, one of the earliest towns in Yorubaland, was at the height of its powers. It had a cultural heritage which made it the cynosure of all eyes. As the torchbearer of Western education, Owo served as the centre of socio-cultural activities and the meeting point of giants in politics. In fact, the Action Group, the most formidable political Association in Western Nigeria of the First Republic, was launched in Owo. As the epicentre of sociocultural and political activities, Owo witnessed rapid development. Through Sir

Olateru, the Saint John/Mary College, the Government Technical College, John Holt Ltd, and a few other development projects were attracted to Owo.

The people held him in high esteem, and he effectively ruled over all the quarters of Owo, namely Igboroko, Ehinogbe, lloro, Isaipen and ljebu quarters. But soon afterwards, the Olowo's authority over the quarters came under fire. The Ojomo of Ijebu quarters, regarded as the second-in-command to the Olówó, became a thorn in the flesh.

Essentially, the Ojomo considered ljebu quarters his domain over which the Olowo had no authority. But for the Olowo the Ojomo's posturing was confrontational. Using his influence in high quarters, the Olowo successfully made a case against the Ojomo whom he accused of trying to separate his quarters from the rest of the Owo town and of undermining the authority of the Olowo. As a form of reprisal, the Western Regional government, in 1953, abolished the title of the Ojomo.

The abolition of the Ojomo title was the watershed of a longdrawn crisis that saw to the deposition of the Olowo in 1968. Following the abolition of the Ojomo title, leaders of thought in Ijebu quarters, who were mostly members of the defunct National Council of Nigerian Citizens (NCNC), decided to join the mainstream of Owo politics. To achieve this goal, they decided to embrace the Action Group (AG). But while Chief Ajasin welcomed the ljebu Community into the Action Group, Sir Olateru opposed their admission. Although Chief Ajasin succeeded in integrating the ljebu community into the mainstream of the AG, the ensuing crisis claimed his headship of Imade College in 1962.

Having fallen out of favour with Chief Ajasin, and Chief Obafemi Awolowo, who supported Ajasin's rapport with ljebu community, Sir Olateru chose to pitch his tent with Oladoke Akintola's Nigerian National Democratic Party (NNDP), which had effective control over the then Western Region. Akintola was the then Premier of Western Region. Sir. Olateru's move was one that angered ardent supporters of the Action Group in Owo. But because of the Olowo's towering personality, they could not mobilize support against him.

But the military intervention of 1966 paved the way for anti-Olowo sentiment. Chief Ajasin formed Owo Community Association which pressed for the removal of the Olowo. With persistent pressures from various quarters, the government of Lt. Col. Adekunle Fajuyi suspended the Olowo from office for six months. The Olowo spent the six-month exile in Ibadan. When at the expiration of the period of suspension he returned to Owo, what he met was a violent confrontation. He ran for his dear life and resumed his forced exile in Okitipupa. The then government of Brigadier Adeyinka Adebayo, convinced that the Olowo was no longer wanted by his people, deposed him in 1968. He was succeeded by Adekola Ogunoye, from the Ogunoye ruling house. Owo has three ruling houses, the other two being Olowo Ajike house and Olateru-Olagbegi house.

Oba Adekola Ogunoye ruled for 25 years. He died on March 29 this year. At his death, the case for the reinstatement of Sir Olateru which has been going on surreptitiously over the years became strident. Representations were made to the state government. Open letters were written to the governor. Meetings were held with interest groups. Some members of the Omolowo, a group of Kingmakers responsible for the election of a new Olówó, met with the government. Even market women were not left out. They made overtures to the State Government on the need to reinstate Sir Olateru. Although there were dissenting voices from some segments of Owo town, the preponderance of opinion, according to Governor Bamidele Olumilua of Ondo State, favoured the reinstatement of Sir Olateru.

Before the Ondo State Government took the bold decision to return Sir Olateru to the coveted stool, the man himself, old as he was, took steps to ensure his reinstallation. Just as Chief Ajasin was the brain behind his deposition, so also was he (Chief Ajasin) the major stumbling block on the way of the return of Sir Olateru to the throne. According to the press secretary to the Ondo State Governor, Mr. Olajide Olusola, Sir Olateru amply recognised this fact. But considering the fact that the two octogenarians have been locked in an epic battle of sorts, Sir Olateru, this time, offered the olive branch. He approached Chief Ajasin and appealed for a change of heart. Chief Ajasin was said to have maintained his stance even after the meeting.

Part of Sir Olateru's desperate move, even at 83, to ensure his return to the throne was done not just for his own sake, but for his children. In Owo, the custom provides that if an Oba is banished from the throne and he dies while still in exile, his children automatically stand disqualified from aspiring to the throne. Sir Olateru was therefore intent on ensuring that whatever misfortune that befell him was not extended to his children.

Ever since the banishment of Sir Olateru in 1968, Owo is said to have known no peace. The town has been divided along many lines. Quarters stood against quarters. Personal relationships among people of contending quarters were discouraged. This situation was part of what government considered before taking a decision on the Owo chieftaincy crisis.

Having considered all this, government, according to Mr. Olajide Olusola, also took a hard look at the circumstances that led to the removal of Sir Olateru as the Olowo of Owo 25 years ago.

In the process, government was convinced that the matter was political and that the AG and the NNDP which were the bones of contention were no longer in existence. Again, government took into consideration the time lag, 25 years, it reasoned was long enough to heal old wounds and therefore considered seriously the need to forgive him. According to Mr. Olusola, Mr. Olumilua personally took up this matter with Chief Ajasin.

To ensure that all sides to the dispute were listened to, government carried out a random survey of the people's opinion. In doing this, Mr. Olumilua said the government's intention was to find out what Owo people wanted. The many years of stagnation which Owo had suffered as a result of the chieftaincy crisis was one which government could not allow to drag on. The need for peace and progress in the ancient town therefore became imperative. Convinced therefore that majority of the people wanted Sir Olateru back to the throne, the Ondo State Governor, through an order made and signed on October 15, 1993, and published in the Ondo State Gazette No. 19 of October 27. 1993 revoked the Olowo of Owo (Deposition) Order No. 17 of 1968 wherein the defunct Western State Government deposed Sir Olateru as the Olowo of Owo.

Consequently, the chieftaincy of the Olowo of Owo was restored to Sir Olateru. Before the order was made, Sir Olateru was made to enter into a bond with the State Government, promising, among others, not to prosecute or pursue further any suit subsisting or pending before any court in respect of any chieftaincy matter or any matters at all against any Owo indigenes, to bring all factions of Owo together under one big family, to devote the rest of his life towards the attainment and enthronement of peace, order, good governance and progress of Owo and Ondo State in particular and that of Nigeria in general, to work assiduously towards the settlement of all outstanding chieftaincy and other disputes in Owo and also recognise and respect the rights, duties and privileges of all chiefs presently in Owo; and perhaps, most importantly to recognise and give respect to the tenure of the late Oba Adekola Ogunoye and not to exhume his remains or do anything that will negatively affect his interest or that of his family as being feared by some people. Sir Olateru accepted that in the event of failure to observe the conditions of the bond, he stood the risk of being deposed and banished by the state government.

In 1968, when Sir Olateru was hounded out of the throne, the people of Owo had no faith in him. They saw in his defection to the NNDP an act of betrayal. They rioted, they looted and they burnt, to bring home their point. Today, 25 years after, the same people of Owo are happy about his return, or so it seems. Perhaps, part of Sir Olateru's trump card lay in the disabilities of his successor Oba Ogunoye, who was an illiterate. Under him, Owo wallowed in intellectual stagnation, dwindling cultural heritage, incessant and murderous chieftaincy wranglings, politics of acrimony, deteriorating educational facilities and moral decadence.

In Sir Olateru, the people of Owo appear to have found a saviour. Today, they look back with notalgia at the past glory of the town. As an expression of their faith in the leadership of the Olowo, Owo has never gone to bed since his reascension on November 2. His re-entry to the Olowo's palace after 25 years of absence from it was triumphant. But the Olowo only made a brief appearance there. He has since returned to his personal house. The palace is being renovated at the instance of the Olowo.

At the hill-top residence of Sir Olateru, it has been pomp and pageantry since his reascension. Hordes of visitors, people who have come to pay their respects, dance groups, women associations, traditional rulers, church leaders, etc., have been trooping in in large numbers to pay homage to the Olowo. In fact, his residence is now a bee-hive of activities. The old man is under pressure. But to stave off part of the heat, the Olowo is usually shielded from visitors until about 11.00 a.m. every morning.

As the celebration goes on, the Olowo appears to think less of the circumstances that led to his removal. Even at that, age has worn his memory thin. He can hardly elaborate on issues, he only drops hints and sometimes makes very categorical statements. His case is made more cumbersome by the intricate nature of the issue that saw to his dethronement. In a chat with him last week at his hill-top residence, the Olowo appeared to have forgotten what really transpired at that time. However, he noted that what happened then was a rebellion against him and said it was difficult to narrate. He appeared to have lost grip of exactly why he was removed from office. For him however, what happened then had a national colouration. It involved the entire Nigeria. It was a matter of people taking sides in issues that did not permit such a devisive approach.

Apart from the devastating effect of age on the Olowo, Sir Olateru today cuts the image of someone that has been sober by experience. His approach to issue appears most philosophical. Most issues hardly excite him. It is perhaps in this light that he would stop at nothing to let his interviewers run away with the impression that his 25 years out of office was uneventful. He did nothing while out of office. He only travelled occasionally outside the country but would not let you believe it was for anything special.

Still relying on his age and wealth of experience, the Olowo tries as much as possible not to relapse into a paroxysm of cheap emotional outburst. Perhaps to dwell on how he felt while out of office would betray his private convictions. Thus, in the manner of a stoic, he summarised his circumstance thus: "Things that cannot be helped must be endured."

Perhaps it was this ability to endure that led to the final triumph of Sir Olateru. Today, he appears to harbour no animosities against any of those responsible for his removal. He has even forgotten most of the very names that worked against him then. But the names of Chief Ajasin and Adeyinka Adebayo have not yet gained entrance into his sub-conscious mind. He mentioned them with ease when he was asked to name some of the actors that worked against him in those tumultous days.

For Sir Olateru, the single most important factor that led to his dethronement was hatred. This hatred lay with the people. Unfortunately however, the government of the day got bitten by the same bug of hatred and acted in concert with the people. That notwithstanding, what Sir Olateru have for his people is a positive plan of action that would usher them into a new era. The dethronement of Sir Olowo was not only a seminal event; it was the first in the history of Owo people. Whatever happened to Owo while he was away was, for Sir Olateru, a yardstick for measuring the quality of leadership offered by his successor. Convinced therefore that Owo witnessed only fracas and disorder during the reign of Oba Ogunoye, Sir Olateru blamed him for his inability to bring peace to his people.

As Sir Olateru settles for a refreshing continuation on the throne he ascended in 1941, voices of dissent are growing strident in Owo. Again, Chief Ajasin is at the forefront. But like his contemporary, the Olowo, age has taken a good toll on Chief Ajasin. Like Sir Olateru who could not bring himself to say all over again the events that led to his removal, Chief Ajasin feels he has over the years, shouted his voice hoarse on the Olowo issue. He hardly has anything new to say. But he grumbled loudly all the same over the restoration of the Olowo title to Sir Olateru. For him, government's decision to reinstate Sir Olateru was an imposition on the people. He noted that the Omolowo whose duty it is to choose a new Olowo were not invited in this case to do their job. Even the head of the Omolowo, he argued, was not involved in the reinstatement of Sir Olateru. For Chief Ajasin therefore, there is everything wrong in what the government has done.

However, Chief Ajasin appeared to accept the situation with resignation. He is however consoled that his views on the matter are in the records. He therefore begged to be left alone especially as he turn 85 in a matter of days.

Like Chief Ajasin, Alhaji S.S. Aralepo, head of the Senior Omolowo responsible for the installation of a new Oba, believes the reinstatement of Sir Olateru was forced on the people by the government. In the same vein, Chief J. A. Aralepo, the Aladesokan of Owo and Secretary to late Oba Ogunoye, feels that the manner in which Sir Olateru was returned to office amounts to an imposition by government on the people. However, if the crowd that troops in and out of the Olowo's personal residence is anything to go by, it will be hard to believe that Sir Olateru's return does not enjoy the popular approval of majority of Owo people.

But for Mr. Olumilua, the re-enthronement of Sir Olateru as the Olowo of Owo was not an imposition. He does not agree with Chief Ajasin and the Aralepo who are insisting on the involvement of the Omolowo. As explained by Mr. Olumilua, Sir Olateru needed not go through those processes because he had gone through all the processes of installation before. On the view that government's order that reinstated Sir Olateru was an imposition, the governor argued that if such a view was accepted, then it would also be correct to argue, that even the original order that deposed the Olowo was also an imposition. That being the case, what his government did was to quash that earlier imposition. As he put it, "you need some imposition to bring peace to society."

Imposition or not, Mr. Olumilua believes that the reinstatement of Sir Olateru was a better option than going through the processes of electing a new Olowo. For one thing, the people wanted him. They felt that they would be better of under Sir Olateru. For another, attempts at choosing a new Olowo would even have factionalised Owo the more. There would be different contending groups clamouring for the exalted throne, and that in the view of the governor, is not healthy for Owo. Moreover, the government is confident about its decision because Sir Olateru, as being feared in some quarters, would not renege on his promises. Mr. Olumilua's view of the Olowo is that of a prominent man, a reputable Oba. A one-time Minister-Without-Portfolio and a sportsman of note.

Moreover, though he (Sir Olateru) was not compelled to sign the document that reinstated him, the Governor is convinced that he would not go back on his words.

Culled from the Guardian of Sunday November 14, 1993

CONTROVERSY BUILDS OVER RETURN BID OF EX-OLOWO

The Ondo State Government is under pressure from powerful but opposing interests over whether a former Olowo of Owo, Sir Olateru Olagbegi, should be restored to the throne from which he was deposed 25 years ago, in succession to Oba Joseph Adekola Ogunoye II, who passed on some time ago.

Although successions in many Yoruba Kingdoms are usually controversial, the present situation in Owo where a strong lobby is being exerted on Ondo State Governor, Mr. Bamidele Olumilua, is informed by peculiar circumstances surrounding the deposition of Sir Olateru.

In the main, the Government is expected to sift through opposing argument on the issue and decide whether:

· It is feasible within the purview of custom and tradition for a deposed king to be reinstated; and

· The 1968 deposition of Sir Olateru was not unduly motivated by political exigency that should be disregarded under the current dispensation

The government may have to appraise the popularity and support enjoyed by Sir Olateru during his 27-year reign (1941-1968). Indicatons are that he still commands the respect and loyalty of thousands of Owo indigenes.

So far, neither the state government nor the 82-year-old former Olowo, who is at the centre of the controversy, has spoken. But their silence only fuelled the controversy.

Chief Michael Adekunle Ajasin, the Asiwaju of Owo and former Ondo State Governor, was recently quoted as opposing moves to reinstate Sir Olateru.

He reportedly said: "No Oba has ever come back after such removal. The people have publicly rejected him. It will be difficult for him to return to the throne. Usually the government does not allow the people who have been deposed to come back because of likely trouble that their return might engender. Emir of Kano, Sanusi, was removed, but when he was allowed to return he lived outside the town. It is not likely that he, Olagbegi, will go back because I have not heard of it in the present-day Nigeria."

The Ajana of Owo and one of the seven kingmakers, supported the former governor's argument, saying: "When Olagbegi was dethroned, all the rites that are normally done for a dead Oba had been performed. Olagbegi has got his chance, and he cannot come back to the throne."

But for Chief Raji Adebayo, the Aragbaye of Igboroko and one of the kingmakers who signed the order of banishment, the action was regrettable: "Now I have resolved to use the last breath in my body to fight for the old man to ascend the throne and right a lot of the wrongs in the town", he said.

The late Oba Adekola Ogunoye was enthroned in 1968 after the dethronement of Sir Olateru who was very influential in the First Republic. He ascended the throne in 1941, and was one of the founding fathers of the former Action Group (AG) headed by the late Chief Obafemi Awolowo, who was the first Western Region Premier.

But Sir Olateru had some sympathy for the late Chief

Samuel Oladoke Akinola's Nigerian National Democratic Party (NNDP) which was then ruling in the region. Some AG members thus allegedly pressed for his banishment by the former Western Region Military Governor, Col. Adekunle Fajuyi, after the military sacked the First Republic.

Fajuyi issued a six-month suspension order on Sir Olateru, but the Oba's return bid after the suspension lapsed was resisted by some indigenes, resulting in chaos in the town.

Although he escaped a riotous welcome, several houses belonging to him and his supporters were torched. Major-General Adeyinka Adebayo, who succeeded Col. Fajuyi, later set up the Bode Kumapayi Commission of Inquiry. Although the commission's report was never published, Sir Olateru was deposed and sent on exile to Okitipupa, and the late Oba Adekola Ogunoye was enthroned within a year.

Culled from The Guardian Sunday May 2, 1993

PRESSURE MOUNTS FOR REINSTATEMENT OF DEPOSED OLOWO

Prominent indigenes of Owo, Ondo State, have intensified campaigns for the reinstatement of former Olowo, Sir Olateru Olagbegi, deposed 25 years ago by the General Adeyinka Adebayo's administration in the former Western State.

A letter sent yesterday through a prominent son of Owo Town, "to the entire Owo people at home and abroad, our dear elders and community opinion moulders," by Concerned Indigenes of Owo, appealed for Olagbegi's reinstatement in the interest of peace.

Titled, "A clarion call for the restoration of peace,

reconciliation and unity," signed by over 20 indigenes based in Lagos including Col. Femi Adekanye, the letter said that Sir Olateru Olagbegi is still alive and capable, (and) he should be reinstated to the throne of Owo in order that reconciliation, unity and peace which we all direly need may be achieved.

"We are convinced and it is our collective belief that there are no problems created by human being that cannot be solved by men of honour and valour," it added

The group appealed to the town's "illustrious leaders," including Chief Ajasin and Sir Olateru, described as "a great leader of men, to please come together again, bury the hatchet in the name of the Almighty God who you both serve and in the greatest and noblest interest of Owo to spend the remaining part of your glorious lives to redeem Owo."

It appealed to princes and persons interested in the vacant stool to understand that "time is on their side and that they should wait a little for we believe that they too have a stake in the unity and peace of Owo."

The letter recalled with nostalgia "our age of gold when the fruits of leadership co-operation produced the very best of achievements in physical progress of our town coupled with personal educational upliftments in our people."

The group described the passing on of Oba Joseph Adekola Ogunoye II last month "as a big blow to the town as a whole" and we feel we still have the joint responsibility to carry on the struggle for the unity and progress of the town where Oba Ogunoye left it.

The dethronement of Sir Olateru Olagbegi in 1968 was a fall-out of the intra-party crisis within the Action Group (AG), the party in control of the former Western Region before the military took over in 1966.

Culled from The Guardian

Tuesday April 13, 1993

OLATERU OLAGBEGI MAY REGAIN HIS CROWN

The Ondo State government has been called upon to revoke the order banishing the former Olowo of Owo, Sir Olateru Olagbegi, since 1968 (25 years ago) to enable him return to the throne.

The Chairman of Owo local government, Dr Adewunmi Abitoye, who made the call in Owo last week, said Sir Olateru's reinstatement became necessary because majority of the people of Owo wants him back on the throne since the demise of the Olowo of Owo, Oba Adekola Ogunoye.

He said the campaign for the return of Sir Olateru has been launched by prominent citizens of the town since last month.

The Council boss added that "since it appeared that practically, all the people of the town now wish for the return to the throne of Sir Olateru who was deposed in 1968, the only option available to the State Government was to revoke the order banishing him."

He believed that there was nothing extraordinary in the wish of the people, adding: "If the people believed the return of the ex-Olowo was what could bring peace to the town, the local and state governments could not do otherwise."

Abitoye said that his council would ensure that peace reigns supreme in the town, saying that this could be achieved by abiding by the wish of the generality of Owo people.

Sources stated that five out of the seven kingmakers of the town are part of those championing the return of the ex-Olowo.

Efforts to get comments on the issue from the first civilian Governor of the state, Chief Michael Adekunle Ajasin, one of the powerful sons of the town, proved abortive, as he was said to be either sleeping or not around each time we called his house on phone.

Culled from Sunday Times

April 18, 1993

IN OWO, A BATTLE FOR THE CROWN

Lofty acacia trees provide shade for the old men and women sitting under them while playing the traditional ayo game on Oke-Ogun, the well paved major street that runs through Owo in Ondo State from the Akure/Owo/Akoko Expressway.

Children cavort on the pavement in front of buildings on the street, neat structures that are an admixture of the old and the new.

In the heart of the town-Oke-Owo- is the Oja Oba, the main market. It is, as usual, a beehive of activities as buyers and sellers haggle over, and shout, their wares at the top of their voices, unmindful of the sweltering afternoon sun.

Owo on that Thursday could have been any town in the country. But while it shares many features with small towns everywhere, Owo is at the same time unique as Yoruba municipalities. For the ancient town of Owo, the headquarters of the Owo Local Government Area, is a border town. As such, its culture is a unique blend of that of Ife and the Bini in neighbouring Edo State. Its language is a peculiar dialect of Yoruba combined with Edo, a development that makes it difficult for most Yorubas to follow it.

Despite its cultural affinities, the town, founded in 1019 AD, is usually tranquil, providing respite from busier and larger urban areas. But beneath this seemingly placid surface is a geyser, threatening to erupt and spew forth its steaming waters with devastating repercussion. For just in front of this bustling market is the Olowo's (the traditional ruler of Owo) Palace, the throne, which has lately been vacated by Oba Joseph Adekola Ogunoye II who recently joined his ancestors after 25 years of a bitter-sweet reign on the throne.

The brewing tension emanated out of the uncertainty surrounding who should mount the throne as the new Olówó, now that Oba Ogunoye, who was installed in August, 1968, in unusual circumstances, is no more. During his reign, Oba Ogunoye was loved by a segment of the town while the other segment hated him. His achievements are thus being viewed in this stereotyped perception. While some sing his praise as a good ambassador of his people, others scorn his achievements with a wave of the land.

Oba Ogunoye was enthroned in 1968 after the dethronement of the ex-Olowo, Sir Olateru Olagbegi, in 1966. Sir Olagbegi, who was very influential in the government of the First Republic mounted the throne in 1941 and was one of the founding fathers of the Action Group (AG), which was headed by the late Chief Obafemi Awolowo, the first Premier of the Western Region.

With the advent of the crisis in the Action Group, and the subsequent emergence of the Nigerian National Democratic Party (NNDP), which was led by the late Chief Samuel Akintola, in power in the Western region, Sir Olagbegi summoned his chiefs and elders for their mandate and also in accordance with his attitude to politics, which was to "support the government of the day, so that amenities might be offered your domain." As a result, he joined the NNDP which was then the government of the day. This action by Sir Olagbegi was met with criticism from die-hard Action Group members of the town who owed their allegiance to the party and were thus poised to forment trouble for the Olowo. Until January 1966, when the military struck, the town knew no peace. It was divided because of partisan politics.

With the soldiers at the helm of affairs of government, those opposed to the ex-Olowo were still bent on punishing him. A clamour for his removal from the throne arose, leading the then Military Governor of the Western Region, Colonel Adekunle Fajuyi, by mid-January, 1966, to issue a six-month suspension order on the Oba. The aim of the suspension was to enable tension and nerves to cool down so that Sir Olagbegi could return to the throne.

Sir Olateru Olagbegi's attempt to come back when his suspension lapsed turned the town into a cauldron of violence. Although he escaped in the riotous welcome, several houses belonging to him and his supporters were razed. Major General Adeyinka Adebayo (rtd), who succeeded Col. Fajuyi, later set up the Bode Kumapayi Commission of Inquiry to investigate the causes of the riot and recommend solutions. Although the commission's report was never published, Sir Olagbegi was deposed and sent on exile to Okitipupa.

Within a year of the deposition, Oba Ogunoye was appointed as the new Olowo. His enthronement was stiffly opposed by the sympathisers of the ex-Olowo who maintained that it was untraditional in Owo for an Oba to reign while another one is still alive. The town became divided and disunited to the point that one group looked at the other with suspicion.

As the succession to fill the vacant throne, which, according to Chief Idowu Ojumu, the next-in-rank to the late Olowo and the head of the regency council, must take place within three months of the burial of the late Oba gradually draws to an end, the big question on the lips of many is: Who will mount the throne? It is indeed a question of: To be or not to be?

"The succession bid had heightened with the emergence of

two groups. While one supports the return of the 82-year old Sir Olagbegi, others would prefer another person to fill the vacant stool."

Chief Michael Adekunle Ajasin, the Asiwaju of Owo and the first civilian Governor of Ondo state, was recently quoted in a report as opposing the move to reinstate Sir Olagbegi. According to him: "No Oba has ever come back after such removal. The people have publicly rejected him. It will be difficult to return him to the throne. Usually, government does not allow the people who have been deposed to come back because of likely trouble that their return might bring. Emir of Kano, Sanusi, was removed, but when he was allowed to return, he lived outside the town. It is not likely that he, Olagbegi, will go back because I have not heard of it in the present-day Nigeria."

When contacted by The Guardian, Chief Ajasin subscribed to his earlier views but refused to be drawn into any further debate on the issue, saying: "As far as chieftaincy matters in Owo are concerned, I do not want to say anything more for the moment."

Also expressing doubt over the possibility of the ex-Olowo's re-enthronement is the Olurogho of Owo, Chief Olusola Bayode, who is one of the Omo-Olowos who are responsible for the screening and adoption of one of the princes as Oba. According to him: "Of the 23 Omo-Olowos, only 15 are still alive and out of this 15, only four are with Olagbegi. To appoint an Oba is the wish of God, and if God does not sanction it, it may not be possible."

Chief Michael Adekunle Ajasin, the Ajana of Owo and one of the seven kingmakers, agree. He told the Guardian that it was not proper in Owo tradition to re-install a deposed Oba. According to him: "When Olagbegi was dethroned, all the rites that are normally done for a dead Oba, such as cutting all the trees in the market and shifting its (market) location to a different location until another Oba mounts the stool, has been performed by the Iloro Chiefs who are in charge of such duties. To us, Olagbegi has got his chance and he cannot come back to the throne."

One of the Iloro chiefs, Chief Aragbagbaye Olanrewaju of Iloro Quarters, confirmed Chief Ajana's claim.

But the Ojomo of Ijebu-Owo, Oluda John Agboola Ojomo, who is also the head of the Omo-Olowos in an interview with the Guardian, waved aside Ajasin's opinion. His words: "Is there any law which says that an Oba having been dethroned cannot aspire to the throne of his forefathers if he is alive and wanted by his people? What is wrong with people like Ajasin is that they do not know the tradition and customs of Owo.

"The Owos do not depose their Obas, rather, they are executed. Olowo Alubiolokun was assassinated at Ogbese, Adara was beheaded and Olowo Alubiolokun was executed with all his sons. But since Olateru is alive and the people are yearning for him, he can always come back. Apart from that, if it is the wish of the people and the Omo-Olowos that Olagbegi should come back, then no obstacle can stop him from mounting the throne."

Oluda Ojomo, who denied holding brief for Olagbegi, said that there are precedents in history where Obas have been dethroned and where it was discovered that such actions were neither traditionally nor politically wise, they were returned after the kingmakers were urged to make the right choice in the interest of peace.

Chief Oludugba Adetula, the Sasere of Owo and one of the kingmakers, was of the view that unless Sir Olagbegi was reinstalled, the town, which has not witnessed much development during the era of the late Oba, may continue to witness retrogression.

According to him, "the only solution to the problems of the community is for the leaders to meet and correct all the anomalies in the enthronement of the late Olowo. Unless the wrongs that led to his installation are put right, we may not achieve much because we are still living with the wrong."

For Chief Raji Adebayo, the Aragbagbaiye of Igboroko, it was remorse and finger biting for the 25 years of Oba Ogunoye's reign. He has his reasons for this belief.

"I was one of those that was hoodwinked into signing the banishment order that saw Sir Olagbegi out of the throne 25 years ago. I did it along with some chiefs because I am not educated and I never knew the real implication. But for the past 25 years this our town has not witnessed any meaningful development, no peace. But Sir Olagbegi has remained loyal and committed to the development of Owo and its environs. He always donates thousands of naira at every launching and endowment fund unmindful of the circumstances leading to his removal besides giving scholarships to needy school children. Now I have resolved to use the last breath in my body to fight for the old man to ascend the throne and put right a lot of the wrongs in the town."

When The Guardian sought the view of the ex-Olowo at his Olagbegi's Rest House on the outskirts of the town, the British Knight declined to comment, saying: "For now I do not want to say anything. When I am ready I shall talk to all the press."

People around him, however pay obeisance to him as if he was still on the throne. One of his wives who spoke to The Guardian, Olori Caroline Olagbegi, said that it will be nice to come back and serve the people once again after so many years. She revealed that the ex-Olowo loves his people dearly and would come back if the people want him. Chief Adetula revealed that moves have been made to the Ondo State Government to revoke the banishment order on Sir Olagbegi. According to him: "It is the wish of the generality of the people of the town that he should be re-installed on the throne."

Sources at the Ondo State Governor's Office in Akure revealed that a powerful lobby group had visited the governor.

The source revealed that if it is the wish of the people that Sir Olateru Olagbegi return to the throne, Governor Olumilua may have to grant their wish. "Since this administration came into office, it has always clamoured that peace should reign supreme throughout the state. If the Owos want Olagbegi, fine they will get him," the source revealed.

Culled from The Guardian

May 1, 1993

ADDENDUM

O.D.S.L.N. 2 of 1993

The Chiefs Edict (No., 11 of 1984)

The Interpretation Law (Cap. 51)

THE OLOWO OF OWO (REVOCATION OF DEPOSITION AND RESTORATION) ORDER, 1993

WHEREAS OLATERU OLAGBEGI was by an order of the defunct Western State of Nigeria deposed on 15th day of February, 1968 from the Chietaincy of Olowo.

WHEREAS the State Government has received several petitions from various interest groups in Owo calling for the revocation of the Deposition Order with a view to restoring Olateru Olagbegi to his throne.

WHEREAS the said Olateru Olagbegi has exhibited soberness and ready to work in harmony with his people and Chiefs.

AND WHEREAS the said Olateru Olagbegi has promised and entered into a bond not to depose or victimise any of his

Chiefs particularly those Chiefs appointed and installed by the late Olowo Oba Adekola Ogunoye.

AND WHEREAS there is a vacancy in the Olowo of Owo Chieftaincy.

AND WHEREAS there is need to restore peace, order amity and progress to the town and its environs and heal all wounds arising out of the deposition of Sir Olateru Olagbegi as the Olowo of Owo.

AND WHEREAS the State Executive Council is convinced that the circumstances leading to the deposition of Olateru Olagbegi from the Olowo of Owo Chieftaincy in 1968 no longer exist.

AND WHEREAS in order to satisfy the yearnings of the majority of the people of Owo who are agitating for the restoration of Olateru Olagbegi as the Olowo of Owo, it is necessary to revoke the Order deposing him.

NOW THEREFORE, I, BAMIDELE ISOLA OLUMILUA, the Executive Governor of Ondo State, in exercise of the powers conferred by Section 21 of the Interpretation law, Cap. 51 Laws of Ondo State of Nigeria, 1978 and by virtue of all other powers enabling me in that behalf, I hereby make the following Order

1. The Olowo of Owo (Deposition) Order 1968 is hereby revoked

2. The Chieftaincy of the Olowo of Owo is hereby restored to Sir Olateru Olagbegi with effect from the 15th day of October, 1993

3. This Order may be cited as the Olowo of Owo (revocation of Deposition) and (Restoration) Order 1993.

MADE at Akure this 15th day of October, 1993.

EVANGELIST BAMIDELE ISOLA OLUMILUA

Governor of Ondo State of Nigeria.

Chapter 10

SIR OLATERU OLAGBEGI IN THE EYES OF THE PRESS

Right from his ascension to the throne, Sir Olateru Olagbegi enjoyed high visibility in the media on account of his legendary activities. He kept a high profile throughout his years on the throne particularly during his active days in the Government of the Western Region as spokesman of the Council of Chiefs and later Minister without portfolio and President, Council of Chiefs. With the controversy surrounding his deposition, Sir Olateru became a regular feature in the Nigerian media and anything said or done by him attracted media comments and focus.

This high visibility surely has both positive and negative effects on the life of the King.

The attempt in this chapter is to recall few of the memorable newspaper comments or articles on the personality of Sir Olateru Olagbegi. The diverse nature of the comments contributes in making the man an enigma that he is.

SIR OLATERU OLAGBEGI-A KNIGHT WITH 160 CHILDREN

Sir Olateru Olagbegi is an angry man. And he has cause to be. In 1966, Sir Olateru was dethroned from the exalted stool of Olowo of Owo, Ondo State and banished. In 1977, he returned to Owo but not to his throne.

But the British knight, who was born with a silver spoon, says his experience has made him richer while his idea of riches is totally different. "I had just six graduate children at the time I was deposed but I have more than 100 graduates now," Sir Olateru told Lagos Life at Owo. That's his idea of riches. "And God will continue to bless me."The merciful Lord has exceedingly done that for him.

Sir Olateru had no fewer than 160 children from 25 wives. And that may not be the exact figure, for tradition forbids him from giving the exact number of his household.

"I will say it's between 150-160 children. I would have loved to tell you the exact figure but let's keep the actual figure for the sake of tradition. I am comfortable financially and spiritually but don't start having notions of my being stinkingly rich. But I will go down on record as one man in the country who has spent the greatest on child upbringing.

"Let's face the fact, I love kids and they are my investment. I prefer spending my money on them than keeping the money in the bank. Tell me any continent that my children are not in throughtout the world and they are all doing worthly things. That is my pride and I am grateful to God."

"Some people may think that with such a large household, Sir Olateru will be finding it difficult to identify members of his family. But he sharply disagree. "Why not, if not? I know all my children by name, facially and through their mothers," he said, adding that each one of them has his traits which make for easy identification."

With the economic crunch, how does he cope feeding his army of children?

"Others might think it's a herculean task but it is not. Maybe, I would have been a billionaire if I don't have all these kids, 'But what will I do with all the money? 'he asked."

Even at 81, Sir Olateru still wanted to go on because according to him: "I am still able to care for them even at my age." At that time, his eldest son, a lawyer was about 50 years old and the youngest was one-and-a-half years old. Sir Olateru even found it more difficult to tell Lagos Life the number of his wives and grandchildren. That would be difficult but I think it is in the region of 250 – 270. You know they are always having kids and I only got to know that number last year during my birthday. As I have said, we don't count wives and children in Yorubaland, so I will only give you a rough estimate. He said that his wives are about two dozen or more and the youngest was 21 years old.

Details of this interesting and refreshingly different encounter with Sir Olateru was published last week in Lagos Life. He talked more about his army of family, his dethronement, banishment and determination to regain his crown. He also has harsh words for Chief Michael Ajasin, General Adeyinka Adebayo and Chief Obafemi Awolowo, all now late, for their respective roles in his travails.

Called from Lagos Life of Thursday, June 13 -Wednesday, June 19, 1991

SIR OLATERU...A SOLOMON OF OUR TIME

"I am sharp upstairs," he said. But he is highly charged too. Because according to him, he had no fewer than 160 children, 270 grandchildren and 25 wives. Even that is a modest estimate as tradition would not allow him to disclose the exact figure, yet he is still producing.

At 81, he (was) damn too intelligent and sharp for his age. Many people in his age bracket have gone senile and turn vegetable but he is hale, hearty and kicking, with no traces of senility. He is deposed, yet, seemed greater even out of the throne. His people still regard him as their king as they keep seeking his fatherly views on issues of particular importance.

But what does he feel about Pa Adekunle Ajasin, Major General Adeyinka Adebayo (rtd) and Chief Obafemi Awolowo? "Biting words. Or what else do you want me to have for those who stabbed me from the back after helping them."But how did the rebellion start? Does he still hope to come back? These and many more issues dominated the more than two hours discussion with Sir Olateru Olagbegi, former Olowo of Owo, one-time Federal Minister without portfolio, former President, Western State House of Obas and Knight of the British Empire, at his Owo country home, Ondo State.

Q: How would you describe your early life?

A: How can you describe your childhood yourself when for most part of it, you hardly know what you are doing? I can only describe the part of my childhood that falls between my school years. Anyway, I was born by the Late Olowo of Owo, Oba Olagbegi I, 81 years ago, precisely in 1910. As a youngman, I went to Owo Government School, left the place and became a teacher for three months and left the place again. I later joined the District Office where I was, till I ascended the throne early in the 40s.

Q: Life as a prince then entailed a lot of privileges. Could you tell us a little bit of those privileges you enjoyed?

A: I know I was born with a silver spoon and I can tell you boldly without mincing words that I turned that silver spoon into a gold spoon with which most of my children were fed. I have never lived with anyone in my life outside my parents and that is why I make sure none of my children ever suffers. I have never wanted anything that I can't buy. I can buy anything I want in life, I am not a money bag or what is the new word being used to describe rich politicians now? But I must confess I am absolutely comfortable because I have been exceedingly blessed by God. As a prince, I was never in want of anything and that is because my father was also a rich man by whatever standard then and my mother was in the palace so I was well treated.

Q: How did you become the Olowo of Owo?

A: That is a very long story. You know, the first requirement for the contestants is that you must be a prince and I was the heir apparent to my father then.

Q: Who and who contested with you?

A: This man, Ogunoye, who is in my palace now contested with me but lost woefully. I was twenty nine and half years when I became the King in 1941 and I was the king for 25 years before those bastards came to drive me out through the backdoor. Before the rebellion, I had been knighted by the Queen of England. I got a long service medal and brought a lot of recognition to Owo town. Till today, Owo is still called by my name. They call it Owo Olagbegi and that is because nobody knows the person occupying my palace now.

Q: Does this mean that you were the most popular Oba Owo ever had?

A: Who else was more popular than me? I brought respect, dignity, development and recognition to Owo. I happen to be one of the first set of Ministers in Nigeria even though without portfolio and we fought for Nigeria's independence together when some of those who drove me out were still cutting cocoa in the farm. Mention the conferences, the 1954, 1956, 1958, etc. I was there. I was at the Lancaster Conference and even the one of 1959 which happened to be the last before independence. So you can imagine what I will feel when a khaki man who does not know his right from the left comes to say I have been deposed, thereby, changing the will of the people. It's bad but it can only happen in Nigeria. Don't forget the fact that I was the first and the last president of the Western State House of Obas comprising the whole Yorubaland which shows the respect I command even then. Who would put that man in my palace now in such position?

Q: What led to your deposition and subsequent exile?

A: The rebellion just started from Chief Michael Adekunle Ajasin, the former Governor of Ondo State and his cohort of friends. It started like a child's play. Then the former Governor of Western State, now General Adeyinka Adebayo (Rtd), asked me out of the town in the interest of peace. I left and after sometime, I came back and some thugs started burning houses. (You remember the Operation Wetie episode of 1966). No fewer than 100 houses went up in flames. So Adebayo said he was going to set up an inquiry and before the inquiry, he dethroned me and asked me to go on exile. Can you imagine that? Khaki power or is it not? Even before being tried at all, I was already being punished, then I knew they were up to something. He asked me to go to the riverine area of Okitipupa during the exile and since then, Owo has never known peace. Anyway, after about 60 days in Okitipupa he set up the inquiry under one Mr. Kumapayi and up till today, the report of the probe which occurred in 1966 has never seen the light of the day. So you can see the hypocrisy and orchestrated plan set up by Adebayo, Awolowo and Ajasin to unseat me.

When leaving Owo, I told General Adebayo that I am sorry for him because he allowed himself to be used. I told him he cannot depose the blood of my father from me. So I will always be a king any day. Go to the town today and ask them who their king is? I am the king of the people. Take it from me

Q: Your argument now is that you were unjustly banished.

A: Pure and simple. If I am guilty, he would have been too happy to publish the report of the inquiry but for about 24 years now, the report is not out. Adebayo and his cohort of friends like Ajasin have done their worst but God is watching and he is blessing me ten-thousand fold because I am 20 times richer than I was when I was deposed and in such manner are my offspring. I had just six graduate children as at the time I was deposed but I have more than 100 graduates now. And God will continue to bless me because the cruel people have done their worst and so, he has decided to make my life better than theirs. Tell me any continent that my children are not in, throughout the world and they are all doing worthy things. That is my pride and I am grateful to God.

Q: Did you consciously set out to become a folklore as you have become today in Owo?

A: I never set out to be a hero but I set out to be myself and being myself happens to attract the love, loyalty, dedication and affection of my people. I was a tennis player and a very good one at that, ever before I became the King and even as a King I was very good and most of my children are good businessmen, academicians, administrators, sportsmen or women, etc. That all the Olagbegis have done one thing to promote the name while none has done nothing to tarnish it. I owe that to God Almighty

Q: Are you saying tennis contributed to your family good name?

A: Yes, because we are a well-known sporting family, one of my children is still representing Nigeria now apart from others who have in the past.

Q: Since you say you can buy anything you want in the world, would you give us a modest estimate of your worth?

A: I am not a multi-millionaire anyway, nor a moneybag, but as I have said earlier on, I am absolutely comfortable to buy whatever I want and whatever I want happens to be very small. I am comfortable financially and spiritually but don't start having notions of my being stinkingly rich. But I will go down on record as one man in the country who has spent the greatest on child upbringing.

Q: Give us an idea of the number of your children.

A: Customarily, we don't say a king has one or 10 children but I have plenty of them.

Q: There was a report which puts them at about 150 children

A: H-m--h since you are so keen, I will say it's between 150 and 160 children. I would have loved to tell you the exact figure but let's keep the actual figure for the sake of tradition.

Q: Is there any special joy you derive from having this number of children?

A: Eeh!! Try it and you'll feel the special power. Nothing is more fulfilling than seeing all your children in high places. The joy of having all this large number of children is in knowing that you are breeding reasonable Nigerians who would be useful to the country, who wouldn't be riffraffs. And for that I am grateful to God for giving me the power to take care of them because all my kids are enlightened and educated.

Q: Do you recognize them facially, by name or by their mother's names?

A: Ah! Ah!! Ah!!! I am sharp upstairs. Even when indigenes of Owo see an Olagbegi they will know him or her by the look. So why wouldn't their father? Why not if not? I know all my children by name, facially and through their mothers. Olaleye! (Calls one of his children. Olori, ko omo Olowo wá nbí (King's wife, bring the king's children here) You can see their look. All have the traces of their father which makes for easy identification

Q: What's the age of your eldest son and the last child?

A: The eldest is close to 50 years or more while the youngest is about one and half years old.

Q: Is there any hope of still having more children?

A: Why not? I will, because I am still able to care for them even at my age. Moreover the mother of my last child Olaleye (Olori Funmi) is still too young to stop child bearing. These are some of the last generations I am having now (calls them out).

Q: Don't you find their upkeep difficult considering the present economic crunch?

A: Others might think it's a herculean task but it is not. Maybe I would have been a billionaire if I don't have all these kids but what will I do with all that money? Let's face the facts, I love kids and they are my investment. I prefer spending all my money on them than keeping the money in the bank or gamble with it, or assemble cars or party about town. I am not that rich but up till now, no complain, so I thank God for blessing me.

Q: How many grand children?

A: H-m-n-h (pause). That would be difficult but I think it is in the region of 250-270. You know they are always having kids and I only got to know that number last year during my birthday.

Q: How many wives gave birth to all these children?

A: As I have said, we don't count wives and children in Yorubaland, so I will only give you a rough estimate. I think about two dozen or more (24).

Q: Who is your first son?

A: The first one is Lawyer Folagbade Olateru-Olagbegi. The one who is the Chairman of Owena Bank is Adeyanju Olateru Olagbegi, Adebanji Olateru-Olagbegi is the Rector of llaro Polytechnic, Rolake plays lawn tennis for Nigeria and Olaleye is the last born.

Q: Let's come back to the rebellion that removed you from the throne. Did the Late Chief Awolowo play any part in it?

A: You see, I feel if I remain alive for a long time, I will return because my people want me back. But as per Awolowo, I don't talk ill about dead people when he is no longer here to reply, and even custom demands that. But if Awolowo were to be alive today, I will talk, but even at that, I am sure in heaven he will know his defunct Action Group started first in my Palace. History recorded it as Owo but it was inside my palace at Owo, not just Owo but let's leave it at that.

Q: Did some members of the AG contribute to the rebellion?

A: Yes they did.

Q: Did it include Chief Adekunle Ajasin?

A: Enh-en, that is their ring leader. He is somebody I helped to go to school. I personally employed him at lmade College as Head teacher or is it Principal they call it now. It is pure backbiting. It is simply biting the hands that fed you and that is one of the worst crimes against humanity. It is like a Brutus stab because here is someone you had helped coming back to unseat you from the seat where you had helped him. Well, I have since left him to his conscience

Q: Have you ever had an occasion to meet him since then?

A: Yes and that was sometime ago. I was expected to be at Imade College for an occasion and he was to be there too but maybe because of my presence he dodged. So after the occasion, I decided to check him at home to ask why he didn't turn up. I know his heart must have missed a thousand beats all together at once when he saw me pulling up in front of his house because he would be confused and asking himself, what has he come to do in my house? I just said M. A. (his initials), why weren't you there and he said because the people they were welcoming would still check him up. I knew that wasn't genuine enough. And as he was seeing me off to my car, I asked him how he feels at Owo since he has not been seeing me and he was spell-bound. After some time, he picked up courage to talk and as he was about explaining what led to my deposition, I tapped him on the shoulder and said, "Don't worry, that is gone with history," and I sped off. Since then, we've never seen each other because I hardly go out.

Q: What of the present Olowo, have you had any occasion to meet him personally?

A: Ah! Ah!! Ah!!! That one, he will run if he sees me. You think he will have the effrontery to face me? Never. I met him at Akure during one fundraising ceremony not long ago. He was already seated when I came with my usual large convoy. Immediately I saw him, I went straight to him and told him that though I know he is silly, I will still shake hands with him but he ran away. He was fidgeting, the tension was too much for him. How would you want a rat to wait for a lion? He can't wait. Never.

Q: Have you forgiven all those who contributed to deposing you?

A: God has taught me never to hate anybody so I don't hate them. I have forgiven them because if they knew I will be as I am today, they would never have done what they did. There are some of them who have come to beg me for their children's school fees, and I gave them.

Q: But most people felt it was because of your involvement in the politics of the First Republic that led to your deposition.

A: Maybe, yes. I happen to be a minister in the First Republic so why should they expect me not to be involved. Was it me alone who was involved? Adesoji Aderemi was a Governor but he wasn't deposed. I went to the House of Chiefs as of right not of chance. Maybe because I do not share their political belief so they felt the best way to deal with me was to depose me. I am sure they must be regretting it today. I am not boasting, I am not their equal now, in everything. You can't see any Oba who would say who is Olateru Olagbegi? Because none was greater than me then. I was the president of the Western State House of Obas and I gave the place a lot of respect. On the throne, I was great, outside it, I am greater. Not in terms of money because I am not super-rich and because that is a small thing but in terms of clout, colour and achievement.

Q: How do you relate to the indigenes of Owo now?

A: The who-is-who in Owo are still with me? Tell me, have you not counted more than two hundred people who have been here since you came here now? Even his chiefs come to tell me they wanted me back. Those who have problems bring them, I solve them for them. They bring their disputes I settle them, yet one oba-on-paper will come and claim he is a king. They, the rebels, want a crony they can push around but they found that I am too great to be pushed. They wanted an illiterate Oba, but found me too learned because they know I can teach them the Queen's language, so bootlickers connived with government agent to use khaki power to dethrone me. If it were a just democratic society, there will be civil riot but soldiers came to Owo to threaten my people with machine guns in order to install the present guy in my place. Out of the 21 kingmakers, they destooled 17 and reconstituted another one with seven members, out of which three people have been destooled again. Does that show a people's King? It never happens in a normal society. They have done all they could to smear my name, but found me too clean to destroy. They said I ordered my police orderly to shoot people. How can I do that when I am not an Inspector General of Police who can control somebody in uniform?

Q: Tell us a bit about your days in exile.

At first, I was thinking about my predicament when a spirit appeared to me and asked me to take heart that what was happening is not of God's making and that I shall triumph and that has fortified me till date. I was never alone so 1 was not dejected. I came back to Owo in 1977. I was in Lagos for nine years, I was in the habit of building houses here and there when one day, I asked myself why are you in Lagos when somebody occupies your palace. Who is bold enough to stop you from coming home? So, I wrote to the government that I was coming home and they fortified this place for my safety and when I entered this town, the crowd that came to welcome me was unprecedented in Owo. Nearly all Owo people took specially made clothes with my picture and name and the bastard in my palace ordered nobody to wear it and there was going to be a bloody clash until he was warned by government that he cannot prevent people from wearing whatever they wanted to wear

Q: Don't you think, returning to Owo would make the Olowo uncomfortable;

A: Why should he not be uncomfortable in my palace and on my throne? Naturally I know he will feel uncomfortable because in Owo, he is a loner. If he is bold enough, let him declare himself ready for a plebiscite to determine the people's King. I will finance it and will want a credible independent organization to supervise it. I know he cannot afford it but let him come out for a test of strength on who the people want as their King.

Q: Have you met General Adebayo since then?

A: Adebayo was here some time ago.

Q: Did he feel sorry for dethroning you?

A: He must be sorry now. There was a time we met at Ife during one launching and he said he is sorry for his actions. And I believed him because if he knew I will live to be great as I am now, they would never have done it then. They have polarized my people. And only my return can unite them as they used to before.

Culled from Lagos Life

Thursday June 20- Wednesday, June 26, 1991

A Colonel To The Rescue

THE Military Governor of the Western State, Colonel Oluwole Rotimi, in his address to the Council of Obas in Ibadan last week told Yoruba Obas that payment of their salaries will hence forth be made a statutory responsibility

The announcement is as much pleasing to the Nigerian public as it is to the Obas themselves. The intention of the Western State Government is to completely insulate Obas from partisan politics and thus improve their lots and restores their dignity.

DAYS OF POLITICS

Prior to this announcement, Obas were paid from local government funds. So bogus was the arrangement that a Chairman of a Local Council could, at will, or at the instigation of a "Leader" somewhere, sit on the salary of the Oba for as long as he pleased.

Which was why it was all too easy for a government in the days of politics to coax an Oba into joining the party in the power. The Oba himself usually would have to be something more than an ordinary member of the party. In most cases he was a "dignified" party field secretary in his area. And what choice did he have, especially that he had to feed his many wives, train his children and live up to the standard his corporate personality demanded.

Ideally, the Yoruba Obas should be the father of their subjects. The Member of Parliament, the Minister, the Commissioner and what have you should pay homage to him in his exalted palace surroundings. But during the civilian government, the position was reversed. A local party leader had enough power and influence to send a maid to the Oba, or by telephone conversation, request him to report at his residence. And God bless the Oba who had enough effrontery to arrive there minutes late, not to mention complete absence!

What exactly was responsible for this desecration of the tradition of chiefs?

In the colonial era, the District Officers or the Residents found in Obas a good instrument of influence on local people.

Despite all we have in the history books about the clashes between colonialists and native chiefs, history has been good enough to imply that the ruse were personality clashes, the chief trying to assert his power on one hand, and on the other hand, the colonialists trying to make the chief accept the sovereignty of the British Monarch over and above everything else.

Be that as it may, the Whiteman recognized the chief as a power, and worked through him to establish a good administration in each area.

Our politicians approached it differently. To get a proper grip on the local population, the head just must be tucked inside the party pockets before anything else. Where there was resistance, the intemperate party leader challenged it with brutal force, ranging from salary cut to banishment.

The Obas were partly to blame for the treatment they received from the politicians. By the frequent and indiscriminate conferment of spurious traditional titles with long-winding and often funny names on one politician after the other, the Obas, by their own hands, prostituted an institution that by tradition should enjoy absolute reverence, dignity and honour.

So much so that at a stage one of the leading Yoruba Obas was obliged to warn on the dangers of making Dick, Tom, and Harry a chief, in this town, that village or a community down the street.

The warning came too late! It had already become an epidemic. A Member of Parliament, a Cabinet Minister, or a Premier was incomplete without the appellation, "Chief." Thus in the old Eastern Nigeria, we had Chief Dr. Mrs. the Honourable Member of Parliament for X town, Dick, Tom. Harry.

By that token many inconsequential "nobodies" started to arrogate to themselves glories and honours it could not under normal circumstances have pleased destiny to bestow on them. They virtually claimed equality with the traditional chiefs, and sometimes with their Obas. They sat at council meetings, conference of the elders, doing most of the talking, taking decisions while the Obas watched in bemused silent.

THE RESTORATION

Some Obas accepted the marvels of the day while others would not watch their position of glory and power gradually taken away from them.

In the conflict that followed, a number of Obas, some of which were first class traditional chiefs, were subjected to unparalleled political savagery by the rulers of the First Republic, especially in the West. The Alaafin, Oba Adeyemi I, was exiled from his throne, and did not come back to his domain until he departed this world.

Oba Adesoji Aderemi, the Oni of Ifè, was removed from the governorship of the Western State when political tide tuned in the West. The Odemo of Ishara, as controversial as he was pleasant, had his salary cut down to a penny a year, a step that perhaps passes for the most ridiculous disciplinary action history has recorded so far.

Oba Akran of Badagry, who as a public officer for several years served the West as Minister with Cabinet rank at the turn of the tide, was tried and convicted for embezzling public funds.

Each of the personalities mentioned above, with the exception of the Late Alaafin, went through the mill but succeeded in overcoming their difficulties by triumphantly scaling over their trying days. Even the Late Alaafin, down in his grave, will today consider his son's installation as the new Alaafin a triumph for him.

There is an Oba, perhaps different in personality, background, and outlook, whose life-history has some basic similarities with the cruel misfortune of the Obas I have mentioned. For all the grandeur, affection, progress and liveliness that characterized his reign, he has been the worst victim of circumstances. He is Prince Olateru Olagbegi, the ex-Olowo of Owo.

His subjects still regard him as the Olowo of Owo. And there is some sense in their insistence on sticking out their necks to see him restored onto his throne.

The Owo people in a petition to Col. Rotimi recently made clear that tradition does not allow the installation of another Oba during the lifetime of the reigning Oba.

If nothing else, this argument should be enough for the restoration of Prince Olagbegi back onto his throne, especially now that we have in the saddle a Governor who by practice has demonstrated his willingness to uphold the traditions and dignity of our Obas.

Sir Olagbegi, to the people of Owo, has been a rare bird. His reign revolutionized the whole institution of Obas and Chiefs both in Owo and the Western State as a whole. His ascension to the throne on March 13, 1941, gave Owo people the first educated Oba in the chequered history of the area. By that date, there were three (primary) schools and no secondary schools in the area. The influential and progressive man that he was, Sir Olagbegi embarked on development programmes of road development, building of more schools and the coming into being of the Imade College, to mention only a few. During his reign many more schools and colleges were built, and the Oba's palace in Owo transformed into a modern edifice housing lawn tennis courts, gardens, orchards and playing grounds.

RIGHTFUL DEMAND

That a man who has put in so much to the development of his town, who by his own singular effort, improved the lot of his people and this endeared himself to them should be thrown out of his domain for no cause other than supporting the government of the day, remains a mockery to the tradition of Obas and Chiefs in Yorubaland. And to think of the fact that this same respected dignitary served the Western State people for fifteen years as Minister-Without-Portfolio highlights the importance of the role he played as an Oba, and the indispensability of the contributions the institute of chiefs still has to play in the future of the state generally.

This is why Colonel Rotimi should consider as soon as able the rightful demand of we (the) people to restore Sir Olagbegi onto his throne in Owo.

Major General Adebayo as Governor of the State realized, albeit too late, the weight of the mistake he made in removing Sir Olagbegi, and therefore made moves to put things right in the dying days of his reign. Although he directed that the prince could now enter Owo, this would appear not to be enough clearance to the noble Sir Olagbegi because, as a peace-loving man, he needs nobody to tell him of the consequence of a 'forced-landing' at Owo. The direct effect of such move will be to create two ruling Obas with two palaces. We will, so to say, be courting yet another disaster in that part of the state.

The experience of Sir Olagbegi in a similar suicidal entry advised by the Government of Major-General Adebayo is too fresh to be forgotten so soon. He has lost properties destroyed by the unkind hands of people pandered by political considerations and actively backed by the forces that should in normal circumstances protect the lives and properties of innocent and law-abiding citizens.

His Excellency the Military Governor of the Western State should consider the case of the ex-Olowo as inseparable from his declared intention of returning the glory of the good old days to the institution of Obas in the State.

If only because there is no parallel to the example offered by the case we have at Owo today.

Not so much for what going back to the throne may mean to Sir Olagbegi but more for what the precedence which the position may create mean to the future of the institution.

Culled from Morning Post April 26, 1971

OLOWO PRAISES WEST NIGERIA GOVT.

OBA OLAGBEGI II, the Olowo of Owo, has commended the Western Nigeria Government for the amenities provided for the farmers of the region.

He was addressing the first Ondo provincial agricultural show and farmers' festival at Akure.

The Oba also congratulated the Western Nigeria Ministry of Agriculture and Natural Resources on the increased number of highly trained members of its staff.

The Deji of Akure, Oba Adesida II, who presided over the show, praised the effort of the Regional Government in encouraging young men "to go back to the land."

This new agricultural policy, the Oba declared, would soon transform the economic position of the country as a whole.

In a message to the show, Chief G. Akin Deko, Western Nigeria Minister of Agriculture, congratulated the people of Ondo Province on the historic occasion.

Culled from Daily Times January 14, 1960

OLOWO AND OJUKWU KNIGHTED

OBA JAMES TITUS OLAGBEGI II, the Olowo of Owo, and Western Nigeria Minister-Without-Portfolio, has been knighted by Queen Elizabeth II in Her Birthday Honours list released for publication early today.

The Olowo, who will be fifty years old next August, thus becomes the youngest traditional ruler in Nigeria to receive the knighthood.

Also knighted are: Marie Charles Emmanuel Clement Nageon de Lastáng, Chief Justice of the High Court of Lagos, Arthur Treham Weatherhead, former Deputy Governor of Northern Nigeria, and Odumegwu Ojukwu.

To be Companions of the Most Distinguished Order of Saint Michael and Saint George: Leonard, George Coke-wallis, Chairman of the Western Region's Public Service Commission, and Dermodat Pelly Murphy, Western Region's Deputy Governor.

To be Officers of the Most Excellent Order of the British Empire; Theophilus Sunday Babatunde Aribisala, Senior Agricultural Officer: Stephen John Henry, West Electoral commission and Joseph Ehaifoghe Imoukhuede, Principal Assistant Secretary in the Premier's Office.

To be a Companion of the Imperial Service Order: Philip Ashby Allison, Conservator of Forests.

To be Members of the Most Excellent Order of the British Empire: Stefan Bergander, Owendoline Vera Clark, Timothy Talabi Dada, the Olotta of Otta; Frank Hollis Longley, Banjamin Olatunji Oguntimehin, Michael Adeosun Oso Olurin, and Cyril Oyebola Phillips.

To be Companions of the Most Distinguished Order of Saint Michael and Saint George: John Horace Party and Peter Hyla Gawne Stalard.

Culled from Daily Times June 11, 1960

THE DEPOSITION OF SIR OLATERU OLAGBEGI II

Ex-Olowo of Owo

"POLITICS with bitterness," that was the pre-1966 rule of the game. Politicians then saw their opponents as bitter enemies. Traditional rulers were not spared in the game. Chief S.L. Akintola, Premier of the Western Region slashed the salaries of some traditional rulers to one kobo a year, while some were completely banished from their domains.

Traditional rulers that played politics either lost their crowns or suffered public disgrace. This readily brings to mind the episode between Oba Akenzua of Benin City and his second-in-command, Chief Humphrey Omo-Osagie (a.k.a B2). The Oba was a diehard Action Group follower, while his chief belonged to the NCNC. The latter with his supporters stormed the palace, disconnected the electricity supply and displayed the Oba's coffin at the ring-road while the Oba was still alive.

Oba of Ishara, Samuel Akinsanya, shared the same fate when his salary was slashed to a penny per year. Sir Adesoji Aderemi, the Late Ooni of Ife too, was not forgotten as his son-in-law, Chief Fani Kayode, publicly disgraced the Ooni and slashed his salary in a like-manner.

It was in this type of mess, Sir Olateru Olagbegi found himself. But, apart from this political problems, other prevalent vices compounded the whole issue.

He, for instance, had a personality clash with Chief Michael Ajasin, the then political leader of the Owos. Secondly, Sir Olateru was not in good terms with his subjects and the neighboring suburb which he subjected to political victimization. Now who is Olateru Olagbegi? Sir Olateru Olagbegi ascended the throne of his forefathers in 1941. He met Owo in shambles, but within a very few years of his ascension, he transformed Owo to one of the best towns in the then Ondo Province. Educationally, Owo town was in the forefront. His ascension to the throne saw the building of Imade College. It was during his reign too that the roads in the town were tarred to his credit.

VICTIMISATION

Politically, he was not lagging behind as exhibited by the launching of the Action Group party in his palace.

Despite all these laudable achievements, what brought him to his knees and subsequently kicked him out of the palace? Like other traditional rulers that involved themselves in politics he suffered political victimization. But he was the architect of his fortunes or misfortunes.

As the Chairman, Western House of Chiefs and as a king in whose palace the party, Action Group was launched, nobody expected that he could easily be bought over to cross carpet. It was a bitter pill that was very difficult for other Action Group members to swallow. He did not merely cross carpet, it was alleged that he wreaked havoc on a small village called Isho, (a distance of eight kilos to Owo) by ordering the police to open fire on the villagers.

Apart from this, it was alleged that he was causing troubles in the town. Wherever two brothers were struggling for a chieftaincy title, he (Olowo) would give it to a junior neglecting the senior one. Due to these actions, his subjects were not happy with him. Again, it was alleged that the ex-Olowo wanted to introduce the system in Benin Kingdom in Owo by installing his first son as "Edaiken," who automatically becomes the king of the town after him. But his subjects resented this move.

The town, Owo, normally and traditionally has two obas. The Olowo as one and the other over the Ijebu quarters of the town. But when Olagbegi ascended the throne, he cancelled the Ijebu Oba of the town. Personality clash played another prominent role in his removal.

Sir Olateru Olagbegi was alleged to have built the Imade College, Owo. In his capacity as the proprietor, he appointed Chief Michael Ajasin as the first principal of the college.

When Olagbegi started to commit atrocities, his subjects were reporting and complaining to Chief Ajasin, the leader. In turn, Chief Ajasin would caution and advise Olateru. At a stage, Chief Ajasin's advice were not heeded again by Olowo. As a result, misunderstanding and crises of confidence sprang between them. Eventually, Sir Olagbegi sacked Chief Ajasin as the principal of Imade College. The relationship between the Oba and Chief Ajasin on one hand was poor while the Oba and his subjects was at the lowest ebb. One of his chiefs still loyal to him, Chief Ojo Elewere, summoned a meeting of all the twenty-four traditional chiefs of Owo and districts on Friday 25/3/66 for their vote of confidence.

But out of fear and an unbridled bias, 20 out of the 24 chiefs stood in favour of Olagbegi. Moving the motion, Chief Elewere said, for the fact that there was no "adverse report against Oba Olagbegi" during his tenure of office as a minister in the suspended government of Western Region and in view of the fact that his 25 years reign has been what was described as phenomenal progress in the history of Owo, the vote should be passed on him.

Exactly one week after the deceitful vote of confidence on Olagbegi, trouble busted out. Houses were set ablaze. Assassination in public places became rampant. There was trouble everywhere.

The then Governor of Western Provinces, Lt. Col. Adekunle Fajuyi, had to impose a curfew on the town. But the curfew imposed on Owo did not solve the problem. Instead, it aggravated it. The whole town demanded that Olagbegi should be removed as Olowo.

There was nothing Fajuyi could do than to suspend Olowo

Olagbegi, at least to allow the dust to settle down a bit. The problem came to a climax when on April 24, 1966, Governor Adekunle Fajuyi embarked on tour of Ondo Division of the Province. On April 30, Adekunle was at Owo. He was welcomed to Owo by thousands of men, women and children carrying placards which read "Olateru must go," "Olowo is no more our king."

To this attitude, the Governor was not happy and he did not hide it when he expressed his embarrassment at the placard carrying exercise, but promised that justice would be done and said, that the complaints against the Olowo of Owo, Oba Olateru Olagbegi, would be investigated.

In his own welcome address, the Olowo, Olateru Olagbegi, asked, among other things, for the provision of more social amenities, the insulation of chiefs from politics, and the filling of vacant chieftaincy titles in Owo Division.

Unfortunately, Fajuyi could not implement his decision before the July 1966 countercoup snatched him away.

Colonel Adeyinka Adebayo had hardly stepped in when the agitation for Olowo's removal sprang up again. At this time Olagbegi was in Ibadan as a result of suspension order clamped on him.

Sir Olagbegi requested from Colonel Adebayo that he would like to go back to Owo, but with police and army escorts, which Adebayo refused to grant him. But told him to go home if truly his people loved him.

Truly, Olagbegi went to Owo, but he was lucky to have escaped death as his subjects revolted and started to shoot guns and invaded the palace. Olowo managed to escape through the backyard and up till today, he has never put on the crown.

Culled from Headlines November, 1990

"OLAGBEGI - AN OBA WITHOUT A THRONE"

"OBASHIP in the political era rarely went to blazes in the hands of some politicians so much so that some Obas were placed on 1 kobo salary per annum - Oba Lamidi Olayiwola Adeyemi, The Alaafin of Oyo, in Oyo Chieftaincy Institution & Modernism."

VISITING Sir Olateru Olagbepi is like paying a visit to the house of a fallen monarch. It is not just simply that the trappings of court and ceremony are not there. It is that one conjures easily from the absence of these and also from Sir Olagbegi's own personal simplicity, dreams of times gone by. But if there is no ceremony, no regality, at least there should be grandeur. There is none of these too. There is only decor and in the simple sitting room, the friendliness and benign understanding of a man who once dined and wined with Kings and Queens.

Posted in front of the small sitting room where the ex-Olowo of Owo resides is only one Secretary (also benignly addressed as Chief) to contain the troops of relatives, towns people, hangers on and others who besiege the ex-Oba daily for favours and to seek help.

When an Ex-Oba falls on bad times, what happens? Legends abound of those who turned fishermen in their desperation, fishing for their subjects what they starved them of in their days of glory. There are others who took to the monastery to make penance and others who were hounded by their subjects for atrocities. Sir Olagbegi's story is none of these. His regal Rolls Royce, though now stripped of its police escorts, is still a beauty to behold. He himself, has personally kept all his charm, his agility, and thanks to his love for sports, his physical appearance. But there is much missing. The home simply is not a home. The residence is too crowded. One wonders how this man who carries a load of financial responsibility on his head without sustenance or government subvention manages to carry on without tiring. A man at crossroads? Indeed. But Sir Olateru Olagbegi's case is an epitome of endurance, of the infinite capacity of man not to give up trying.

NEWBREED:

The Olagbegi myth still burns on. Indeed, you are not the only holder of a chieftaincy title who, due to the circumstances of politics, or any other reason lost his crown in the civilian era. Yet while many of these have been forgotten, your own situation continues to elicit massive mixed feelings. Why is this so?

SIR OLAGBEGI:

When a man is loved, he continues to be loved. Nothing is well done until it has been rightly done. The whole affair was mishandled from the beginning. When justice has not been done, people will continue to ask why. Of all the first class Obas I am the only one who has suffered such monstrous injustice. My people still want me back, the elders, the kingmakers and everyone else. The public does not still know different from what others have done.

NEWBREED:

Would you say then that the inaction with regard to the resolution of this problem is not entirely devoid of politics?

SIR OLAGBEGI:

Indeed, there is much politics involved in the matter. Government has done what they ought not to do from the beginning. If they should act rightly, they would abide by custom and take what the kingmakers have said. But even now when after much footdragging, my people have suggested a plebiscite to decide who is more acceptable, the government of the day is still soft pedalling.

NEWBREED

It is the view that your enforced reinstatement may lead to widespread disorder in Owo area.

SIR OLAGBEGI:

If the government is to fear a breakdown of law and order, who is the government then? All we now want is justice.

NEWBREED:

What happened to the Commission of Enquiry set up in 1968 after the riots following your return?

SIR OLAGBEGI:

This is an interesting question. Even before that enquiry was set up following the disorder, there had been pronouncement of an enquiry into the whole matter. Before this had materialized, the Adebayo government said I should go back, which I did. But following my return, the opposing faction, went on the rampage which led to a breakdown of law and order. Yet surprisingly, instead of Governor Adebayo making haste to bring to book all those involved, he merely promised an inquiry into the matter and quickly banished me to Okitipupa for some 13 months. It was while there that the Special Commissioner for the enquiry, Mr. Ikumapayi, came to hear my side of the story. Unfortunately, the finding of the enquiry up till tomorrow has not be published. Up till now, my people are agitating to know the findings of the Commission. Personally I want to know where I went wrong. This has proved futile. Yet the biggest irony is that we live under a military regime which is no respecter of personalities. If justice is not done in the military era, only God knows what would happen when the military makes its exit.

NEWBREED:

So for the nine years in which you have been banished from your throne, how have you managed to sustain yourself and meet your huge financial commitments?

SIR OLAGBEGI:

I have not been given a penny by the government. I have been living and sustaining my obligations through the help of God, my people, my children and my farms. Being here with me for barely a few hours, you yourself must have seen how they continue to troop in and out.

NEWBREED:

In his book, "Oyo Chieftaincy Institution and Modernism," Oba Lamidi Olayiwola Adeyemi noted that Obaship in the political era nearly went to blazes in the hands of some politicians so much that some Obas were placed on 1 kobo salary per annum. Can you recall the circumstances of some of these? Why was their remuneration reduced to 1 kobo?

SIR OLAGBEGI:

I cannot recount political acts of victimization, I only remember that the Odemo of Ishara was only one of many who suffered at the hands of mercenary politicians. I myself, in the wake of the events that led to my dethronement, held a press conference at the time and asked that I should not be reduced to a 1 kobo per-annum chief. There are too many such sordid atrocities to recount here.

NEWBREED:

Thus, would you on looking back agree that there are certain things which you did but should not have done?

SIR OLAGBEGI:

I have not regretted any of my actions. Nothing there was which I did either for my people or in politics which I have regretted. No Oba can say conscientiously that he agitated for the progress of Nigeria than I did. My belief is that anyone should support and follow the government of the day. And that is what I did. I followed the government of the day.

NEWBREED:

What do you think you should have done which you did not?

SIR OLAGBEGI:

I should have been able to help my people better which I didn't. Since my exit, things have gone worse for my people. Owo cries for development, yet up to now, no one seems much concerned. The people themselves could take it upon themselves to embark on development projects but unfortunately, they find it difficult to reconcile themselves with the traditional goal and leadership of a usurper.

NEWBREED:

How does it feel to live now like an ordinary mortal without trappings of court and its attendant ceremonies?

SIR OLAGBEGI:

I miss my home, my people and my children. Otherwise I apply my energies into constructive avenues. I enjoy my lawn tennis and other games. Once a sportsman, always a sportsman. A sportsman should take life as it is and not what it should be.

NEWBREED:

I have heard rumours that some of your wives have begun to desert. Is this true?

SIR OLAGBEGI:

Not a single one of my wives has left. Once an Olori always an Olori. All my wives are with me-but we are not together. Some are in Ibadan, others in Lagos and some at home.

NEWBREED:

Would you be good enough to disclose the number of your wives?

SIR OLAGBEGI:

Customarily, this is not allowed.

NEWBREED:

What about the number of your children? I understand, there are so many and their presence so permeated Nigerian society that if ever they think about organizing a coup, they have among them capable men to man all essential services.

SIR OLAGBEGI.

That is interesting (laughing). I cannot tell you the exact number although there are more than a hundred. I have children in primary 1 - 6, secondary I to 5 and in the Universities, children from first to final year. I have seven children in America, four children in Britain, one son in Russia and few others in other European countries. Here at home, my children and their accomplishments would constitute a pride to any father.

NEWBREED:

The role of traditional rulers is undergoing severe strains in the course of building a modern Nigeria. As I see it, in the 80's the Obaship would have ceased to mean much to anyone. Do you agree?

SIR OLAGBEGI.

I agree that traditional rulers will reign but not rule. But Obas will continue to exist. Not that they will be ruling as our forefathers ruled.

Nevertheless their cultural heritage will enable them to wield influence among the people. Yet if government intends to do anything to retain the importance of Obas, the first step will be for it to take over from the local councils the burden of paying them.

NEWBREED:

One grave consequence of such a measure will be for the Chiefs to become agents of government.

SIR OLAGBEGI:

What is wrong with Chiefs joining hands with the government in effecting measures in the interest of the people? But the chief advantage of governmental payment of salaries will be to reduce the dangers of political strangulation. In the civilian era the Councils were instrumental organs through which chiefs were treated as play things by political parties. If the Chief disagrees with the party controlling a particular council, he automatically lost favour with the council and consequently his remuneration is withdrawn.

Thus as a result, the Obas, in fear, were compelled to follow the party sheepishly. But it would be a different thing if any Oba has the confidence that he has a share in the government and is not exposed to pressure.

NEWBREED:

It is not Council strangulation alone which has helped to reduce the power of natural rulers, indiscriminate conferment of chieftaincy titles on undeserving public figures. What are your views on this?

SIR OLAGBEGI:

You never change society. Every society has its own honours. The Queen of England confers honours on worthy individuals annually. Here at home, we have our national honours which are conferred on deserving citizens for significant contributions. While I agree that there may be cases of indiscriminate conferment, I think that the existence of honours is a vibrant stimulus to a people to be industrious and patriotic.

NEWBREED:

You still look quite agile and sporty for your age? Have you got the elixir of life?

SIR OLAGBEGI:

I also do not have the answer to age. All I have done is to keep up with sports.

NEWBREED:

So finally, after all these years, with attitudes crystallized up to this point do you personally think it will be easy to return to your throne?

SIR OLAGBEGI:

Indeed there will be no easy solution when the government of the day wants to shelve the truth. Yet I have never for once given up hope that there can be solution. Even in the Nigerian context history is there to vindicate my hope. Many years ago, the Olu of Warri was deposed and banished to Ogbese in the Mid-West for political reasons. When the Military Government came to power, it set up an enquiry into the circumstances of his banishment. He was vindicated and is now back on his throne. The demand for his return was as strong as in my case. In the West, the Aseyin of Iseyin, was also banished to Okitipupa because of a usurper. When the Military Government investigated the matter in 1967, he was re-instated. So who says there is no darkness before light?

*Culled from **Newbreed Magazine*** April 1975

TO MAKE OWO BEAUTIFUL

HIS Royal Highness, Oba Adekola Ogunoye, the Olowo of Owo, recently "entered the ceiling" at a good, ripe age. A more colourful description, which came into currency when the Benin throne became vacant for the ascension of His Royal Highness Omo N'Oba Erediauwa II (long may the Oba live) would be that the Olowo has "joined his ancestors."

Both phrases express the fond belief rooted in tradition that an Oba does not physically die even at his demise. He merely moves away from the throne, presumably in an "upward" direction, to create room for those who would later join him as ancestors.

Such notions have been preserved as a fence around the values which the traditional rulership represents throughout the country. Even in these so-called modern times, the traditional palace continues to be the repository of the culture of a community, as well as the reference point for the mores of the people.

This fact was quickly realized by the early colonialists who blandly exploited the situation through the "indirect system of governance." Having installed themselves in the position of the "final authority," they first "recognized" or appointed the natural ruler, and then installed him as the "native authority." Thus he was officially confirmed in a position that was rightly his, or was procured for him, only to become a cat's paw in the implementation of the white man's policies.

All that should have ended naturally with the departure of the colonial masters. But, unfortunately, the politicians who took over the reins of powers had learnt their lessons very well by the time the country became independent. They also vigorously pursued the policy of keeping the traditional rulers in the reduced circumstances of the glorified agents of the power-structure in control over various areas of government administration. They punished any Oba who was insubmissive but openly showered favours on those in whom they were well pleased. With high turnover of incumbents in the seat of power, the wheel of fortune was frequently spun to dislodge many a crown that was earlier regarded as secure.

The fearsome instrument of dethronement was fashioned by the British to effect the ultimate measure of reprisal against insubordination from any local authority. Some titans of our history, like King Overamwen of Benin, King Jaja of Opobo and King Kosoko of Lagos, dared the colonial overlords and suffered that fate. But such incidents were spread over several decades up to the time of the banishment of that glamorous Ondo Prince, Oba Fidipote. However, the dreaded weapon of summary removal from the throne was fiercely wielded almost routinely by the political chieftains of the First Republic in certain parts of the country, as the baton of power changed from one hand to the other.

The traditional stool of Owo was thus caught in a crossfire of contending interests in which advantages swiftly shifted from one side to the other. What was right suddenly became what was reprehensible. What was sound then became hollow...fair is foul and foul is fair. This progressive area was soon embroiled in a king-size controversy, in more than one sense of the term, before the people even knew it. But again, it was the age-old outcome of proverbial elephants at war: the grass underneath the ponderous skirmish is the main casualty. On the long run, the real victims of the problems thus created in Owo have been the decent citizens whose social lives were riven with disaffection and disputes, the nature of which had never visited their land.

Of course, the central figure of the imbroglio, Sir Olateru Olagbegi, who was then the Olowo of Owo, consequently lost his throne. But he remains one of the towering figures of the history of development in Owo. As the first educated occupant of his ancestral palace, his destiny as a crowned head was outlined from birth and this inspired his upbringing. The young prince was cosseted in public, but he was made to learn the discipline of responsibility as he grew older.

It is no wonder that when he came on the throne, his one consuming passion was to be positioned at par with the developed areas of Yorubaland. Places like Lagos, Abeokuta and Ibadan, boasted of secondary schools, pipe borne water, electricity and good roads among other social amenities. The young Olowo set about the acquisition of these facilities with unstinted enthusiasm and consummate charm.

As a young man, he was startlingly handsome and highly cultivated for his class. He was therefore able to use his personal influence to usher in considerable development into the land. And the Owo people took him to their hearts with pride as their potentate. He was more than that. He made them look beautiful to the outside world as a worthy representative, for the Owo people have always been a lovable and loving community.

"The time has now come for them to live up to the noble qualities of their intrinsic nature."

Undoubtedly, the homecall of Oba Adekola Ogunoye, himself a man of sterling attributes, has plunged the Owo people into some sorrow even if the bereavement may be bearable to a certain extent. However, the sad occasion also offers a unique opportunity for reproachment which, enabled by maturity, can only produce grand results of reconciliation. We call on all the leaders, not only of Owo but throughout Yorubaland, to rise to the task now. In particular, the traditional rulers must feel fully involved because they are. What they do for their royal brother now, they must realize, they do only for themselves. It could have happened to anyone.

The issues leading to the deposition of Sir Olateru Olagbegi were no more than an offshoot of the virulent crisis which split Yorubaland clean through in the sixties.

The forces at play were very powerful and relentless. The encounter was with no holds barred. But the protagonists have left the stage. The theme is exhausted. All that the aftermath has to offer are lessons. In that vein, several men of goodwill have been able to come together to restore peace, even where the conflict was between people of different dialects within the Yoruba community. How much more appropriate the establishment of amity would be among the elements of a single unit is patently unarguable.

Sir Olateru Olagbegi, through divine mercy, still lives. His recall to the throne of his forefathers is bound to bring back the wholesome feeling of peace and brotherhood which must be the heart-felt desire of the majority of Owo people. A lot of what they consider with great pride in their homeland today emanated from the enlightened rein of the old man. It is only fair that he should, in the fullness of time, "enter the ceiling" to join his ancestors from the throne which he rightly inherited from them.

Culled from The Vanguard April 19, 1993

...AND THE OBA WAS BANISHED! WHEN OLATERU OLAGBEGI LOST GRIPS ON HIS PEOPLE

Owo, one of the most ancient Yoruba towns, was founded in about 1019 A.D. From Lagos, Owo is 400 kilometers (250 miles), and it is situated in the tropical rainforest belt of Ondo State, on 183 mm (600 feet) above the sea level.

Owo has many features that truly make it ancient-respect for traditions, generously accommodating, peace loving and tough; but behind these virtues is a transparent evidence of long cases of rebellions.

The traditional head is known as the Olowo. In the days of yore, whoever puts on the mantle of Obaship was regarded as the traditional representative, or a deified oracle. Hence, the Olowo is addressed in eulogy as "Kabiyesi, Igbakeji òrìṣà." Whatever he decreed was final. But then this was when he enjoyed absolute loyalty from his subjects. When things turned sour, the same subjects could turn rebellious against his reign and rule.

Till date, Owo has had twenty nine Olowos. Each of them

encountered one type of rebellion or the other, during his reign. Most of them weathered the storm and triumphed. But the history of Owo revealed that three of those previous 28 Olowos disappeared from the thrones during the storm of rebellion.

The first of these three who did not survive the tempestuous rebellion was Oba Alubiolokun. It occurred in the year 1690 and he was the 17th Oba on the Owo throne at the time. Before he was dethroned, he both reigned and ruled for almost half of a century, because he ascended the throne in the year 1643. When the turbulence got to the climax, Oba Alubiolokun was thrown into River Ogbese.

The second Olowo to fall from grace to grass was Oba Adara. He was enthroned in 1876. His offence was that he was allegedly dealing in slavery and slave trade. It was alleged that the Portuguese and American slavemasters were using him as their outpost to promote their illicit slave business. Owo children were alleged to be sold into slavery. Others were exchanged for such things like looking glasses and umbrella. An agitation was organized against the practice by the entire citizenry. The Oba proved obdurate in slavery.

A rebellion was raised against Oba Adara. He saw the issue from one angle but his subjects viewed the practice from another. Oba Adara regarded slavery as a lawful commercial enterprise designed to enrich himself over and above his poorer subjects, while the subjects believed that slavery and slave trade was an illegal and immoral business which tended not only to depopulate Owo, but to profane the tradition and, therefore, bring disgrace to the people.

There was a rebellion. This rebellion reached such irretractable crescendo that Olowo Adara was assassinated in the year 1880. His body was dumped into the forest on the outskirts of Owo town for "feeding" the gods.

The third Olowo of Owo to be removed from the throne was Olowo Aladetohun. He was the successor of Oba Adara, as he ascended the throne in or about 1880 or 1881. Things went apart between him and his subjects nine years after he became the Oba. His palace was razed to the ground with fire by his Owo people. In the provocation which ensued, all the male descendants of his family were murdered in cold blood.

Characteristically Owo, right from its inception in about 1019 A.D., has been a cesspool of chaos, political or royal. In the 20th century Owo, the dethronement of Sir Olateru Olagbegi II made another addition to the long series of cases of rebellions in the town. The Owo crisis had its genesis in the politics of the old Western Region. In the days when the proscribed Action Group of Nigeria was at the pinnacle of its power and popularity in the region, Oba Olateru Olagbegi II, like most of his brother Obas, was not only a custodian of his people's customs or traditions, but he was also an ideological supporter of that political party.

In the mid-1950s, Sir Olagbegi summoned all the chiefs and elders to his palace for a meeting. By the time these elders were aware that they were at a political meeting, they had sworn to secret oaths to be loyal supporters of the banned Action Group. In Owo, like any part of the country, or of the world, swearing to an oath was revered, feared and strictly obeyed. Its breach was feared to have damnable consequences like death or illness. Therefore, the Owo chiefs and elders made up their minds right from the onset to adhere to the requirements of the sacred oath which they swore to in the Oba's palace.

On the advent of the A.G. crisis in 1962, there were factions within the party. One toed the leadership line, while the other faction supported the party's deputy leader. The latter faction formed the Nigerian National Democratic Party which was led by Chief Samuel Ladoke Akintola the then Premier of the region. Sir Olateru Olagbegi expressed his conviction in the old saying that what was good for the goose was good for the gander. In other words, if he could summon his chiefs and elders to register supports, by way of swearing to an oath, for the Action Group as the government of the day, nothing hindered him from displaying similar solidarity for the newly formed NNDP which "controlled" the day's government. Sir Olagbegi, therefore, summoned the chiefs and elders for the second time in eight years (1954 and 1962) to support the NNDP.

The people declined on accounts of the glaring double dealings, more so as the elders had earlier sworn to sacred oath to adhere to whatever the Action Group might stand for. The elders and chiefs disobeyed their Oba; they feared the evil consequences of the earlier oath of 1954 on themselves and their children's children. They had earlier evoked the spirits of the gods of their ancestors to descend on their children if they ever changed their decision to breach the oath.

During the Morgan Chieftaincy Review Commission, Sir Olateru Olagbegi testified. He was led in evidence by his lawyer son, Mr. Fola Olateru-Olagbegi. "During the political crisis in the former Western Region, I was mandated by my people to support Chief Ladoke Akintola, the then Premier and leader of the banned Nigerian National Democratic Party ((NNDP)." In 1960, Sir Olagbegi was a Minister-Without-Portfolio in Akintola's government. The decision of the Owo chiefs and elders to honour the 1964 oath, rather than breach it, marked the genesis of the debacle in Owo. In spite of the elders' disobedience to his entreaty Sir Olagbegi joined the NNDP. In the words of Olagbegi himself to the Press: "My attitude to politics is simple. Support the government of the day, so that amenities might be offered to your domain."

Contrary to the feelings of his subjects, the ex-Olowo decamped to the NNDP which characteristically embarked on the victimization of the supporters of all other parties. This victimization of the AG and the NCNC members by the NNDP angered the masses. The result of the episode was that Sir Olagbegi, who was once loved and respected by his subjects, lost popularity among them.

Such was the situation in Owo when the Army struck on January 16. 1966. The victimized supporters of other political parties who refused to go with him into the NNDP organized what was known as "Olagbegi-Must-Go" campaign, which reached such magnitude that on June 15, 1966, the military government of the West, under Col. Fajuyi, issued a suspension order on Sir Olagbegi. The order was to last for six months after which the nerves could be allowed to cool down enough for him to return to the throne.

After six months, on December 15. 1966, the suspension order was revoked. By then the much dreaded commotion in Owo had subsided. Some of his subjects were prepared to accept him, while others were unprepared to do so. By then tongues started to wag that in 1924 similar six-month suspension order was clamped on Olowo Olagbegi l, who incidentally was Sir Olateru Olagbegi's father. The intention of the colonial government then was to prevent bloodshed during the reign of Olagbegi I when his subjects allegedly rebelled against his authority. Elders in the town who were at the prime of their youths at that time recalled that it was a case of history repeating itself. Opposing factions to Sir Olagbegi's return used all means at their disposal to keep him off from the throne.

Governor Adeyinka Adebayo, who succeeded Col. Fajuyi, was unwilling to do anything which would give the indelible impression that his government was deliberately imposing Sir Olagbegi on his subjects. A decision to accord him any escort would indicate that he was being imposed on the Owo people.

The Military Governor wisely decided against this. Adebayo's policy was that if the subjects wanted him, the Olowo should return and be received enthusiastically. But if trouble erupted, it followed that he was unwanted by his subjects.

Thursday, February 8, 1968, marked a turning point in the annals of Owo town and of Sir Olagbegi for, it was on that fateful day that the knighted Oba Olateru Olagbegi returned to Owo Town. Sensing that the epoch-making return might provoke miserable consequences, Sir Olagbegi disguised. Despite the disguised appearance, the town was turned to a cauldron of violence. Although he escaped unscathed in the riotous welcome about 60 of the buildings which belonged to him and his ardent supporters in the town were reduced to ashes while about 40 others were damaged.

Gravely disturbed by this discordant development in Owo, the Military Governor, Major-General Robert Adeyinka Adebayo, set up Bode Kumapayi Inquiry to investigate the causes and possible solutions to the unrest. Before Sir Olagbegi was deposed on February 8, the report of the Kumapayi Inquiry was never published. He was deposed and exiled to Okitipupa where he was from 1968 to March 18, 1969. In sanctioning the deposition order, Governor Adebayo, said: "Sir Olagbegi was more a politician than a traditional ruler." Within one year of the deposition, a new Olowo was appointed.

August 7, 1968, was another milestone in the history of Owo. That day witnessed a declaration under which a new Olowo was appointed. It was known as The Olowo Chieftaincy Declaration of 1968. On

August 22 the Ministry of Local Government approved the appointment, the name of the Oba-designate was Obayoriade Ogunoye. He was not without opposition. Sir Olateru Olagbegi's supporters challenged the election.

Series of objections were raised against the August 7, 1968 Declaration. In the first place, it was argued by Olagbegi's men that the 1968 Declaration bore the signature of Mr. M. L. Famakinwa, who was said to be the Secretary to the Chieftaincy Committee of Owo District Council. The said signature was however strongly refuted by Mr. Famakinwa that he retired from the District Council since 1963 and as a result he could not have signed the declaration documents.

In the second place, the 1968 Declaration provided that the Ajagbusiekun House would be the Ruling House. According to Olagbegi's faction, such provision in the Declarations was a bold effort to prohibit the families of twelve deceased Olowo from ascending the throne anymore. Oba Ajagbusiekun was the 13th Olowo of Owo.

In the third place, by the earlier Chieftaincy Declaration of 1967 there were 20 kingmakers. But that of 1968 reduced these 20 Kingmakers to seven (7) made up of only senior chiefs. The contention of Olagbegi's faction was that such drastic reduction had no historical justification. Rather, the reduction should not be below 12 Kingmakers according to tradition, the reduction to seven(7) was seen as a design to eliminate those members who might be for Sir Olagbegi.

In view of the said irregularities in the 1968 Declaration, it was obvious that the appointment of Ogunoye was destined to encounter serious oppositions.

On February 7, 1980, one protest letter was signed by 23 prominent citizens of Owo, and published as an advertisement in the Daily Times of Saturday, April 5, 1980. The letter requested the former Governor of Ondo State, Chief Michael Adekunle Ajasin, to look into the circumstances which surrounded the dethronement of Sir Olateru Olagbegi II. In the letter, the signatories claimed that the banishment of Sir Olagbegi from his throne was not an end in itself as the banishment of an Oba had been a temporary measure, during which period no other person should ascend the throne. Citing instances, the signatories mentioned a number of Obas who underwent similar experience at one time or the other but were eventually allowed to return to their thrones.

Mentioned in the letter were the Alake of Egbaland, Sir Ladapo Ademola who was banished to Oshogbo; the Saki of Arigidi, Oba Olanipekun; also Olagbegi I who was banished to Akure in 1924, and Olu of Warri, Oba Erejuwa. In the case of Warri, when the vacancy was filled and was discovered to be contrary to the Itshekiri tradition, the deposed Olu was reinstated. It was argued by them that the case of Sir Olateru should not be an exception, more so because by installing Oba Ogunoye II as the Olowo in 1968, the traditional owo rites were not adhered to. The letter asserted that Owo customs and traditions were raped by installing an Olowo while one was living and that The Olowo Chieftaincy Declaration of 1957, was abrogated to suit the imposition of Oba Ogunoye.

About a couple of weeks after the publication of Sir Olateru's version, another faction which styled itself as "Owo Community" published a rejoinder in the form of an open letter to Chief M. A. Ajasin. It was rebutted in the "Open letter" dated April 21, 1980, by the Owo Community that the references made to the named obas in their respective domains were cases of mere suspension and not banishment. It went further to list those Obas who were actually dethroned and never allowed to return.

Such Obas were ex-Ogoga of lkere, Ondo State; the ex-Osemawe of Ondo, Ondo State; Mr. Babatunde, ex-Olukare of Ikare, Ondo State; Oba Adeyemi, the late ex-Alaafin of Oyo, Oyo State; the ex-Emir of Kano, Kano State; and Timothy Fadina, the ex-Olota of Ota, Ogun State. The open letter urged the then Governor to regard the case of Sir Olateru Olagbegi a closed chapter in the history of Owo.

The advertised open letter to former Governor Ajasin in the Daily Sketch of June 19, 1980 ran thus: "After the deposition of the ex-Olowo of Owo, now Prince J. T. Olateru Olagbegi, in 1968, his post as the Olowo of Owo became vacant. A meeting of the Senior Omolowo was convened to appoint a successor; and the meeting was held in the house of Chief Suberu Aralepo, the head of Senior Omolowo.

There were three contestants and the other Senior Omolowo

decided to elect one by casting their votes. In the election, some of the Senior Omolowo who were present and were signatories to the previous petition of February 7, 1980, cast their votes for Ogunoye and placed him in the majority. The chiefs who voted for Ogunoye but later turned round to sign a petition in support of Olagbegi were Ojigbo, Oguabumaiye, Ojo Adefen, Ekongba and Oludasa. They played double dealings.

After the election, Oba Ogunoye was presented to the kingmakers with Chief J. Ajidasile, the Osere of Ehinogbe, as the chairman. The other three members were Chiefs Akowa, Ajana and Elerewe. At the meeting of the kingmakers, Chief Elerewe abstained from voting to confirm the acceptance of the Olowo elect while the others unanimously approved the appointment of Adekola Ogunoye as the Olowo of Owo. Adekola Ogunoye was presented to the people of Owo by Chiefs Osere and Akowa at Owo Town Hall for installation as the Olowo of Owo in accordance with the approved Olowo's Chieftaincy Declaration.

In 1971, these were the comments made by Chief Akowa and Chief Oshere, following the unprecedented peace which reigned after the installation. Chief Daramola Akowa: "I don't want Sir Olateru to come back to the throne. The ex-Olowo saw himself as the big boss whose every word should not be challenged. Chief Oshere of Ehin-Ogbe Quarters: The present Olowo has not given us any cause to regret his obaship. Many of those who are calling for the reinstatement of Sir Olateru Olagbegi merely do so in their own interest.

The behaviour of Chiefs Oshere, Akowa and Elerewe led some people to demand for their removal. The requests were tabled before the Council of Oba and Chiefs in the then Western Region and enquiries were conducted both at Ibadan and at Owo, and the following recommendations were made: (a) That Chief Joseph Ajidasile Olakunori, the Oshere of Ehin-Ogbe be suspended for six months (b) That Chief Adafen Daramola, the Akowa of iloro be suspended for six months. (c) That Chief Abraham Ojo, the Elewere, be deposed.

The recommendations were upheld by the Military Government of the then Western State and was accordingly published in the Western

State of Nigeria Gazette No. 13. Vol. 25 of March 25, 1976. Before the implementation of the above orders, new states were created. The above named chiefs were reported to have appealed to the then Military Governor of Ondo State, Wing Commander I. D. Ikpeme.

In 1977, when the ex-Olowo, Sir Olateru Olagbegi wanted to return to Owo, a delegation of Owo Community protested to Governor Ikpeme, on discerning the imminent troubles that could result by his return. The Military Governor assured the delegation of complete peace.

In another open letter which was also advertised, a group which was known as The Owo Parapo Association, of which Mr. Olanitori Olafemi Arowaji was the Secretary, alleged in paragraph 5 of the letter advertised in the Daily Sketch of July 15, 1980, that the election for the installation of the incumbent was not freely done. It was alleged that thuggery and vandalism were introduced during the election of the new Olowo.

With the incessant chieftaincy disputes in Ondo State, the military regime thought something should be done. Therefore the Morgan Chieftaincy Review Commission was set up during the governorship of Wing Commander Ita David Ikpeme. The commission was to undertake a thorough review of the Chiefs Law (Cap. 19) Of the Western Nigeria. It was a four-man commission which was headed by Mr. Justice Adeyinka Morgan. Other members were Dr. Femi Anjorin, a senior lecturer in history at the University of Ife. Chief J.O. Akindolire, a high chief at Ile-Oluji, and Chief Bode Kumapayi, the Permanent Secretary in the state's civil service.

At the time, there were 17 local governments in Ondo State which the commission was to examine. Its terms of reference were:

(1) To investigate the customary law pertaining to the appointment of all recognized chieftaincies in each local government areas: make recommendations as to the possible changes in their existing chieftaincy declarations pertaining to such office, and to suggest guidelines in the preparations of such documents.

(2) To investigate the status of each traditional ruler and other important chiefs in each local government area and make

recommendations, including the wearing of paraphernalia of office and order of precedence

(3) To undertake a thorough review of the Chiefs Law (Cap. 19) of the Laws of Western Nigeria, and make recommendations as to possible changes thereto with a view to speeding the filling of chieftaincy vacancies and other ancillary matters: and

(4) To make such other recommendations which the commission may deem fit in regards to chieftaincy matters and generally.

The four-man Review Commission resumed sitting at Owo on November 28, 1977. They were given four months to complete their assignment. Sir Olateru Olagbegi came to Owo from exile after 11 years, to submit his memorandum to the Commission. He, in turn, received notification to appear before it for evidence. In an interview with journalists at Owo, the ex-Olowo said: "The government edict says anybody interested should submit memorandum to it. Olagbegi family is interested, and as the head of that family, I have complied with the edict's directive. As the custodian of Owo tradition for several years, I will lay bare what we feel is good for Owo and assist the commission." He was escorted to Owo by about 500 policemen.

In those days, the jurisdiction of any Olowo was very wide. By tradition, the Olowo of Owo was the only consenting authority in the appointment and installation of community heads in his area of jurisdiction. Olowo's areas of jurisdiction included the whole of the former Owo Division made up of Isho Emure, Ipele, Iyere, Ute, Okeluse, Idase, Ipemo and some other smaller towns.

At one of the sittings of the commission, a 117-year-old traditional chief and kingmaker, Chief Owashoju Ariyo, who claimed to have been chief since 1941, urged the Commission to reinstate the ex-Olowo of Owo, Sir Olateru Olagbegi. Led in evidence by a counsel, Mr. Taiye Omonijo, Chief Ariyo deposed that it never occurred in the history of Owo for another Oba to be enthroned in the lifetime of the incumbent holder. According to the witness, two previous Olowos, Oba Ogejan, and Oba Magele, who were suspended from the throne one after the other never, had their vacant throne filled in their lifetime. The filling of the Olowo stool in the lifetime of Sir Olagbegi, according to Chief Ariyo, was the cause of the internal rancour in Ondo State.

Another witness, Chief Ariyo Adeleye, said that no Olowo of Owo could claim to be above discipline from his subjects. In his statement, he deposed that two recalcitrant Olowos had, in the past, been banished before Sir Olagbegi II. He offended the people and they deposed him.

Chief Gabriel Oludasa, another witness, disclosed that since 1957, Owo had always had 13 Omo-Olowo and 20 kingmakers. The Omo-Olowo were many, but 13 of them were their representatives who were recorded in the 1957 Olowo Chieftaincy Declaration. "At the dethronement of Olagbegi, the Olowo Chieftaincy Declaration was amended without consultation with the Omo-Olowo. This amendment was another cause of the internal unrest at Owo."

In his own evidence, the ex-Olowo called for a plebiscite to determine whether or not he was still wanted by his people. Led in evidence by his lawyer-son, Prince Fola Olateru-Olagbegi, the ex-Olowo said that during the political crisis in the former Western Region, he was mandated by his people to support Chief Ladoke Akintola, the then Premier and leader of the banned Nigerian National Democratic Party (NNDP). Before then, Sir Olagbegi claimed that the late Prime Minister, Sir Abubakar Tafawa Balewa, implored him to mediate in the dispute between the proscribed Action Group and the NNDP.

The ex-Olowo further said: "On the procedure of vying for the throne in Owo, interested candidates would first of all present themselves before the Olori-Ebi, the head of the family. But in this modern age, interested candidates could present himself through a letter to the head of the family. By tradition, only the Olowo of Owo was entitled to wear a beaded crown in the whole of Owo Division. On the demise of an Olówó, the inner-council of Chiefs, headed by the Ojumu and other Ọmọ-Olówó, would take over the administration of the town until another Olowo was appointed. It is not in our tradition to have a single regent on the demise of an Olowo, like in other places.

Giving his own evidence then, Mr. Michael Adekunle Ajasin, a community leader at Owo at the time and also the Chairman of the Owo Local Government, told the Morgan Commission that he was unaware that a Chieftaincy Declaration should be made during an interregnum. He said: "I did not know when this became a convention. It was late Alhaji D. S. Adegbenro, a Minister for Local Government in the defunct Western Region, who approved the 1957 Olowo of Owo Chieftaincy Declaration."

At one of the sittings, it became necessary to tender a copy of the 1957 Chieftaincy Declaration. The Morgan Commission was told that the document could not be found. As the document in dispute was vital to the findings of the Commission, efforts were made to send a delegation to Oyo State Governor's Office in Ibadan to search for it. The Permanent Secretary in the Ondo State Governor's Office, Mr. Ayo Ogunlade, told the commission that the document was missing.

Similarly, the original minutes which were taken at the meeting when the Declaration was made in 1957 could not be found. Following a frantic search however, the document was found, and tendered. It was the true certified copy of the declaration. It was tendered by Mr. Ayo Ogunlade, Permanent Secretary in the Political and Economic Department of the Ondo State Military Governors Office. On September 6, 1980, however, the Ondo State Governor, Chief M. A. Ajasin, appointed Mr. Justice T.A. Oluwole as the Chairman of the Chieftaincy Review Commission.

This was because the Morgan Commission did not finish the enquiry because of ill health and therefore, could not submit any report. Mr. Justice Oluwole was to continue from where Mr. Justice Adeyinka Morgan left off. Other members of the Commission included Mr. J. A. Ogundele, Permanent Secretary in the Governor's office, Mosignor Oguntuyi and Chief J.A. Ojomo. Dr. P.A. Oluyede served as counsel to the Commission.

The Oluwole Commission submitted its Report in February, 1981. It took evidence in respect of 42 chieftaincy disputes in the entire Ondo State. Still not satisfied that he was not being reinstated, Sir Olateru Olagbegi on February 5, 1981, filed a suit at the Akure High Court to challenge his deposition order of 1968. The case came up for hearing in February, 1981.

Sir Olagbegi swore to an affidavit which said that the orders which first suspended him from office in 1966 and then deposed him in 1968 were unconstitutional, illegal, null and void. He argued that the present incumbent Oba Ogunoye was installed contrary to the customary law of the town. Those who were joined in the suit were the Attorney-General and the reigning Olowo of Owo, Oba Adekola Ogunoye II.

In the suit of February 5, the Ondo State Deputy Solicitor General, Mr. E.O. Olamosu, standing in for the Attorney- General, argued that the mode of commencing action by originating summons was irregular; it should commence by writ of summon. He further submitted that the action was stale. Moreover, he said that the 1979 Presidential Constitution "did not review a right that was barred." Mr. Olamosu, therefore, urged the court to strike out the case.

In his submission, Chief Rotimi Williams, for ex-Olowo Olagbegi, argued that the objection which was raised by the defence counsel were too late. He argued that the object of an originating process was to bring the opponents to court. Chief Williams added that since they were present in the court, it would serve no useful purpose to strike out the action.

On March 16. 1981, Justice Olakunle Orojo, Chief Judge of Ondo State, ruled that the suit which was filed by the ex-Olowo was irregular. In his ruling, Justice Orojo said that he was not satisfied by the way in which the action was filed before him. He remarked that the action was not brought by a writ, rather it was brought by an originating summons, pointing out that such process was irregular.

Justice Orojo, however granted the plaintiff the permission to regularise his originating summons to conform with a writ of summons and serve the defendants within the following 14 days. He awarded a cost of N100 to each defendant.

In the subsequent action which Sir Olagbegi filed seeking court declaration that his deposition was null and void, Justice Orojo struck it out. In addition, the former Olowo was to pay N1.000 as costs. In his ruling. Mr. Justice Olakunle Orojo upheld the provisions of the Chiefs Law under which the former Olowo was suspended and deposed. The counsel for the ex-Olowo, Prince Fola Olagbegi, signified his intention to appeal against the ruling.

The ex-Olowo went to the Appeal Court, praying it for an

injunction to restrain Oba Ogunoye from parading himself as the Olowo of Owo, or from performing the traditional functions of the office of Olowo and from making use of the official residence of the holder of that title.

On January 19, 1983, the Federal Court of Apeal dismissed the suit. Sir Olagbegi's appealed, challenging the validity of his deposition, and seeking for a declaration that he was still the Olówó. It was dismissed. In the judgment which was delivered in Benin City by Justices Mamman Nassir, President of the Court, and assisted by Justice, B.0. Kazeem, S.J. Ète, A.G.0. Agbaje and R.O. Okagbue, the Federal Court of Appeal rejected all the grounds of appeal and the arguments which were advanced in support of Sir Olagbegi's case and thereby confirmed the judgment of the Chief Judge of Ondo State in favour of the Attorney-General of Ondo State and Oba Adekola Ogunoye.

The Federal Court of Appeal further stated that the 1979 Constitution of the Federal Republic had no retrospective effect to deprive the government of Ondo State and Oba Adekola Ogunoye of the acquired tested right and the protection not to be sued or taken to court under the Constitution of the federation and of the constitution of Western Nigeria 1963 and the Chief's Law of Western Nigeria.

The Federal Court of Appeal held that the chiefs law of Western Nigeria 1959 was applicable to Ondo State in respect of all chieftaincy matters. Prior to the coming into effect of the 1979 Constitution in the absence of any expressed provision to that effect. It then awarded a cost of N800 against Sir Olagbegi.

Culled from the Headline

July, 1984

OLOWO DANCES FOR DR. AZIKIWE

The Olowo of Owo, Sir Olateru Olagbegi II, yesterday danced for the Governor-General as part of the elaborate programme arranged to mark his first official visit to Owo.

At a stage during the three hours the Governor-General stayed at Owo, Sir Olateru played lawn tennis for him. Replying to an address of welcome read by the Olówó, Dr. Azikiwe warned against attempts to achieve political ends by the use of violence.

Commenting on the portion of the address which referred to the travesty of Nigeria by the activities of over-zealous politicians, Dr. Azikiwe said: "All I need say here is that we in Nigeria believe in governments by the ballot box and not government by bullets.

"We believe in the virtue of parliamentary democracy which we inherited from our former rulers".

"We believe in the freedom of individuals under the rule of law."

"In these days of increasing international tensions, it is essential that we should endeavour to protect our national unity which has wielded and through the strains and stresses of the first 30 months of our independence," he added.

In their own address of welcome, the people said that as one of the emergent nations of Africa, there was much task ahead in building Nigeria into a truly independent country.

They expressed the belief that with Dr. Azikiwe in the forefront, followed by a team of Ministers, headed by God-fearing Sir Abubakar Tafawa Balewa, the task would be accomplished within a reasonably short time.

The people of Ondo have demanded that any president chosen when Nigeria becomes a republic should play an executive role side by side with other presidents in Africa.

This was contained in an address of welcome presented to the Governor-General during his visit there yesterday.

Culled from Daily Times July, 1962

FOUR DAYS TO WEST ELECTIONS
OLOWO OF OWO DEFENDS ROLE OF WESTERN OBAS

SIR Olateru Olagbegi, Olowo of Owo and Western Nigeria Minister-Without-Portfolio, has defended the role of Western Obas and Chiefs in the politics of the region.

In a statement in Ibadan yesterday the Olowo said: "Certain leaders of the NCNC have in the past week or so been associated with statements which suggest that the party regards the question of chieftaincy as one of the major political issues in the forthcoming elections".

"According to Press reports, the NCNC has pledged itself to the establishment of a Panel of Chiefs which will be responsible for various aspects of the chieftaincy institutions in the Region. I have found this a rather curious statement and I think it is fair to say that the so-called pledge is calculated to confuse issues and to mislead the public".

"Now, all those who have any knowledge of the administration of this Region will be aware that there is already in existence a Council of Obas and Chiefs established by law and responsible for advising the Governor in any matter which might raise a question of public policy concerning chiefs or any class of chiefs in the Region. Members of this Council are drawn from amongst the Chiefs themselves and the Council is presided by one of the chiefs in the Region. Members of this Council are drawn over by the President of the House of Chiefs. In no instance has the present Government decided upon a particular course of action in any matter relating to the exercise or discharge of any power in relation to any chief or chieftaincy without prior consultation with the Council of Obas and Chiefs".

STATUTORY PROTECTION:

"It is clear therefore that already, chiefs in this Region and the traditional institution which they represent, have received adequate statutory protection and we also have an efficient and representative machinery of one of the most cherished institutions in our land.

"It is perhaps not generally known that in the Eastern Region, where the NCNC is in power, the Minister of Local Government has a free hand in dealing with the appointment and discipline of chiefs. The Minister's powers in this respect are absolutely unfaltered and he need not consult any chief or body of chiefs. The public can draw the obvious conclusion from such a practice".

"Turning to the Northern Region, we see that although there is in existence a Council of Obas and chiefs, the Council is presided over by the Premier of the Northern Region in person. It cannot be said, in the circumstances, that the Council of Obas and Chiefs in the Northern Region enjoys anything like the freedom and impartiality that characterises its counterpart in the Western Region".

"The present Government of the Western Region has, from time to time, given practical demonstration of its belief in, and regard for, the institution of chieftaincy: The most eloquent example of this sincerity of purpose is to be found in the recent appointment of an Oba as the Governor of the Region. The chiefs in the Western Region know that their affairs are well secured both by Constitutional provisions and the enactments and practices of the present Government".

"In those local government councils, the Western Region where members of the NCNC constitute the majority, they have shown persistent disrespect and hostility towards Obas and Chiefs. For example, the Owa of Ilesha, the Olubadan of Ibadan, and the Oba of Benin know from practical experience that they can expect nothing but insult and humiliation from the hands of the NCNC. In one instance, the party went so far as to deny the payment of salary to one of these Obas and in many other instances the party has attempted to reduce the salary of a number of Obas and Chiefs in the Region. These facts speak for themselves and we need to entertain any doubt that given the opportunity, the NCNC will pursue precisely the same policies on an enlarged scale."

The NCNC issued the following statement at Ibadan yesterday:

"One of the worst diseases of the Action Group Government is squandermania. The Western Region is very rich in natural resources and each year over £10 million are collected from export and import duties and the Federal Government pays to the Western Regional Government another £6 million as statutory grants.

"Also, five years ago, when the reserves of the Central Marketing Board were shared out to the Regions, the Western Region Government received £34 million, more than any other Region of the Federation. But today, according to the Approved Estimates of the Action Group Government, the Public Debt of the Western Region is now £11million.

"Where has all these money gone into?

"Let the Action Group answer this question.".

Hansard-Western State House of Assembly

EPILOGUE

EXCERPTS from Memorable letters to Sir Olateru Olagbegi, after his reinstatement to the throne

---

"It is but one evidence of your many landmark achievements to have re-ascended the throne after twenty-five years break, a rare feat in history be it ancient or modern."

Chief H.B. Chanrai,
Bamokun of Lagos, 12th Nov,. 1993

"Looking back over the years, the one and only important thing one can say is that God is great, merciful and above all, just. Those of us who know the history of your unjust deposition must consider ourselves lucky to be alive at this time and to see justice done."

Chief Ayo Rosiji
Apapa, Lagos 1st Nov., 1993

"Your reinstatement is an eloquent testimony of the selfless service which you rendered to humanity especially the people of Owo during your early tenure. They have craved for your return and divine will has thus prevailed. They remember your first twenty-five years of peaceful and prosperous reign and ask for a repeat that should be totally devoid of any rancor and acrimony."

Ibrahim A. Coomassie, NPM,mni
Inspector-General of Police. 16th Nov,. 1993

"Since it has pleased God to demonstrate His Special love for you not only by sparing your life this 25 years but bringing you back to the throne, I beseech you by the mercies of God to show love to all your subjects and all people, irrespective of what anyone may have said to or about you."

The most Rev .J. Abiodun Adetiloye
Archbishop, Metropolitan
Primate of all Nigeria
8th November, 1993

"If God has spared your life and health to see your restoration after a quarter of a century, I feel sure you will use the opportunity to reunite the Chiefs and people of Owo for whom as you know my family and have always had an abiding affection."

Chief Anthony Enahoro, CFR
Benin City 18th Jan,. 1994.

"As two of your most loyal friends and admirers, Mrs Adebo and I wish to convey to you our warmest congratulations on your restoration to the throne of your fathers and our prayers for your happiness and God's Guidance through the rest of your days."

Chief Simeon Adebo
Okanlomo of Egbaland
Abimbola Lodge, Ibara, Abeokuta
6th November, 1993

"The Occasion has clearly demonstrated the love of Owo people for social justice, peace and enduring progress. I am confident of the fact that your reign would usher in the long awaited and much deserved economic and socio-political development of Owo in particular and unity among the Yorubas in general."

Alhaji Chief (Dr) W.I. Folawiyo, OFR
Baba Adinni of Nigeria
Chairman, Yinka Folawiyo Group.
4th Nov,. 1993.

A

Abeokuta **51, 102**

Aboluwodi **52,136**

Action Group Party **150, 230**

Adara, Olowo **6, 244**

Adekunle Fajuyi, Lt. Col. **69, 76**

Adesoji Aderemi (Sir) **221, 226**

Adetokunbo Ademola (Sir) **99**

Ademola Ladapo (Sir) **42**

Adeyinka Adebayo Gen, **76, 82**

Ajaka, Olowo **15,**

Ajasin, Micheal Adekunle **48, 117**

Ajegbere **13**

Akintola S. L. Chief **69, 77**

Aribo Chief **75, 131**

Alaafin of Oyo **233, 250**

Alademeji Prince **33**

Alubiolokun Olowo **6, 8, 149**

Amaka, Ojomo **16**

Ameri **25**

Aragwagbaiye **52,**

Ashara MB **1,3**

Alanleye Olowo 7, 21

Awolowo, Chief Obafemi **57, 111**

Azikiwe, Dr. Nnamdi **258**

B

British Council **53**
BBC **180**

C

(1) Captain Rowpal **6**
(2) Canon Akinyemi **121**
(3) Chiefs Edict **124**

D

Daily Times **96, 142**
David Jemibewon **142**
Deji of Akure **95, 144**

E

Eduma **5**
Egbe Omo Oduduwa **48**
Elewere Chief **231**
Elewuokun Olowo **6, 61, 146**
Enahoro Paraketo (Chief) **33**
Ewi of Ado Ekiti **14**

G

Gowon, General Yakubu **33, 86, 97, 154**
Government Primary School Owo **30**

H

Hansard **261**
Herbert Macauley **6**
House of Chiefs **50, 59, 129, 271**

I

Idaniken **70, 130**
Ido-Ani **6**
Igogo **4, 11, 127, 146**
Ile-Ife **1, 3**
Iloro **3, 13, 52, 174**
Imade **3**
Imade College **16, 150, 190, 320**
Isuada **5, 12, 160**

K

Kabba **6**
Kam Salem (Alhaji) **81**
Kumapayi Commission of Inquiry **108, 114, 166, 235**
King Kosoko of Lagos **241**
King Overamwen of Benin **241**

L

Lagos Life **212, 213**
Leo, Zodiac **26, 27**

M

Morning Post **63, 84, 227**
Morgan Commission of Inquiry **129, 150**

N

NNDP 190, 204, 246
N.C.N.C. 54, 59
Newbreed Magazine 240
Nigerian Tribune 173

O

Oba Akoko **7**
Oba of Benin **2, 5, 260**
Oba Iso **6**
Obas Conference **50**
Obasanjo Olusegun Gen. **101**
Oduduwa **1, 2**
Ogedenge, Ilesha **6, 260**
Ogunoye I, Olowo **7**
Ogunoye Adekola II, Olowo **99, 175,190**

Ogunoye Majekodunmi **95**

Ogun Odi **5**

Ogbon Ogwata **7, 11**

Ojugbelu **1, 2**

Ojomo chieftaincy **14, 19, 73, 119**

Okiti Asegbo **3**

Okoro S.R.B. **137, 164**

Olagbegi **1,6,7,18,21**

Olowo Chieftancy Declaration **162, 248**

Oloba **6, 120**

Olowos **3, 14, 41, 62, 149, 244**

Oludanre **2**

Oludipe **15, 25**

Olu of Warri **141, 158, 240**

Olumilua, Bamidele **175,181,191, 208**

Omo-Ori-ite **34**

Omolowos **17, 142, 174**

Omode Owa **5**

Ooni of Ife **14**

Ooni Commission of Inquiry **17**

Ondo State Government **175, 191, 208**

Oro **5**

Oronsen **4, 9, 11**

Owo Commercial College **16**

Owo Council Secretariat **56**

Owo Divisional Appeal Court

Owo Government School **7, 36**

Owo Kingmakers **123, 142, 154**

Owo Native Administration **21, 36**

Owo Polytechnic **7**
Owo CMS School **30**
Owo Treasury **36**
Owo Town Hall **56, 251**
Osemawe of Ondo **17**
Osuporu **75, 94, 159**
Oyo Empire **9**

P

Post Office **7, 11, 57**

Q

Queen of England **239**

R

Rerengenje, Olowo **4, 11**
River Ogbese **8**

S

Saraki, Dr. Olusola **104**
Sasere of Owo **207**
St. John College **39**
St. Mary College **39**
St Louis Combined Hospital **4**
Sunday Times **175**

Sunday Star **83, 138**

T

The Guardian **197, 206, 208**
Tribune **155**

U

Uka Masquerade **5**
Ute **7**
United Kingdom **53**

V

Vanguard **163, 182, 188, 243**

W

Western Regional Government **55, 261**
Western Regional House of Chief **55**
Woman's World **79**

ABOUT THE AUTHOR

Dr Olusola Oloidi is the Pastor-In-Charge of RCCG, Strong Tower Resource Center, New Jersey, USA since July 2002. He is also a Provincial Pastor, Province 9, RCCGNA, Region 6 and a Certified Pastoral Counselor with Certification in Intimate Partner Violence.

A Licensed Family Therapist with more than 20 years experience in reputable agencies and he co-founded Harmony Family Services, Inc with his wife, Pastor (Mrs) Olubunmi Oloidi. They have been married for more than 35 years. Dr Oloidi is a Faculty member and Director of Counseling at the Redeemed Christian Bible College and Seminary, Texas, USA.

He has a Master of Science Degree in Pastoral Counseling and Doctoral Degree in Transformational Leadership. He is an active member of many Counseling Professional Associations in USA

Lightning Source UK Ltd.
Milton Keynes UK
UKHW021430030122
396549UK00005B/399